PARADOXES OF STRATEGIC INTELLIGENCE

PARADOXES
of
STRATEGIC INTELLIGENCE

Essays in Honor of Michael I. Handel

Editors

RICHARD K. BETTS
Columbia University,
New York, NY

THOMAS G. MAHNKEN
US Naval War College
Newport, RI

Routledge
Taylor & Francis Group

LONDON AND NEW YORK

First published in 2003 in Great Britain by
Routledge
2 Park Square, Milton Park, Abingdon, Oxon, OX14 4RN
711 Third Avenue, New York, NY 10017, USA

Routledge is an imprint of the Taylor & Francis Group, an informa business

British Library Cataloguing in Publication Data

Paradoxes of strategic intelligence: essays in honor of Michael I. Handel
1. Military intelligence. 2. Surprise (Military science)
I. Betts, Richard K., 1947– II. Mahnken, Thomas G., 1965–
III. Handel, Michael I.
355.3′432

ISBN 0-7146-5471-X (cloth)
ISBN 0-7146-8376-0 (paper)

Library of Congress Cataloging-in-Publication Data

Paradoxes of strategic intelligence: essays in honor of Michael I. Handel /
editors, Richard K. Betts and Thomas G. Mahnken.
    p cm.
    Includes bibliographical reference and index.
    ISBN 0-7146-5471-X (cloth) – ISBN 0-7146-8376-0 (paper)
    1. Military intelligence. 2. Deception (Military science) 3. Surprise
(Military) science 4. Handel, Michael I. I. Handel, Michael I.
II. Betts, Richard K., 1947– III. Mahnken, Thomas G., 1965–

UB250.P34 2003
327.12–dc21

                                                        2003046153

Typeset by Servis Filmsetting Ltd, Manchester

Publisher's Note
The publisher has gone to great lengths to ensure the quality of this reprint
but points out that some imperfections in the original may be apparent.

To Jill, Yael, Benjamin, Ethan, and Sarah Handel

Contents

Preface

This volume is a tribute to the life and work of Michael I. Handel, one of the world's leading theorists of strategic surprise and deception. Handel was fond of paradox. Indeed, it formed the foundation of his view of strategy and intelligence. Nothing illustrates this better than his essay 'Intelligence and the Problem of Strategic Surprise', which forms the first chapter of this volume. The fact that many of the volume's other contributors echo this chapter's themes is a testament to the influence of Handel's approach. His influence on the study of intelligence was great, though less than it might have been had he not died early, at the age of 58, in June 2001.

Born on 1 November, 1942 in Haifa, in what was then British Palestine, Handel was the only child of refugees from Hitler's Austria. Most of his extended family perished in the Holocaust. After undergraduate studies at the Hebrew University of Jerusalem in the 1960s he came to the United States to study for a PhD in the Government Department at Harvard. He completed the degree in 1974. In addition to serving as a Teaching Fellow at Harvard in this period, he taught briefly at the University of Massachusetts at Boston. His dissertation became his first book – *Weak States in the International System* (London: Frank Cass, 1981) – a project that began a long association with this British publisher.

Before completing his dissertation Handel published a monograph, *Israel's Political-Military Doctrine*, Occasional Paper No. 30 (Cambridge, MA: Harvard University Center for International Affairs, 1973), one of the first major analyses of Israeli strategy. This appeared on the eve of the October War in the Middle East. Like many Israelis, Handel was shocked by the Arabs' successful surprise, and turned his attention to analyzing the political, technical, and psychological reasons for the Israeli intelligence failure. He published his findings in a monograph – *Perception, Deception, and Surprise: The Case of the Yom Kippur War* (Jerusalem: Hebrew University, 1976) – and as an article in *International Studies Quarterly*.

The project on the Yom Kippur War started Handel on a life-long career in theorizing about strategic surprise, misperception, and intelligence warning, and their effects on international politics and military strategy. His second book was *The Diplomacy of Surprise: Hitler, Nixon, Sadat* (Cambridge, MA: Harvard Center for International Affairs, 1981). He published a Davis Institute monograph, *Military Deception in Peace and War* (Jerusalem: Hebrew University, 1985), an article on diplomatic surprise in *International Security*, and three major edited volumes: *Strategic and Operational Deception in the Second World War* (London: Frank Cass, 1987); *Leaders and Intelligence* (London: Frank Cass, 1989); and *Intelligence and Military Operations* (London: Frank Cass, 1990). Other work on the subject appeared in his collection of essays, *War, Strategy, and Intelligence* (London: Frank Cass, 1989).

In the mid-1980s, Handel convinced Frank Cass to publish a new journal called *Intelligence and National Security*. A number of scholars tried to dissuade him, fearing that there would not be enough high-quality academic analyses in the newly developing field to sustain a journal beyond several issues. He persevered, co-edited the journal with Christopher Andrew of the University of Cambridge, and proved the skeptics wrong by establishing it as a prestigious outlet for historical and theoretical studies of the subject.

After Harvard, Handel took up his academic career in Israel, becoming a tenured member of the faculty of international relations at Hebrew University. He had become a US citizen at the time he finished graduate school, however, and felt steadily drawn to the United States. At the end of the 1970s, he returned to do research on a Ford Foundation fellowship at MIT, married an American, Jill Schindler, and returned briefly to Israel. In the early 1980s, he and his growing family once again came back to the United States on a research fellowship at the Foreign Policy Research Institute in Philadelphia, and this time they stayed for good. Handel became a professor at the US Army War College in Carlisle, Pennsylvania. There, he instructed the elite of the Army officer corps and organized conferences that brought together military leaders, historians, political scientists, and intelligence officials. In 1990, he moved to the Naval War College to join the Department of Strategy and Policy, which is known for its unique critical mass of high-powered civilian faculty in military and diplomatic history and strategic studies.

Handel was a political scientist, but one perched halfway between that discipline and history. In his work he sought patterns and generalizations, but was always anchored in the careful study of great international events of the past 200 years – most of all, the epochal issues associated with World War II. He was instinctively and determinedly theoretical, but skeptical of the recently dominant theoretical trends in mainstream political science. He lived in the world of books more than of journal articles. He was devoted to teaching and won several awards for his performance. His beard and occasionally bohemian idiosyncrasies, and most of all his intense, no-nonsense, argumentative style, marked him as something of a character in the military environments in which he taught. His teaching method was Socratic, which proved a particularly salutary and often novel experience for the legions of officers who passed through his seminars.

Like so many of the statesmen and commanders he studied, Handel was caught by surprise. Never having been seriously sick, he went for a checkup, had some tests, and was abruptly told that he had a few months to live. When they heard the news, his colleagues and superiors in Newport moved to dedicate the Naval War College's annual conference to him. Proving that it is difficult to deceive the deceiver, he soon learned of the supposedly secret project. True to form, Handel took over the planning of the agenda and the contributors, and finished shaping the conference shortly before he died.

The other essays in this volume reflect the topics that Michael Handel explored throughout his professional career. The chapters by Richard K. Betts and Woodrow J. Kuhns explore the pathologies and paradoxes of intelligence analysis. Betts explores the politicization of intelligence, a theme that Handel examined in his article 'The Politics of Intelligence'. Much as analysts and policymakers would wish otherwise, Betts notes that there is an inherent tension between the objectivity and influence of intelligence estimates. Kuhns examines the contribution of epistemology to intelligence analysis. He argues that we know a lot less than we should about the record of successes and failures of intelligence estimates, and suggests ways to improve both our knowledge of the analytical track record and the performance of intelligence prediction.

The chapters by James J. Wirtz, John Ferris, and Uri Bar-Joseph examine surprise and deception from both theoretical and historical perspectives. Wirtz uses Handel's theoretical work on intelligence failure as the starting point to derive a theory of surprise. As Wirtz notes, surprise may paradoxically favor the attacker initially but in the long run hasten his defeat. He also discusses ways to mitigate the threat of being victimized by surprise. Ferris' chapter explores perhaps the premier case of deception in wartime: Britain's development of deception operations during World War II. Bar-Joseph examines why Israel was surprised by the outbreak of the 1973 October War. Handel was also interested in how changes in technology might influence surprise and deception in the future. The final chapter, by Mark M. Lowenthal, explores this theme.

Handel's other main body of professional work was the analysis and exegesis of the writings of Carl von Clausewitz, the greatest philosopher of war. Although Clausewitz, ironically, deprecated the importance of intelligence (one of the few errors for which Handel took him to task), he was painfully aware of the complexity of war, and his theory struggled with internal tensions and apparent contradictions. Many of the latter are better understood, when considered carefully, as insights into paradox. In this, the two main strands of Michael Handel's work came together. Moreover, Clausewitz's classic *On War* was an unfinished work – as was Handel's prematurely shortened professional life.

Acknowledgements

The essays in this volume were written for an international strategy conference held in honor of the late Michael I. Handel during November 2001, at the United States Naval War College in Newport, Rhode Island. Michael Handel taught during the last decade of his life in the Naval War College's Strategy and Policy Department. He was our esteemed colleague and close friend. When Michael discovered in early 2001 that he was seriously ill and had only a short time to live, we wanted to find some way to express our admiration for his life's work and our gratitude to him for the way he enriched our lives. One of the traditional ways to honor a distinguished scholar, of course, is for his colleagues and students to join together in presenting him with a book of essays. We thought that this tribute would be a fitting way for our department to honor Michael, who has made such a valuable contribution to the study of strategy through his writings, lectures, teaching, and conferences. When we approached Michael about our plans, he embraced the entire project, and during his final illness played a major role in organizing the effort. Michael liked to encourage the study of strategy by bringing together scholars for gatherings marked by the lively exchange of ideas. His whole-hearted enthusiasm for this project was a tonic for those of us who deeply admired his work and would soon mourn his passing. The conference and this volume, by his involvement in their conception, bear Michael's direct imprint. Our first debt in producing this volume, then, is to Michael Handel himself, whose teaching, scholarship, and intellectual rigor provided a model to us all.

At the Naval War College, the administration gave their complete support to Michael and us in carrying out this enterprise. The then Dean of Academics, Charles P. Neimeyer, the then Provost, Rear Admiral (ret.) Barbara McGann, and the President of the Naval War College Foundation, Rear Admiral (ret.) Joseph C. Strasser, provided generous funding and administrative support for the conference. Later, Alberto Coll, Dean of the Naval War College's Center for Naval Warfare Studies, gave additional funding, without which the conference could not have taken place. Michael's friend, Mary Estabrooks, working in the office of the Dean of Academics, made the wheels of the administrative bureaucracy turn for us. Anita Rousseau, also in the Dean's office, ably assisted us in making this conference a reality. Meanwhile, William Spain, the Assistant Dean of Academics, oversaw the smooth running of the conference. The President of the Naval

War College, Rear Admiral Rodney Rempt, presided over the conference's proceedings and graciously welcomed its participants to his home.

George Baer, then chair of the Strategy and Policy Department, supplied ever-useful advice for orchestrating the conference and gave his full backing for the project. The current chair, Tom Nichols, has also supported this major effort by the Department to honor Michael. From within the Strategy and Policy Department, Carol Keelty helped in the daunting task of bringing together for the conference scholars from Europe, Israel, Canada, Australia, and across the United States.

The response to our invitation from Michael's friends was overwhelming, with the result that they have produced three volumes instead of one in honor of Michael's memory. These three volumes reflect some of the diverse interests and themes of Michael's work. John Maurer of the Strategy and Policy Department edited *Churchill and Strategic Dilemmas before the World Wars*. Michael's long-time friend, Richard Betts of Columbia University, and Thomas Mahnken, from the Strategy and Policy Department, edited *Paradoxes of Strategic Intelligence*. Bradford Lee and Karl Walling, also from the Strategy and Policy Department, edited *Strategic Logic and Political Rationality*.

Credit, too, for bringing these volumes to print belongs to Michael's publisher of long standing, Frank Cass, and to his son Stewart Cass. Michael himself had approached Frank and Stewart Cass, wanting them to publish these volumes. Stewart took the time to attend the conference, and his sound guidance and enthusiastic backing have greatly assisted us in our work. No authors could ask for a more congenial publisher.

Finally, Michael's partner in life, his wife Jill, helped us at every stage of this project. Jill faced the adversity afflicting her family with courage and constancy, caring for Michael during his final illness while tending to the needs of their four children. The presence of Jill and her older children at the conference lifted the spirits of its participants, and she has supported us in the subsequent preparation of these volumes for publication. These volumes, then, represent not only a tribute to Michael and his life's work but to Jill's bravery.

Notes on Contributors

Uri Bar-Joseph received his PhD from Stanford University in 1990. At present he is a senior lecturer in the Division of International Relations at Haifa University. His fields of interest are national security, intelligence, and the Arab–Israeli conflict. In addition to numerous articles on these subjects, his books include: *The Watchman Fell Asleep: The Surprise of the Yom Kippur War and Its Sources* (Hebrew, 2001, under translation into English); *Israel's National Security Towards the 21st Century* (ed., 2001); *Intelligence Intervention in the Politics of Democratic States: The USA, Britain, and Israel* (1995); and *The Best of Enemies: Israel and Transjordan in the War of 1948* (1987).

Richard K. Betts is the Saltzman Professor and Director of the Institute of War and Peace Studies at Columbia University. He was a Senior Fellow at the Brookings Institution and taught at Harvard and Johns Hopkins universities. Betts served as Director of National Security Studies at the Council on Foreign Relations, and on the staffs of the original Senate committee investigating the US intelligence community and of the National Security Council, and was a member of the National Commission on Terrorism and the National Security Advisory Panel of the Director of Central Intelligence. Among his several books is *Surprise Attack* (1982).

John Ferris is the author of *Men, Money and Diplomacy: The Evolution of British Strategic Policy, 1919–1926* (1989) and of 40 articles on British intelligence, strategy, operations and diplomacy, and editor of *The British Army and Signals Intelligence during the First World War* (1992). He is Professor of History at the University of Calgary.

Woodrow J. Kuhns is Deputy Director of the CIA's Center for the Study of Intelligence. He received his PhD in political science from Penn State University in 1985 and then joined the CIA as an analyst in the Directorate of Intelligence. He later served as the CIA's representative on the faculty of the Naval War College and as a member of the CIA History Staff.

Mark M. Lowenthal serves as the Assistant Director of Central Intelligence for Analysis and Production and is also Vice Chairman of the National Intelligence Council for Evaluation. He previously served as Staff Director of the House Permanent Select Committee on Intelligence and as Deputy Assistant Secretary of State for Intelligence.

His textbook, *Intelligence: From Secrets to Policy* (1999, 2003), is in its second edition. He received his PhD in history from Harvard University. He is also an adjunct professor at the School International and Public Affairs, Columbia University.

Thomas G. Mahnken is a professor of strategy at the US Naval War College. He is a graduate of the University of Southern California and holds a PhD from the Paul H. Nitze School of Advanced International Studies of the Johns Hopkins University. He previously served in the Pentagon's Office of Net Assessment and as a member of the Secretary of the Air Force's Gulf War Air Power Survey. He is the author of *Uncovering Ways of War: US Intelligence and Foreign Military Innovation, 1918–1941* (2002).

James J. Wirtz is a Professor and Chair of the Department of National Security Affairs, Naval Postgraduate School, Monterey, California. He received his PhD from Columbia University and he was a John M. Olin Fellow at the Center for International Affairs, Harvard University. His works on intelligence include *The Tet Offensive: Intelligence Failure in War* (1991, 1994) and *Strategic Denial and Deception* (2002), which was co-edited with Roy Godson. He is currently working on a book about contemporary balance of power politics and on the *Encyclopedia of Weapons of Mass Destruction*.

1

Intelligence and the Problem of Strategic Surprise

Michael I. Handel

. . . The textbooks agree, of course, that we should only believe reliable intelligence, and should never cease to be suspicious, but what is
the use of such feeble maxims? They belong to that wisdom which
for want of anything better scribblers of systems and compendia
resort to when they run out of ideas.

(Clausewitz, *On War*, Book One, Ch. 6)

. . . the general unreliability of all information presents a special
problem in war: all action takes place, so to speak, in a kind of twi-
light, which, like fog or moonlight, often tends to make things seem
grotesque and larger than they really are.

Whatever is hidden from full view in this feeble light has to be
guessed at by talent, or simply left to chance. So once again for lack
of objective knowledge one has to trust to talent or to luck.

(Clausewitz, *On War*, Book Two, Ch. 2)

The study of strategic surprise can be rather disappointing for those who
have always assumed that a better *theoretical* understanding of the subject
at hand would logically lead to the discovery of more effective *practical*
means to anticipate strategic surprise and alleviate its impact. Thus far in its
application to the real world, improved insight into the causes and pattern
of strategic surprise has made only a negligible contribution to the search
for ways to warn of a sudden attack in an accurate and timely fashion. If
anything, the scrutiny of this phenomenon in recent years has chiefly served
to explain why surprise is almost always unavoidable – and will continue to
be so in the foreseeable future – despite all efforts to the contrary.

Strategic Surprise as a Force Multiplier

From a military point of view, the advantages to be derived from achieving strategic surprise are invaluable. A successful unanticipated attack will

facilitate the destruction of a sizable portion of the enemy's forces at a lower cost to the attacker by throwing the inherently stronger defense psychologically off balance, and hence temporarily reducing his resistance. In compensating for the weaker position of the attacker, it will act as a force multiplier that may drastically reverse the ratio of forces in the attacker's favor. Stated in more general terms, the numerically inferior side is able to take the initiative by concentrating superior forces at the time and place of its choosing, thereby vastly improving the likelihood of achieving a decisive victory. Clearly, then, the incentive to resort to strategic surprise (as well as to deception) is particularly strong for countries that are only too cognizant of their relative vulnerability. Stronger armies, however, lack the 'natural incentive' to employ such methods, and must therefore make a conscious effort to exploit the full potential of strategic surprise if they are to maintain a superior position and achieve more decisive results at a minimal cost.[1]

Although strategic surprise in modern military history has seldom failed in terms of its initial impact, surprising the enemy *per se* does not necessarily mean that the attacker has reaped the fullest possible benefits or will be assured ultimate victory. (There is, in fact, no positive correlation between the initial success of a strategic surprise and the outcome of a war.[2]) One reason for this is that the attacker is often so amazed by the effectiveness of his own attack that he is caught unprepared to exploit fully the opportunities it presents. For example, the Japanese did not follow up their success at Pearl Harbor with repeated attacks on US oil depots and other naval and air installations in Hawaii, nor did the Allies take advantage of the opportunities produced by their surprise landing in Anzio. The same holds true for the Egyptian and Syrian armies in their 1973 attack on Israel: rigidly adhering to the original plan of attack, they prematurely halted their advance following the first phase of the attack, when they could have continued to make considerable progress at little cost to themselves.

The benefits accruing from a strategic surprise will be maximized to the degree that plans for the attack are flexible, and more initiative is delegated to field commanders, who are also encouraged to improvise and accept risks. (The Germans very successfully exploited the surprise gained in the opening of their attack on Norway and the west in 1940, and in the earlier stages of their attack on the Soviet Union in 1941, although they failed in this respect during the Ardennes offensive in 1944. In another instance, the Israelis came close to fully exhausting the potential of their unanticipated attack on Egypt in the opening phase of the 1967 war.) Thus, accomplishment of the surprise itself is only the *first* phase of planning; the *second* must consist of detailed preparations for the best possible exploitation of the projected surprise attack; frequently, this objective can be produced through a maxi–max (high risk–high gain) strategy as practiced by the Germans in Norway, the Japanese in Singapore, MacArthur in Inchon, and the Israelis in 1967. While the first phase, as we shall see below, rarely fails, the second one poses serious, sometimes insurmountable problems. Yet the whole *raison d'être* of launching a strategic surprise will collapse if the first stage cannot be followed up by the second.

Surprise in Historical Perspective

Although surprise has always been possible on the *tactical* level, its feasibility on the *strategic* level is a relatively new historical phenomenon of the twentieth century. Before the technological-industrial revolution, the rapid movement of large troop formations over long distances in a short period of time was virtually impossible. The slow pace of mobilization, not to mention that of troop concentration and movement, provided ample clues as to an adversary's offensive intent. Furthermore, such evidence could be gathered in time to countermobilize and make all preparations necessary to intercept the expected attack. This was recognized by Clausewitz, who believed that strategic surprise was of greater theoretical interest than practical value.

> Basically, surprise is a tactical device, simply because in tactics, *time and space* are limited in scale. Therefore in strategy, surprise becomes more feasible the closer it occurs to the tactical realm, and more difficult, the more it approaches the higher levels of policy . . . While the wish to achieve surprise is common and, indeed, indispensable, and while it is true that it will never be completely ineffective, it is equally true that by its very nature surprise can rarely be outstandingly successful. *It would be a mistake, therefore, to regard surprise as a key element of success in war. The principle is highly attractive in theory, but in practice it is often held up by the friction of the whole machine* . . . Preparations for war usually take months. Concentrating troops at their main assembly points generally requires the installation of supply dumps and depots, as well as considerable troop movements, whose purpose can be assessed soon enough. It is very rare therefore that one state surprises another, either by an attack or by preparations for war.[3]

Indeed, Clausewitz was convinced that, *in his time*, strategic surprise was not powerful enough to overcome the inherent advantages of the defense.

> The immediate object of an attack is victory. Only by means of his superior strength can the attacker make up for all the advantages that accrue to the defender by virtue of his position, and possibly by the modest advantage that this army derives from the knowledge that it

is on the attacking, the advancing side. Usually this latter is much overrated: it is short-lived and will not stand the test of serious trouble. Naturally we assume that the defender will act as sensibly and correctly as the attacker. We say this in order to exclude certain vague notions about sudden assaults and surprise attacks, which are commonly thought of as bountiful sources of victory. They will only be that under exceptional circumstances.[4]

In the past, surprise was thus confined to the tactical and grand tactical levels. With the advent of technology came the ability to achieve strategic surprise, as well as a change in the modes and aims of surprise, which, in its strategic form, is a much more complex phenomenon. Surprise could now be achieved simultaneously on several levels: in *timing*, the *place* of attack, *rapidity* of movement, the use of *new technologies delivery* and *weapons systems*, the frequent appearance of new doctrines and innovative tactics to match the new technologies, as well as in the choice of the political-military goals for war itself.[5]

The beginning of the railroad era, shortly after Clausewitz's death, touched off the revolution in mobility in warfare. Half a century later, the combustion engine further expanded the flexibility of movement and maneuver while obviating the necessity of dependence on railroad tracks for rapid mobility. The introduction of tracked vehicles and tanks by the end of the First World War improved the possibility of movement over difficult terrain, thus bringing the revolution of movement on land to its logical conclusion. Such trends conducive to strategic surprise were even further boosted by the development of air power, which added a third dimension of movement across all natural barriers, in all directions, and in very short periods of time. Air power brought to near perfection the possibility of success in the use of strategic surprise. Readying air power for the initial strike did not require an unusual concentration of forces, since it was based on the use of forces in being. Furthermore, the transition from peace to war was instantaneous, while the firepower that could be concentrated and unleashed was tremendous. Air power was particularly suitable for the attack of targets such as headquarters, communications centers, airfields, fuel depots, bridges, roads and other choke points vital for a counter-mobilization and the effective management of the defense against surprise attack. Moreover, it surpassed all other types of power in the ability to effect deep penetration bombardments and airborne attacks and/or provide support for deep penetration operations in land warfare.

In general, the existence of a variety of means of transportation made possible an accelerated pace in the initial mobilization and concentration of troops for the attack. This, in turn, improved the likelihood of achieving a breakthrough to be followed up by deep penetration into the adversary's territory. In addition, supplies could now be transported to the attacking forces more rapidly and over longer distances, thereby widening the range of options for maneuvering on the battlefield. When employed in conjunction with the enormously increased capacity of conventional firepower, the efficient, rapid means of transportation multiplied the power with which one could attack at a selected point and catch one's adversary completely off guard. Time and space, to use Clausewitz's apt phrase, had now been compressed.

In the twentieth century, technological surprise has become one of the most formidable forms of surprise in war. The unexpected appearance of new weapons in massive quantities, and/or their use in an innovative way, can be of decisive importance. Among some of the better known technological surprises, the first massive use of gases and tanks in the First World War and the appearance of and, even more so, the methods of use of the radar and radar counter-measures in the Second World War, are outstanding. The use of gliders by the Germans during their attack in the west in 1940 on the Belgian fort of Eban-Emael, the performance of the Japanese Zero and the Russian T-34, the British code-breaking effort and the strategic and tactical use of Ultra and the American atomic bomb are also among the best known surprises of wartime.

Technological surprises can be divided into two categories. The first involves the secret development of 'one' large system which is not deployed on the battlefield itself, such as Ultra and the atomic bomb. This type of technological surprise is extremely difficult to discover or anticipate. The second category involves the massive battlefield deployment of a new weapon system, such as the Zero or the T-34, which takes considerable time and is difficult to conceal. Yet very much like all other types of strategic surprise and for the very same reasons discussed below, technological surprise never fails. Given the rate of technological change since the end of the Second World War and evidence from recent wars, there is little doubt that technological surprise and deception will play a much more critical role in future wars.

As technological developments made unprecedented contributions to the feasibility of strategic surprise, the warning time available to the intended victim decreased dramatically. During the opening phases of the war at the very least, it significantly enhanced the power of the offense over the defense. The possibility that an unanticipated attack could quickly determine the outcome of an entire war thus became a very serious threat to the survival of states, especially in an ideologically competitive political environment.

In this manner, then, advanced military technology unintentionally opened up a highly destabilizing pandora's box. The fact that any country could clandestinely mobilize its armed forces and/or gain a tremendous advantage by simply starting to mobilize its forces first, created a situation in which *the reciprocal fear of surprise attack*[6] could, under crisis conditions, trigger automatic mobilization responses, loss of control, and pre-emptive attacks (i.e., become a self-fulfilling prophecy). Having produced optimal conditions for strategic surprise, technology emerged as one of the principal destabilizing factors in the international system of the twentieth century.

This trend reached its acme with the invention of modern nuclear weapons and ICBMs, whose staggering concentrated firepower, capable of being activated in minutes, meant that a strategic surprise could be both the beginning and the end of a war. That which Clausewitz considered to be a strictly *theoretical* possibility – the idea that a war might be decided by 'a single short blow'[7] – has become part of reality. Technological progress in the last hundred years or so has reduced the time required for concentrating troops or launching weapons for a strategic surprise from months to weeks, to days, and ultimately to hours or even minutes (see Figure 1).

A significant by-product of the military-technological revolution was the tremendous increase in the importance and number of functions assigned to military intelligence. The connection between the rise of technology and that of military intelligence is a subject that has received very little attention from military historians.

In times of little technological progress or change, intelligence and up-to-date information were not of paramount importance, because the behavior and strength of one's adversary did not change very frequently. The shape of each war differed only marginally from that of earlier wars. This is *not* the case in a world of rapid technological change, where each new weapon and the continuously changing rates of military industrial production may give the innovator a critical unilateral advantage almost overnight. For the first time in history, intelligence itself has become a major defensive weapon. Furthermore, most of the technological innovations and preparations for war continue in peacetime, indicating that intelligence work has become as important in peacetime as it is in war.

Although military technology has revolutionized almost every conceivable aspect of military performance, the one area in which it has, ironically enough, made little progress is that of anticipating surprise attack. The warning gap between the attacker and defender has remained as wide as in the past and still favors the offense over the defense. This will continue to be so, mainly because intelligence work, despite its access to electronic monitoring equipment, high-powered computers, and satellites, to name a few, is still based upon the human factor. As it is labor-intensive, intelligence work must reflect human nature, not technological excellence. The quality of results achieved in the world of intelligence and strategic warning in particular depends upon finding solutions to human problems which sometimes defy technological (or for that matter, any other) solutions.

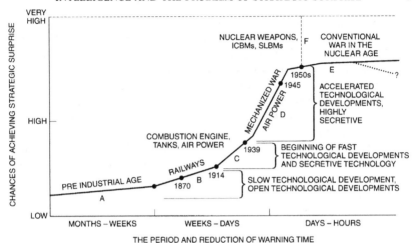

Notes:

A. Pre-industrial age. Slow mobility, limited fire power. Chances of a successful strategic surprise very low. (1870)

B. Railway age. Increased mobility, mobilization. Slow increases in fire power. Chances of a successful strategic surprise low but possible. (1870–1916)

C. Combustion engines, tracked vehicles and tanks, rise of air power and fire power. Mechanized warfare blitzkrieg. Chances of strategic surprise high. (1916–1939)

D. Further improvement in mobility and fire power. Chances of strategic surprise high – but also improvements to intelligence. (1939 to present)

E. Development of nuclear weapons and later ICBMs and SLBMs par excellence the weapons of strategic surprise. War can be decided – theoretically and practically – in minutes. (1945 to present)

F. Improvements in conventional mobility and fire power. Increased importance of air power. High chances of success for strategic surprise – but slowed increase given the technical developments of reconnaissance (air photography, satellites, electronic intelligence). Potential for surprise is somewhat leveled off by reconnaissance and familiarity with tactics of blitzkrieg. Yet, despite all the technological improvements that may help the defense, the basic problems of anticipating an attack are perceptual and psychological and remain without a satisfactory solution.

Figure 1   Strategic surprise in historical perspective: the decline of warning time

Among these are problems of: human psychology and politics; wishful thinking; ethnocentric biases; perception and misperception of reality; conflicting interests; political competition over scarce resources; organizational biases. As long as men interact with machines in the decision-making process, the quality of the decisions made will be most heavily influenced by the human factor, the complexities of which can be explained but not done away with.

In the past, it has often (either explicitly or implicitly) been assumed that intelligence work can be pursued by professional, detached experts working within an objective environment, and that they will be able to present the truth, as best they can determine it, to the policymakers. The policymakers in this scenario will of course recognize the quality and relevance of the data provided them, and will use this information in the best interest of their country (as they identify it). This 'purely rational decision-making model' and belief in the viability of a 'strictly professional intelligence process' is nothing but an idealized normative fiction. And yet many scholars and even some experienced intelligence experts continue to believe in the possibility of creating – through the 'right' reform – the perfect intelligence community.

Like Clausewitz's war in practice, the real world of intelligence is rife with political friction and contradictions, an environment in which uncertainty is the only certain thing.

Intelligence work can be divided into three distinct levels: *acquisition* (the collection of information); *analysis* (its evaluation); and *acceptance* (the readiness of politicians to make use of intelligence in the formulation of their policies).[8] As suggested earlier, past failures in avoiding surprise cannot be blamed on a dearth of information and warning signals. Consequently, one must look to the levels of analysis and acceptance for an answer.

The major problems stemming from these two levels can be discussed under three principal categories, two of which are primarily related to the analytical process. These are, first, the methodological dilemmas inherent in intelligence work and problems of perception and second, explanations corresponding mainly to the level of acceptance. The third category includes organizational and bureaucratic problems.

A. Methodological Dilemmas and Problems of Perception

1. Signals and Noise

Basically, information collected by the various intelligence acquisition modes can be divided into two types: correct and incorrect, or as they are called in intelligence jargon, signals and noises.[9] Although this dichotomous method of classification is of great theoretical value, in reality it is usually impossible to distinguish between signals and noises. Instead of falling neatly into one of the two categories, much of the information is a combination of both elements and therefore cannot be considered either completely reliable or totally unreliable. In attempting to determine the reliability of any single piece of information, analysts need to corroborate it with many other bits of data. The analysis and evaluation process is further hampered by the often contradictory nature of the information, which defies simple quantitative analysis. (This statement is not meant to suggest that a sophisticated quantitative analysis has a better substitute.) Much of the important data acquired do not lend themselves to a quantitative presentation because the criteria used to determine their selection, categorization and corroboration are ultimately determined by human beings, who cannot detach themselves from their ethnocentric biases, preconceived ideas and concepts, and wishful thinking. Much of the criticism directed at the use of quantitative methods in the social sciences, particularly in international relations, is even more applicable to intelligence work. In many facets of intelligence work, there is often no substitute for the experience and intuition of the expert. Intelligence must, as a result, generally be described as an art despite the many scientific disciplines that make critical contributions to its success.

It has been observed that 'if surprise is the most important "key to victory", then stratagem is the key to surprise.' The ever present possibility of deception further complicates the already difficult task of the intelligence analyst.[10] Deception can be defined as the deliberate and subtle dissemination of misleading information to an intelligence service by its adversaries.

Since the deceiver intends to present noise as highly trustworthy information, most successful uses of stratagem are based on the supply of largely accurate and verifiable data to the adversary. Having worked hard to obtain this information, the adversary is psychologically predisposed to believe it. In view of the aforementioned danger, the intelligence analyst regards most information as suspicious until proven otherwise. This is especially true under two circumstances: (a) when the intended victim of deception frequently makes use of it himself, as he will be more sensitive to its possible use by an adversary; (b) any intelligence organization that has been duped once tends to become overcautious. The latter situation can be summarized by this paradox: *The more alert one is to deception, the more likely one is to become its victim.*[11] And the better the information appears to be – the more readily it fits into a neat pattern – the greater must be the caution of the analyst. For example, Belgian intelligence obtained German plans for the invasion of the west when a German aircraft carrying two staff officers made a forced landing in Belgium on 10 January 1940. Upon receiving the information, the British and French would exclude the possibility that it had been planted for their benefit.[12] The danger here is that the better the information is, particularly when based on one source, the less credible it may seem to be.

Deception, and uncertainty in general, create an environment in which almost all information, at least in the short run, is accompanied by a question mark. This gives rise to yet another paradox.

'As a result of the great difficulties involved in differentiating between "signals" and noise in strategic warning, both valid and invalid information must be treated on a similar basis. In effect, all that exists is noise, not signals.'[13] Attempts to separate the noise from the signals are aggravated by the fact that *the collection of additional information also contributes more noise to the system, and the higher the amount of data collected, the more difficult it becomes to filter, organize and process them in time to be of use.*[14]

The collection of information is of course only a necessary but not a sufficient condition for the success of an intelligence organization. A balance must be struck between the collection effort and the analytical process. If an intelligence organization operates an excellent acquisition and collection mechanism but lacks enough qualified experts to process the information *in time*, its excellence in collection may come to naught insofar as warning of a strategic surprise attack is concerned. The emphasis on acquisition in the United States and the USSR has resulted in American overreliance on technological intelligence and, in the case of both countries, led to the collection of so much data that their analytical capacities have no doubt been seriously taxed.

2. Uncertainty and the Time Factor

From the preceeding discussion, it is clear that the analytical process of distinguishing between signals and noises requires *time*. Normally, a certain amount of time elapses (A–B on Figure 2) before the intelligence organization of the 'victim' gains some inkling of the attacker's plans. The lead time of the would-be attacker (A–B) shrinks in direct proportion to the degree of excellence of the prospective victim's intelligence service. By the time the defender seriously begins to consider the possibility of an attack (at point B), the attacker is well ahead of him in his preparations for war. (Point BB represents the attacker's lead time.) But even then, the defender-to-be is not yet convinced that he will be attacked; therefore, despite the initial warning, he does not fully mobilize (point C). While the attacker continues his preparations, which become increasingly difficult to conceal from the defender's intelligence, the 'victim' may gradually become persuaded of the gravity of the threat and begin to mobilize his own forces (point D). Meanwhile, the attacker has already completed his preparations and launches his attack (point E). Represented by gap F, the time lag between the preparations of the two adversaries depends upon the warning received by the defender and his speed of mobilization. While the defender's actual warning time was B–E, he might require more time (B–H) to complete his mobilization. (G represents the forces the defender managed to mobilize before the attack took place.) This sequence of events is typical of a strategic surprise that is not 'out of the blue'. It offers some explanation as to why surprise is not absolute, since the defender

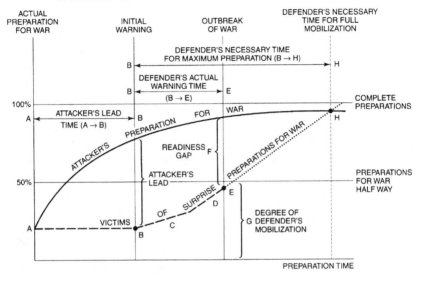

Notes:
A. Attacker starts preparations for war.
B. Defender issues initial warning, but is uncertain of the real probability of war.
C. Due to uncertainty the initial phase of preparation proceeds relatively slowly.
D. As the probability of war increases and becomes more certain the defender accelerates preparations.
E. War breaks out (e.g. surprise attack). Defender's preparations incomplete and lag behind the attacker.
F. The readiness gap favoring the attacker.
G. The degree of mobilization completed by the defenders at the time of attack (E).
H. At this point the defender may have reached his highest level of preparations. Line A↔B represents the *attacker's lead time*; line B↔E represents the *defender's actual warning time*; line B↔H represents the time the defender needs to complete his preparations. The greater is B↔H minus B↔E the more intense is the impact of the surprise attack.

Figure 2   The normal warning and preparation gap between the attacker and defender (this chart empirically reflects most cases of strategic surprise attacks)

normally manages to mobilize at least some of his troops. In many instances, the defender's preparations have been under way for a matter of hours (B–E), while the time required for full mobilization (B–H) can be measured in days or even weeks. The ratio of the defender's actual mobilization (G) to the readiness gap F (or the attacker's degree of preparation for war) is a good conceptual indicator of the intensity and effectiveness of the ensuing surprise attack.

Two possible exceptions to this otherwise typical sequence of events should be mentioned. In the first situation, the defender, having acquired definitive, fully credible information concerning an imminent attack, may therefore decide to launch a preemptive attack even before his own forces have been fully mobilized. He may thus seize the opportunity to begin the war on his terms by immediately using the most flexible and readily available forces at his disposal (e.g., the most suitable would normally be the air force) to attack although his own actual preparations are less than 50 per cent completed. This, for example, would have been the case in the Yom Kippur War of 1973, when the Israelis acquired incontrovertible information warning of an impending Egyptian-Syrian attack. Immediately placed on alert, the Israeli Air Force was instructed to make preparations for a preemptive strike on Arab troop concentrations. The attack was cancelled at the last moment, however, because of political considerations. Under such circumstances, the defender calculates that making the first move will allow him to cancel out, if not surpass, the attacker's advantage.

The second exception occurs in prolonged crisis situations when one side is the first to mobilize fully but then decides to delay his attack. The opponent may then catch up and perhaps reach the point where he can launch his attack first. This type of scenario occurred before the outbreak of the First World War, and again when Egypt mobilized first in May 1967 but allowed the Israelis eventually to exceed Egypt's own preparations and launch a preemptive surprise attack on their own.[15]

3. Intentions and Capabilities

All information gathered by intelligence concerns either the adversary's *intentions* or his *capabilities*.[16] Although this sounds simple enough, the actual sorting, evaluation, and corroboration of the information is an extremely intricate and time-consuming process which involves many interrelated steps. An error of judgment in one phase may set off a chain reaction of other mistakes, causing potentially serious analytical distortions.

Perhaps the most fundamental problem concerns the difference in the collection and analysis of the two types of information. Needless to say, it is far simpler to obtain information about capabilities than about intentions. *Capabilities* can be material or non-material. Material capabilities, that is, weapons, their performance specifications, and quantities are not easy to conceal. Non-material capabilities such as the quality of organization, morale, and military doctrine are more difficult to evaluate in a precise way, although considerable knowledge about them can be obtained. A pitfall to be avoided at all costs is concentrating on the measurable and quantifiable while neglecting the less precise, non-material ones.

Political and military *intentions*, on the other hand, are much simpler to conceal; only a handful of leaders, and at times a single leader (e.g., Hitler, Stalin, Sadat) will shape the strategy of a state. Intentions can be

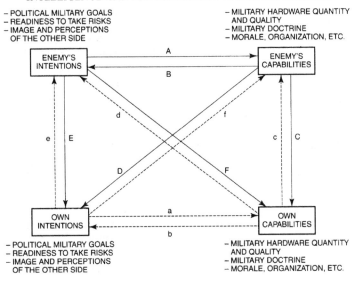

Figure 3   The complexity of the estimative process

changed at the last minute, and defy evaluation in the absence of direct access to the adversary's political-military elite. Yet even the most secretive leaders can provide intelligence analysts with clues to their intentions in their earlier memoirs, speeches, briefings in closed or open circles, and the like. In addition, a better understanding of the adversary's intentions can be developed through the careful corroboration of all evidence with his capabilities (see Figure 3). In the long run, if a leader harbors offensive intentions, he will have to invest in and expand his nation's capabilities (arrow A). This would range from heavy investments in military hardware to a preference for long-range offensive weapons over short-range defensive weapons. Limited capabilities may, however, force leaders to choose a defensive strategy in the short run. For example, Hitler needed to build up Germany's military strength before actively pursuing a policy of breaking away from the Versailles Treaty, reoccupying the Rhineland, or annexing Austria or the Sudetenland. In the absence of such strength, Hitler had to conceal his intentions behind the rhetoric of his peace offensives.[17] The process is further complicated by the fact that the adversary may claim that he merely needs to have capabilities comparable to one's own (arrow C). Thus, Hitler demanded equality with, or disarmament for, everyone else, even as he was announcing German plans for conscription and rearmament. At other times, the adversary may augment his capabilities in response to his perception of the hostile intentions of other nations (arrow D). Such actions and reactions are intrinsic to every arms race.

Furthermore, an adversary may assert that he is gearing his intentions to one's own (arrow E). And actual or perceived changes in one's own capabilities as evaluated by the adversary may trigger a change in his intentions out of fear and suspicion (arrow F). This can heighten antagonism and, in extreme cases, ignite a preemptive war. The description of the evaluation process thus far indicates that one must not only have a thorough grasp of the opponent's intentions and capabilities as such, but also an understanding of how he reacts to and perceives the observer's own intentions and capabilities. A similar mirror image process occurs on the observer's side (arrows a,b,c,d,e,f). To complicate matters, there is no direct correlation between capabilities and intentions; that is, a country with weaker capabilities may nevertheless decide to go to war. There may be a gap or time lag between the two (e.g., a leader might have aggressive intentions without adequate capabilities, or vice-versa). Finally, the evaluation process as outlined above requires exacting coordination and a lengthy period of time for the analysis.

Although capabilities and intentions should undoubtedly be subject to equally careful collection and analytical efforts, it seems more prudent to emphasize the study of intentions for the following reasons.

(A) An adversary can still decide to attack even though his capabilities are relatively weak (1) if he miscalculates the strength of the intended victim (as did the Germans in their attack on the Soviet Union in 1941, or the Arabs in their underestimation of Israeli capabilities in 1967); (2) if he is more interested in applying political pressure or making political gains even at the cost of a military defeat; (3) if he gambles that his surprise attack will have a force multiplier effect sufficient to compensate for his inferior capabilities.

(B) War and surprise attack are determined not by the existence of capabilities *per se*, but by the political intention to use them. The mere possession of superior, equal, or inferior strength is therefore less important. A corollary of this is that, while the adversary's intentions can be influenced at any point (i.e., he can be deterred from taking action), it is impossible to have comparable impact on capabilities immediately before the outbreak of war.[18] Since it is, of course, much easier to obtain information on capabilities than intentions, the temptation to concentrate on that which is simpler to identify or measure must be consciously resisted.

4. The Tricky Business of Estimating Risks

Boldness in war . . . has its own prerogatives. It must be granted a certain power over and above successful calculations involving space, time, and magnitude of forces, for wherever it is superior, it will take advantage of its opponent's weakness. In other words, it is a genuinely creative force.[19]

Procedural, analytical and methodological difficulties constitute only a small fraction of the problems involved in the intelligence estimation process. Other, no less complex problems must also be discussed briefly. The first of these concerns the element of risk assessment in the planning of military operations.[20] The contradictory nature of risks in military operations adds another dimension of uncertainty to all intelligence estimates. Assuming rational behavior on the part of his opponent, the intelligence analyst can supposedly predict that a very risky operation, which may entail very high costs and uncertain benefits, will not be implemented. Conversely, he might assume that an operation involving low risks and high benefits will be selected. Although correct in theory, this premise is unreliable in practice. In the first place, that which is considered a high risk in one culture may be acceptable in another. The danger, therefore, is that the analyst's cultural values will be projected upon the adversary. In the summer of 1962, after US intelligence had received numerous reports that the Soviet Union was installing offensive missiles in Cuba, the National Security Council requested a National Intelligence Estimate (NIE) on the subject. 'In early fall 1962, the NIE was completed. The estimate stated that it was highly unlikely that the Soviet Union would pursue a policy of such high risk as the placement of offensive missiles in Cuba. The estimate was made on the assumption that such a course of action would be irrational (at least from the American intelligence community's frame of reference).' Second, what sometimes appears to be great risk for an adversary may actually be less hazardous as a result of developments unknown to the intelligence analyst.[21] Before the Yom Kippur War, Israeli intelligence overestimated the risks the Egyptians would face from the superior Israeli air force. (So, by the way, did the Egyptian planners. They anticipated some 10,000 casualties in the initial crossing of the Suez Canal. Actually, they suffered about 200 casualties. Overestimating the risks caused them to adopt, perhaps wisely, a very cautious strategic plan.) Certainly no rational Israeli planner would go to war against an enemy who maintained control of the skies. The Israelis were unaware that the Egyptians had reduced much of this threat from the air by building an extremely powerful anti-aircraft defense system consisting of anti-aircraft guns and surface-to-air missiles.[22] The intelligence analyst may also underrate the readiness of the enemy to take risks by assuming that his adversary knows as much as he does about his own strength. In 1941, the Russians may have felt confident that the Germans would not attack because of the extent of Russian strength. But they did not know that German intelligence had, in light of the Red Army's performance in Finland, grossly underestimated Russian strength by as much as 100 divisions on the eve of Barbarossa.[23] In this manner, excessive secrecy can undermine deterrence and lead to negatively reinforcing fallacious estimates. On such occasions, the attacker-to-be underestimates his victim's strength, while the victim, sure of his own position, is more likely to be taken by surprise.

The assessment of a specific risk is further complicated by the estimated impact of the strategic surprise itself. Although the Germans in 1941, the Japanese in 1941, and the Israelis in 1967 knew that their respective adversaries possessed greater capabilities, they calculated that a successful strategic surprise would be the force multiplier needed to redress this imbalance. This expectation thus lowered the anticipated risks for the attacker. In contrast, the defender frequently underestimates the impact that a surprise attack could have, and is, instead, confident that his retaliatory strength and capacity to respond would not be diminished by such an occurrence (e.g., the USSR in 1941, Israel in 1973).

In many instances, the stronger defender, who is interested in perpetuating a status quo that works in his favor, does not fully comprehend the potential attacker's desperate frame of mind. On the eve of Pearl Harbor, the United States was unaware of the degree to which Japanese military and political leaders felt cornered. These leaders were cognizant of the United States' superior war potential and knew that unless the United States was ready to accept Japanese terms after the initial campaign, Japan could not win in the long run. Nevertheless, the Japanese felt they had no choice but to attack. For similar reasons, in 1967 President Nasser of Egypt did not realize how desperate the Israelis felt, while in 1973, the Israelis failed to understand how the lack of progress on the diplomatic front since 1967 caused mounting frustration in the Arab world, culminating in the decision to resort to war regardless of the *military* consequences.

Estimating risks requires an intimate grasp of the adversary's culture and capabilities, his political and psychological frame of mind, and above all, what he knows and feels about the defender. Such detailed knowledge of one's opponent is rarely available, and even if obtained, it is easily distorted by many perceptual biases.

Finally, the paradoxical nature of the calculus of risk should be considered. Superficially, it is rational to assume that very high risk strategies, whose apparent chances of success are low, are normally unacceptable whereas lower risks would be readily taken. In reality, such assumptions may be less than rational: an attacker can calculate that because attacking at a certain place or time would involve high costs, his adversary would rationally conclude that the probability of his choosing this strategy is extremely low. Paradoxically then, opting for a high-risk strategy might be less foolhardy than is first assumed. This was intuitively understood by many of the great captains of war and is associated with some of the most decisive strategic and tactical victories throughout history. The invading Allies' choice of Normandy as their landing beach despite its lack of harbors and greater distance from their starting point than other possible landing sites (Pas de Calais); MacArthur's 5000-to-1 gamble at Inchon;

and Israel's attack on Egypt in 1967 and rescue operation in Entebbe in 1976 are but a few examples of maxi–max strategies that actually reduced the risks involved.

There is no *rational connection* between the degree of risk on the one hand and the choice of strategy on the other. The temptation to choose a high-risk–high-gain strategy is always present. Perhaps the only logical observation that can be made regarding this strategy, on the basis of historical evidence, is that, while it can prevail in the short run, it is bound to fail in the long run. Napoleon and Hitler are the best known practitioners of this approach.

In war . . . 'The idea that something "cannot be done" is one of the main aids to surprise . . . Experts tend to forget that most military problems are soluble provided one is willing to pay the price.'[24] But once someone is prepared to pay a high price, it may be added, his price is actually reduced. This leads to the following paradox: '*The greater the risk, the less likely it seems to be, and the less risky it actually becomes. Thus, the greater the risk, the smaller it becomes.*'[25]

5. Why Mobilization can be Self-defeating

The uncertain, politically sensitive nature of intelligence work is accentuated (perhaps more than in any other type of politico-military decision) by deliberations concerning whether or not to declare an alert or mobilization. This is the most critical policy recommendation an intelligence organization will ever have to make. If correct and timely, it may save many lives and significantly increase the chances of a vulnerable state's survival; if ill-timed, it can set off an uncontrollable chain of events, and possibly lead to war through miscalculation. In the long term, such a grave mistake can also have harmful repercussions upon the ability to make correct decisions in the future.

Every mobilization involves heavy political, material and psychological costs in addition to greatly increasing the danger of war. A status-quo-oriented country (such as the US and NATO, Israel in 1967 and 1973), which does not intend to go to war by its own initiative, will therefore try to avoid mobilizing except in the most extreme circumstances; at times, such a nation can bring even more harm upon itself by taking precautionary mobilization measures which eventually do not end in war. A single alert, let alone a series of alerts or a prolonged period of high alert which is not followed by war will have a decisively *negative* impact on future decisions. A series of false alarms will undermine the credibility of the intelligence organization (the so-called cry wolf syndrome); and by the time subsequent decisions on similar matters have to be made, prolonged periods of mobilization and the routinization of alerts will have brought about 'alert fatigue'[26] (i.e., condition the high command and troops to a state of alert and therefore progressively erode their readiness for action). A continual or 'permanent' state of alert can therefore be self-defeating.

The predicament of intelligence organizations is that many alarms which are deemed false in retrospect may have actually been justified. Although the cause for alarm is usually known, the defender's intelligence may find it much more difficult to produce a *timely* explanation (before the next crisis occurs) as to why the predicted attack failed to materialize. Three basic reasons for this can be set forth.

One. The enemy did not plan to attack in the first place. This is the outcome of an intelligence failure stemming from faulty information, an incorrect analysis, and/or a low threshold for mobilization (see ensuing discussion on worst-case analysis). In view of the normal reluctance to declare alerts or to mobilize, this type of faulty estimate is actually not very common. Of much greater interest and complexity are the remaining two explanations.

Two. The enemy had decided to attack, but canceled or delayed the D-Day at the last minute for reasons such as bad weather, unsuitable political conditions, dissatisfaction with the plan of attack or the military doctrine, or a high level of alert on the defender's side. The best-known example of this sequence of a planned attack, followed by a countermobilization and then the deferring of the attack, is Hitler's series of decisions to launch an offensive in the west: attacks were planned and then cancelled in November 1939 and January 1940, while the attack was finally carried out in May 1940. Before each of the planned offensives, a number of timely and, in retrospect, reliable warnings were received by British and French intelligence. Yet the Allies lost their confidence in some reliable sources of information (such as Colonel Oster of the Abwehr) because the predicted attacks did not take place. By 10 May, the day the Germans at last launched their offensive in the west, the Allies were completely surprised despite the multitude of warnings they had received but brushed aside.[27]

A failure in prediction does not necessarily mean that something is amiss with an intelligence service or the information it has gathered. On the contrary, a *correct* prediction can be based on faulty information or a flawed analysis. For example, on 25 September 1962, the US intelligence community agreed 'on balance' that the Soviet Union would *not* install missiles in Cuba which were capable of reaching the United States. 'The reason the intelligence community gave for its "on balance" conclusion that the Soviets would not place "offensive" missiles in Cuba was that according to its analytical framework, the Soviets were not prepared for this kind of confrontation . . . In the event the Soviets got their confrontation and found a way to withdraw the missiles . . . The intelligence community was wrong but for the right reasons: Khrushchev had miscalculated.' Referring to this, an American former senior intelligence officer said, '. . . While it is most blessed to be right, it is more blessed in our business to be wrong for the right reasons than it is to be right for the wrong reasons.[28] In other words, a very small number of even significant intelligence failures may not constitute proof that something is intrinsically wrong with an intelligence organization; only a higher incidence of repeated failures indicates that reform or reorganization might be required.

The rush to investigate the performance of intelligence organizations after each 'failure' may not only be unjustified, but also counterproductive. The absence of a direct correlation between the quality of intelligence and its actual results may be further illustrated by the fact that the more nearly 'perfect' the operation of an intelligence system, the greater the reliability which decisionmakers attribute to the information received. Therefore, an 'imperfect' intelligence system is the safest, since decisionmakers are more wary of the data distributed to them.[29] The saying that 'there is no failure like success' comes to mind. The continual success of an intelligence organization reduces the incentive for improvement, and thus aids in the concealment of less salient weaknesses. Failure or defeat, on the other hand, are catalysts for improvement. The unquestioned reputation of British intelligence during the First World War diminished British competitiveness between the two world wars, causing a decline which went unnoticed for some time. Accordingly, it can be suggested that *the greater the credibility of an intelligence agency over time, the less its conclusions are questioned, and the more serious the risk in the long run of overrelying on its findings.*[30]

Three. Even more difficult to cope with is a situation in which the enemy prepares for an attack, and the defender reacts by mobilizing upon receiving a timely warning. The would-be attacker may then be deterred after realizing that he can no longer reap the benefits of surprise. The prospective attacker might also fear that his secrets have been betrayed, giving the adversary precise knowledge of his plans. But even after such events have occurred, the defender's intelligence can be hard pressed to determine whether the predicted attack was deterred by his counter-mobilization (which would justify similar measures in the future), or whether there was no attack planned in the first place. This, for instance, was the dilemma faced by Israeli intelligence in the wake of a mobilization in May 1973 that was not followed by an attack. This is summarized by the paradox of the self-negating prophecy: *Information on a forthcoming enemy attack triggers a counter-mobilization, which, in turn, prompts the enemy to delay or cancel his plans. It is therefore extremely difficult – even in retrospect – to know whether or not the counter-mobilization was warranted.*[31]

The methodological problems discussed thus far have no perfect solutions. The intelligence expert is constantly searching for a better way to overcome the difficulties he faces. Other than acquiring more and better information in real time, this search involves three basic strategies. The first is to 'purge' the intelligence process (as much as possible) of human biases and perceptions, the second is a more costly approach in which the analyst takes all threats seriously and implements the necessary precautionary measures; and the third strategy, to be discussed later, calls for certain organizational reforms designed to improve the objectivity of the intelligence decision-making process by either reducing negative political influences or increasing the variety of participants and input involved in the process.

Indicators and Warnings

The most familiar methodological device neutralizing the effect of the human element on the analytical intelligence process is the development of a detailed list of Indicators and Warnings (I & W). In theory, this is a simple and elegant solution. 'Essentially, the purpose of the method [is] to help the warning analyst pick and choose the significant from the massive amounts of ambiguous and possibly conflicting data that would be abundantly available in crisis situations. To do this, the analyst need only ask three simple questions: is it *necessary* (i.e., mandatory rather than optional to *prepare* for an attack); is it *unambiguous* (i.e., a move one takes only to prepare for war rather than for other purposes as well); and can we *monitor* it (i.e., can we observe the indicator we seek).'[32] Warning indicators might include, for example, the cancellation of all leaves; large-scale simultaneous maneuvers by several bordering countries; the intensification of, or unusual reduction in, wireless communication; the departure of foreign military advisors; distribution of live ammunition among units; mobilization of reserve units; the opening of civilian and other shelters; the clearing of minefields and certain roads; and emptying large refineries of highly flammable materials.

Naturally, even a detailed set of warning indicators does not always speak for itself. If the changes occur slowly over a long period of time (acclimatization),[33] they may be overlooked. Experience has shown that political leaders and analysts, if their concepts exclude the possibility of an imminent war, will go out of their way to dismiss as harmless all of the warning signals (e.g., the adversary is mobilizing defensively because he fears an attack; or he is preparing for extensive maneuvers; there are *other*, contradictory signals; it's a game of nerves and bluffs intended to shore up his bargaining position). 'Even the best I & W scheme can only tell you whether and to what extent a government is prepared or preparing to act. It cannot tell you why or what its intentions are . . .'[34] Moreover, if the adversary knows which indicators a given observer considers to be warning signals, he can deliberately manipulate such indicators in order to deceive the observer.[35] Of all methodological devices intended to aid in the avoidance of strategic surprise, paying close attention to indicators and warnings appears to be the most promising.

In addition to simpler types of warning indicators, a number of other kinds of developments merit close observation. These include situations in which the adversary and/or the observer are frozen in a hopeless and unacceptable political deadlock which may encourage the resort to war (Japan in 1941; the Arabs in 1973; Argentina over the Falkland Islands in 1982). The conclusion of a military treaty between former enemies (e.g., the Ribbentrop–Molotov agreement in 1939; Egypt and Jordan in May 1967), as well as the appearance of new leaders, unusual domestic pressures, and unexplicable anomalies in an adversary's pattern of behavior are also developments that should not escape scrutiny.

Worst-case Analysis

A less elegant and more costly strategy essentially involves lowering the threshold for taking precautionary measures in response to emerging threats. This method may prove to be more attractive to the intelligence community. As a result of continuously monitoring the actual and potential threats posed by the enemy, and because of their professional socialization, intelligence (in particular senior) analysts are a cautious and pessimistic lot. The degree of pessimism and extreme caution is exacerbated by a major intelligence failure such as the inability to anticipate a strategic surprise. This is likely to result in the adoption of a 'worst-case' approach, which can be described as the attitude that it is most prudent to base one's assumptions and analysis on the worst that the other nation could do; to assume, when presented with ambiguous evidence, that a threat will be carried out, even if the weight of indicators to the contrary appears to be greater.[36] According to Ken Booth,

> the worst case is more easily definable than the probable case, and so provides a firmer basis for a policy prescription. Worst-case forecasting also frees individual analysts from blame if things go wrong. This is another reason why the tendency is always to think the worst. To base a policy on a less than worst-case forecast will turn out costly if the prediction is wrong. To underplay what turns out to be a real threat may bring defeat: but to overestimate, and perhaps provoke, a potential threat into an actual one, might only increase tension. In the past, when war was a less serious business, it nearly always made sense to defer to the alarmist. In the context of a nuclear confrontation, the balance of the argument should logically change. Risks should be taken for peace rather than war . . .[37]

The psychology behind the worst-case analysis is obvious, as is the play-it-safe, bureaucratic attitude, and at times the political desire for increased defense budgets or fear of failure. But the worst-case approach in its crude form may exact a heavy price.

1. It can be extremely expensive in terms of the cost of frequent mobilization and higher military expenditure.
2. It may bring antagonistic feelings to the boiling point, and prove to be a major destabilizing factor when both opponents adopt a worst-case approach. Under such conditions, one party might mobilize prematurely, which could prompt an identical move by the other, and then result in preemption and a war that no one wanted. (Reciprocal fear of surprise attack played an important role in the loss of control over mobilization and counter-mobilization before the First World War; the almost simultaneous German and British invasions of Norway; and the 1967 Six Day War.)[38]
3. In the event that this approach does not contribute to the loss of control or escalation, it may touch off many mobilizations and alerts that do not culminate in conflict, thus encouraging susceptibility to the 'cry wolf' syndrome and ultimately defeating its own purpose.
4. Frequent and facile resort to worst-case analysis can become an easy escape from analytical responsibility and reduce the quality of threat analysis.

Yet in spite of the social, material, and political costs of mobilization, it is advisable for more vulnerable states – those which are considerably weaker than their adversaries, lack strategic depth, or maintain only small armies – to lower somewhat their threshold for mobilization. The danger and costs entailed could be minimized by introducing a flexible, modular, multi-stage alert and mobilization system. If alerts and mobilizations occur repeatedly, care must be taken not to relax one's vigil. When survival is at stake, fewer risks should be taken. The high cost of false alarms is still lower than that of being caught unprepared.

Preconceptions, Ethnocentrism, and Misperception

> I'll believe it when I see it.
> I'll see it when I believe it.[39]

Given the urgent nature of much of intelligence work as well as the general process by which human learning takes place, all analysis must inevitably be based on preexisting concepts concerning, for example, the adversary's intentions or his capabilities and military doctrines. The concepts, belief systems, theories and images comprising the framework for the assimilation of new information can be old or new, detailed or sketchy, rigid or flexible, static or dynamic.[40] If a long-held concept has served well as a basis for interpretation and prediction and is rooted to the fundamental belief systems of a country, it is likely to be less open to adaptation stemming from new evidence. Therefore, the more successful a concept has proven to be as a tool for explanation and prediction, the less its fundamental premises will be questioned. But since few areas of human or political activity remain unchanged in antagonistic situations, its very success is eventually bound to be self-negating. If, however, a concept is not founded on any deep-rooted beliefs, and if it has had limited success as a basis for explanation and prediction, then it will be easier to change.

Each of these ideal types has its strong and weak points. A rigid concept provides continuity and a solid foundation from which to take action. The danger is that its adherents tend to ignore contradictory evidence; furthermore, the concept may become obsolete, thus endangering policies and strategies which are detached from reality. Commonly-held concepts that have resulted in the failure to avoid strategic surprise range from the belief in one's own power as an effective deterrent posture, and the idea that a war will be preceded, as in the past, by a crisis or ultimatum, to the conviction that without air or sea superiority certain actions are highly unlikely. Other concepts have held that Nazis and Communists would never have enough common interests to reach an agreement (believed by the British and French before the Ribbentrop–Molotov agreement); that no Arab leader would publicly negotiate an agreement, not to mention a peace treaty, with the Israelis (a concept accepted by all intelligence services);[41] and that the Soviet bloc was a monolithic state-system controlled from Moscow (a Western belief during the 1950s and early 1960s).

In contrast, open-ended ideas do not provide enough basis for action or longer planning, as continuous change can bring about confusion and paralysis. For this reason, the majority of erroneous concepts tend to emanate more from the rigid than from the flexible end of the scale.[42]

Generally speaking, perceptual errors are the result of either projecting one's own culture, ideological beliefs, military doctrine, and expectations on the adversary (i.e., seeing him as a mirror image of oneself) or of wishful thinking, that is, molding the facts to conform to one's hopes.

Psychological, cultural, and anthropological studies of perceptual errors have arrived at similar conclusions: human perceptions are ethnocentric. They see the external world inside out, which typically involves the projection of one's own belief systems, and by definition causes the underestimation, if not denigration, of the opponent's culture; motivations; intentions; material and technological achievements; and capacity to identify with others. According to Kenneth Booth, ethnocentric biases are, to a certain extent, unavoidable because they also serve a positive function as a defense mechanism in conflictual situations; if a group were to understand its adversary's motives and problems as well as its own, it might become demoralized.[43] Arising between different racial, religious, linguistic, economic and political groups, ethnocentric biases furnish powerful explanations for most strategic surprises. The Americans by and large believed that the Japanese (and the Vietnamese) were technologically inferior and lacking in determination in comparison to themselves; the Germans believed that the Russians or Slavs were racially inferior and from this extrapolated that they were also organizationally, technologically and motivationally inferior. In 1947–1948 and 1967, the Arabs viewed Israel as weak and demoralized only to discover the opposite; while, by 1973, the Israelis had begun to believe in their own superiority as a result of past victories. In each of these cases, subjective oversimplifications of reality led to the underestimation of the adversary's will to resist, which in turn was responsible either for a hasty decision to open or to become involved in a war, or for a war that could have been avoided had the costs and consequences been more realistically calculated.

Correction of ethnocentric biases is the obvious answer to this problem, but the various measures that can be taken to this end are complex and should not be regarded as pat solutions.[44] The most general suggestion is 'know thine enemy'. This stresses the need to intensify one's knowledge of the adversary's language, culture, political culture, ideology, and so on. Of course, this is always easier said than done, since even in the largest, most ethnically diverse society there are few who are intimately familiar (in the Weberian sense of 'Verstehen') with other cultures; moreover, such experts are not necessarily available for intelligence work. As it is self-evident, this point need not be elaborated upon here.

More original is the suggestion calling for intelligence organizations to spend more time studying their *own* culture and society in depth in order better to comprehend (a) how the adversary reacts to or perceives the observer; and (b) how one's own environment can bias the perception of another society. The need to know 'thyself', according to this approach, is as essential as knowing the enemy. In view of this country's experiences, it is not surprising that this proposal should come from an Israeli former senior intelligence analyst, Zvi Lanir.[45] After the Yom Kippur surprise attack in 1973, many Israeli intelligence analysts concluded that one of the principal causes of their misperception was the unconscious projection of Israeli society and its contentment with the status quo on their Arab neighbors.[46] This was largely based on an inflated sense of self-confidence coupled with a lack of self-criticism, all of which culminated in delusions of grandeur and wishful thinking. According to Lanir, 'the subject matter of the basic national intelligence research – as a necessary condition for its success – will include not only the study of the adversary, but also the study of oneself as related to the adversary. The recommendation is *not* to study primarily the daily tactical moves – but for a deeper understanding of [one's own country's] trends in policy and principles shaping the policy.'[47]

Although original and interesting, this proposal is, however, highly impractical for the following reasons. (a) Intelligence organizations often lack the resources necessary properly to analyze the adversary's intentions and capabilities, let alone to study their own society. (b) Whether intentional or not, the examination of one's own society and its politics will inevitably involve subjective political views and values, and thus contribute to the politicization of the intelligence community. Such studies are likely to alienate leaders (unless the observations made are very flattering) and therefore will become totally unacceptable from a political point of view. (c) It is unclear why it can be assumed that the perceptual distortions which lead to the misperception of other societies will suddenly disappear during the examination of one's own society. There is no reason to suppose that greater objectivity can be attained by those who study their own country.

Perceptual analytical distortions can be formed by either individuals or organizations. The perceptual errors of an individual can at times be critical, but the mistake of a low-ranking individual is more likely to be counter-balanced and corrected by others working on the same problem at various levels within the hierarchy. On the other hand, an individual at the top of the political or military hierarchy is not subject to such corrective procedures, which means that his errors in judgment are much less likely to be rectified. Therefore, individual decisions taken in the lower echelons can be examined most profitably in a bureaucratic, organizational context, while top-echelon decisions can be understood best in a psychological setting.

B. The Politics of Intelligence

In his seminal work, *The Soldier and the State*,[48] Professor Samuel P. Huntington develops two ideal types of interaction between the civilian government on the one hand, and the military professionals on the other. He refers to the first type of interaction, which is more normative and idealized, as 'objective control'. 'The essence of objective civilian control is the recognition of autonomous military professionalism.'[49] In this relationship the military stands ready to carry out the wishes of any civilian group, while the civilians allow the military to perform its duties or advise the government according to its best professional judgment. Here, a sharp distinction is made between the professional world of the military and the civilian world of politics. The two groups therefore are able to interact to their mutual benefit, and the military recognizes its duty to obey the government, yet each group preserves its functional independence, thereby permitting achievement of the highest possible level of national security. The pattern of objective civilian control is, however, virtually nonexistent in the real world of politics and competition.

The actual relationship between the military and the civilian government is more accurately described by Huntington's model of 'subjective control', which involves the maximization of civilian power in relation to the military; reduces the professional autonomy of the military; leads to civilian interference in professional military affairs; and politicizes the armed forces by employing the services of the military for narrow partisan interests. In the long run, a pattern of subjective control may reduce the likelihood of having the best possible national security.

We can consider the intelligence community either as part of the military establishment or as a discrete professional group whose relationship to the civilian could be considered close to one of Huntington's ideal types.

The relationship between the intelligence community and the civilian authority also requires a continuous search for a careful balance between the professional independence of the former and the authority of the latter. For the civilians in authority, the temptation to exploit the intelligence community's control over information for the furtherance of political interests may be even greater than any desire to control the military.[50]

Violation of the intelligence community's professional autonomy occurs not only for the sake of gaining access to critical information possessed by the intelligence community, but because it is an important stepping stone in facilitating subjective control of the military in general. Furthermore, the position of the intelligence community is rendered even more sensitive to outside interference by the desire of the *military* professionals to influence and control it in order to promote their special interests *vis-à-vis* those of the civilian authorities. The professional autonomy of the intelligence may thus be compromised, and is constantly challenged, from these two directions.

Intelligence–Leadership Relations

> Intelligence is the voice of conscience to a staff. Wishful thinking is the original sin of men of power.[51]

> The unresolvable tension between policy-making and intelligence rests in part on an unresolvable definitional problem. For no one agrees on what is policy and what is intelligence.[52]

The correct and timely analysis of the information acquired by intelligence organizations is only a necessary, but not sufficient, condition to guarantee the success of the intelligence community. One of the most critical phases in the entire cycle of intelligence work lies in convincing the military and political leadership to make the best use of the information and analysis supplied to them.

Much depends on whether leaders are open-minded and encourage criticism and accurate, though unpleasant, information. Leaders in a democratic system are generally more inclined to consider a wider variety of opinions than those who have always functioned within authoritarian or totalitarian political systems. In authoritarian countries, where the

climb to the top is an unrelenting struggle for power, habits of cooperation and openness are usually less developed. The prevalence of a rigid
influential doctrine, religious dogma, or ideology naturally restricts openness to variety, criticism, and the consideration of contradictory ideas.
Leaders in totalitarian countries ordinarily have little tolerance for ideas
that deviate from the 'party line', since they are seen as personal criticism
– a dangerous element undermining the existing ideology. Among other
reasons, this explains why the intelligence systems of the democracies, on
the whole, performed better than those of the totalitarian nations during
the Second World War.[53]

What has been said up to this point does not imply that relatively open-
minded people who are capable of cooperation cannot rise to the top in
totalitarian systems or that authoritarian-style, narrow-minded leaders
cannot emerge in democracies. Ultimately, the idiosyncracies and personality of each leader play a decisive role. From the vantage point of intelligence organizations and their capacity to cooperate with a leader, two
ideal types of leaders can be considered.

Leaders such as Hitler or Stalin could not tolerate information which
contradicted their own beliefs or policies. When such structures are
imposed, however, strategic intelligence is of very limited use. Hitler once
told Ribbentrop that 'when he had to make great decisions, he considered
himself the instrument of the providence which the Almighty had determined. He . . . [added] that before big decisions, he always had a feeling
of absolute certainty.'[54] Having no habits of cooperation and orderly
staff work, to put it mildly, Hitler insisted on imposing his ideas on
others. Early success in the face of the opposition of senior military commanders and foreign policy experts had convinced him that his intuition
was infallible. A look at the leaders and military assistants closest to
Hitler – men such as Jodl and Keitel in the OKW, and Ribbentrop,
Göring, and Goebbels – reveals that almost all of those with whom he
had any contact were sycophants. Ribbentrop and Göring (as well as
others in Hitler's coterie) carefully ensured that he received only the
reports that confirmed his beliefs and images. At no point, even after the
most serious defeats, did Hitler encourage another type of reporting.
Good intelligence existed but was circumspectly filtered. 'In light of
Hitler's preconceptions and distorted images, one must question the usefulness of foreign reporting even if it had been one hundred percent
correct.'[55] Although Hitler and possibly Stalin are extreme examples, the
danger involved in distorting information to suit a leader's policies exists
in every type of government and between all leaders and their lieutenants.
In Donald McLachlan's words, 'wishful thinking [is] that ever-lurking
temptation for politicians dealing with military affairs – and for serving
officers involved in politics . . .'[56]

Hitler made most of his important decisions without consulting anyone. (This was also true of Egypt's President Sadat.)[57] The members of his entourage often were as surprised as the victims of his moves were, particularly during the period of diplomatic surprises in the 1930s which, unlike his subsequent military surprises, required no material preparations. Such decisions, generally made on the spur of the moment, are very difficult to anticipate. Intelligence agencies are oftentimes called upon to issue warnings *before* the adversary's leader has made up his own mind. The psychoanalytical study of leaders is beset by uncertainty and speculation. '. . . If our own predictions are based on a "rational" move it is because we know that irrationality can lead to deviant behavior in *any direction* and is inherently unpredictable and that irrational behavior is, in the end, the admission of failure equally for he who commits and he who predicts.'[58] This observation is an exaggeration: irrational or deviant behavior is not random, and in fact normally follows a regular pattern (e.g., Hitler, DeGaulle, Sadat and their frequent use of surprise or their identification with the state and tendency to take high risks; Begin's legalistic mind; Chamberlain's 'rationality' and aversion to taking any risks). It can be difficult to make day-to-day predictions of an irrational leader's behavior, but in time a general pattern of behavior will gradually emerge, thereby helping the observer to gauge some of the leader's reactions and readiness to take risks, if not to make more precise forecasts.[59]

An 'atomistic' style of leadership reaches more severe proportions when accompanied by dogmatic adherence to an ideology (especially if the ideology is irrational). Hitler dismissed intelligence reports on American or Soviet behavior as an overestimation of Jewish, Bolshevik-Slav, or plutocratic groups that were racially or politically inferior and therefore could not be as motivated or efficient as German Aryans.[60] Similarly, Stalin's adherence to Communist ideology, which viewed the world in zero-sum-game terms, led him to believe that any British or Western intelligence supplied to him could not be genuine (reports concerning, for instance, a German plan to attack in 1941); Stalin refused to believe that delays in opening the second front in Europe stemmed from *real* difficulties and not from anti-Soviet sentiments.[61]

Although encouraging a modicum of inter-organizational competition can be beneficial, Hitler's proclivity for pursuing a divide-and-rule policy was counterproductive in its politicization of German intelligence. An intelligence organization desiring recognition from the Führer had to furnish him with the information that he wanted to hear. The dynamics of this competition encouraged a rapid deterioration in the quality of German intelligence and fostered mistrust between the various agencies.

In contrast, the *relative* openness of Roosevelt, Churchill, or Truman to intelligence reports seems to have yielded better results. From his early days at the Admiralty in the First World War, to his daily use of Enigma intercepts during the Second World War, Churchill certainly paid careful attention to intelligence reports.[62] His work habits have been described in this somewhat idealized way:

> We see Churchill following up daily on the performance of his subordinates. We see him emphasizing the importance of science and technology in the development of new weapons. We note his skills in using information acquired through the interception and decoding of German communications, and his success in keeping the knowledge of that decoding a secret. We note how effective was Churchill's insistence on transmitting instructions in writing, on keeping orderly track of every decision and on tracing the progress of decision to action. Such habits make for efficient administration . . .[63]

Yet, unlike Hitler, '. . . he displayed constant interest in the latest information about the enemy . . . He made it a matter of principle that he should be supplied with such intelligence "raw" – that is not in the doctored pieces of staff assessment but as it had come to hand. Thus he felt, often with good reason, that in his central position he was exceptionally equipped for keeping himself "in the know". All that was romantic in him, moreover, thrilled with excitement of intercepted signals, Delphic reports from the agents, the broken codes, the sense of participation. This knowledge is essential if one is to understand his decisions, and at the lower level his impatience with his commanders.'[64] His insatiable appetite for raw intelligence tempted Churchill too often to become his own intelligence officer – a dangerous practice which no head of state should take upon himself.[65]

On the negative side, Churchill did not hesitate to interfere in the direction of military operations against the better professional opinion of his military advisers.

In the words of Major Sir Desmond Morton, Churchill '. . . was a *politician* who wanted to be a soldier'.[66] And, while he interfered too much in military operations, he never committed Hitler's error of assuming direct command of an army in action. Although Churchill did not always feel comfortable among colleagues with superior intellects, unlike Hitler 'his chiefs of staff were professionals of exceptional calibre. None were puny or pusillanimous . . . Pound . . . Dill . . . Alanbrooke, Portal and Cunningham . . . They were a different team from Hitler's entourage – the subservient lackeys, Keitel, Halder, Jodl, Zeitzler and the transient subordinates, their opinions disregarded, uncertain of their tenure, their very lives dependent on a master's whim.'[67]

When critical issues were at stake, Churchill's military advisors did not hesitate to argue with him. In such cases, if they were persuasive and persistent enough, their opinions prevailed[68] (e.g., Dowding's insistence against Churchill's judgment that no more Hurricane fighters should be sent to France in a Cabinet meeting on 15 May 1940). 'Churchill's disqualifications

as a warlord were manifold – disqualifications both intellectual and tem-
peramental . . . he succeeded in spite of them. Hitler's defects of character
were of fundamental significance: Churchill's peripheral.'[69]

In reality, Churchill's handling of intelligence was far more complicated than is commonly realized. As an intelligence consumer Churchill
stands somewhere in between the cooperative and non-cooperative type of
leader. On the one hand, he appreciated the importance of intelligence
work more than any other leader during the Second World War and made
an immense contribution to its development; on the other, he did not hesitate to ignore it when it did not suit his strategy and too often tended to
become his own intelligence officer. Though authoritarian in his attitudes
toward his subordinates and advisers, he nevertheless assembled an outstanding group of professional advisers whose counsel he continuously
sought during the war. Despite the many mistakes he committed which
could have been avoided by more closely heeding his intelligence advisers,
his overall record as an intelligence consumer was impressive. For him,
more than for any other leader in modern times, strategic intelligence was
the key to victory.

Beyond the problem of a leader's psychological profile, there are other,
more general political behavioral patterns that can influence his attitude
toward intelligence. For example, once a leader has invested substantial
energy in promoting a particular policy direction – especially when his
prestige is on the line or he has acted against the advice of his aides – he
will be that much more reluctant to admit defeat even when presented
with contradictory evidence. Under such circumstances, the most attractive course of action may be to ignore contradictory data and insist that
subordinates supply him with the 'right' information.[70] The greatest
danger is present at the stage in which the leader supplants serious
deliberation with wishful thinking. Chamberlain and the advocates of
appeasement policies long resisted the overwhelming evidence that their
policies actually encouraged Hitler's aggressiveness and appetite. Leaders
in democratic systems are particularly vulnerable to such wishful thinking before elections.

There is no perfect remedy for the problems discussed in this section.
Whether operating within an authoritarian or democratic political system,
the intelligence community normally can do very little to encourage the
leader to develop a more cooperative and receptive attitude toward intelligence work. Two suggestions can be made in this context: one is that
more time be devoted to the 'education' of leaders on this subject before
they rise to power. Obviously, this would not be easy, and it is often too
much to expect to change the working habits of leaders. The second suggestion is directed primarily at the intelligence community. It concerns
making the operation of this organization more effective by gearing its
presentation, arguments, and showmanship to the specific character of the

leader.[71] Learning how to work with a leader may be a lengthy task that raises some ethical questions and cannot always achieve the desired results.

Intelligence Advisers and Leaders

So far we have discussed the critical impact of the individual leader on the intelligence process. Each leader, however, is always influenced by his close advisers, whose interaction with him is of decisive importance. The effectiveness of this relationship will therefore also be influenced by the character of the head (or heads) of the intelligence community. Is there a positive or negative chemistry between them? Do they complement or contradict each other in temperament, character or ambition? Can they cooperate with and respect each other? Do they share a common ideology and/or a common social or professional experience?

To answer those questions we must also know something about the intelligence adviser. Is he a man of absolute integrity to whom ambition is secondary to service? Does he put his objectivity and professional judgment above all else or is he primarily interested in maintaining the confidence or friendship of the leader as a means of gaining influence? Did he become a leader in the intelligence community because of his political connections and views, or because of his professional achievements and experience? Is he prepared to resign if his professional views are either ignored or consistently not accepted?

The number of possible combinations between the character of the leader and that of his intelligence adviser(s) is very large indeed. Some of the better-known examples include: President Kennedy and McCone; President Johnson and Rostow; Presidents Johnson and Nixon, and Helms; Churchill and Godfrey; Hitler and his advisers. Though Churchill probably found Godfrey stubborn and argumentative, his relationship with Menzies, head of the SIS, was excellent. Menzies, who assumed control of the SIS at a low point in its influence when its very survival was in question, made every effort to cultivate the best possible working relations with the Prime Minister; Churchill was provided with daily Ultra intercepts which always included some spicy titbits to be used as 'ammunition' in his arguments or conversations with other senior advisers. In this manner, Menzies was gradually able to inspire the Prime Minister's confidence in SIS and consolidate its position.[72]

Another perhaps less well-known twosome was that of Defense Minister Dayan and head of Israeli Military Intelligence, Eli Zeira. In this case, it has been argued that since both of them had been combat commanders and were 'heroic types' they suffered from similar perceptual defects; the fact that they reinforced each other's views may have been a major cause of the failure to take seriously the numerous warnings preceding the surprise attack of the Yom Kippur War.[73]

The above discussion leads to a number of observations.

First of all, a high degree of rapport between the leader of a state and his intelligence advisers is of the greatest importance – for without a good relationship, the effectiveness of the intelligence community will diminish considerably, regardless of how good the quality of its work is.

Second, having political finesse, tact, salesmanship and other related qualities is of critical importance for the leaders of the intelligence community. Unfortunately, however, the professional analyst, educated to prefer truth to tact and objectivity to political influence, may often lack the necessary qualities. It would therefore be difficult to find a head of intelligence who is both a first-rate intelligence expert and an intuitive politician. In fact, the qualities which a highly qualified intelligence expert must possess stand in contradistinction to those required to achieve political influence. Political qualifications, in the above-mentioned sense, are therefore a necessary if not a sufficient condition for an intelligence adviser. In addition to his political skills, he should preferably have the professional experience necessary to understand the problems and intricacies of the intelligence profession.

Third. Experience has shown that leaders tend to choose Directors of Intelligence who share their political views, if not other common traits of character (e.g. Carter–Sorenson, Carter–Turner, Reagan–Casey, Dayan–Zeira). The danger of this natural tendency is that the intelligence adviser is less likely to challenge the views of the leader or come up with a fresh, alternative way of viewing a situation. In the end, better cooperation is achieved at the expense of the quality of intelligence estimates.

Fourth. While there is no doubt that better intelligence estimates with a wider spectrum of views will be considered if the political leader and his intelligence adviser have different or even contradictory views, it is also clear that their relationship is bound to deteriorate sooner or later. The result is that the leader will tend to ignore the intelligence estimates presented by an adviser he does not or cannot cooperate with, and the product of the specific intelligence organization he represents will be lost. Usually, the intelligence adviser will notice that he is being ignored and is making increasingly smaller (if any) contributions to the decision-making process.

This tension between the capacity for cooperation between political leaders and their intelligence advisers on the one hand – and the need to present objective if objectionable estimates on the other – has no simple solution in the real world of the politics of intelligence. The ideal, of course, would be to have a secure and open-minded leader seeking the advice of an intelligence expert with political finesse, who knows his leader's wishes and policies but who has enough courage and skill to give him the most realistic estimates possible. In the real world, the combination of a dogmatic, stubborn leader who prefers to indulge in wishful thinking and an 'intelligence waiter' prepared to serve up the most expedient intelligence palliative is probably more likely to occur.

Political and other biases can also be introduced into the professional intelligence community from below, as will be explained in the ensuing discussion of the organizational and bureaucratic elements underlying strategic surprise.

C. Organizational and Bureaucratic Explanations

Complex systems are simply not responsive to warnings of unimaginable or highly unlikely accidents. Because they are complex, organizational routines must be carefully followed and off-standard events reinterpreted in routine frameworks.[74]

Much of an intelligence organization's professional integrity depends upon the degree to which freedom of expression and criticism are encouraged, whether the system of military and civil administration is based on merit, whether corruption and favoritism are common, the quality of the educational system, and the history of military involvement in political matters. Of course, the control of information and the possibility of manipulating it ('massaging information') to promote the intelligence community's political influence or beliefs is an ever present danger which gives rise to some serious ethical questions. (Were British intelligence analysts during the late 1930s justified in privately supplying Churchill with information he could use against the Government's appeasement policies? Was Colonel Oster of the German Abwehr morally correct when he notified Allied intelligence of Hitler's plans to attack Norway and the west? Should the CIA have leaked to the public some of the conclusions reached during the Vietnam War regarding its futility?) Despite the powerful temptation, intelligence analysts ought to resist direct involvement in policymaking when, for example, after a briefing, they are asked by senior politicians, 'OK, that's your analysis. What would you do about it?' The temptation can be overpowering for the intelligence officer, but his reply should be 'Sorry, sir, that's your business,' even though he might have a pretty clear idea of what to do.[75] This is the point at which many a good intelligence officer has committed himself actively to one policy or another, with the result that his objectivity and judgment were severely impaired.

The purely 'rational' or 'professional' behavior of any organization is modified by many factors such as parochial views, organizational interests and survival, the need for cohesion, and *esprit de corps*.[76] The neutral intelligence process, unencumbered by such complications, is a theoretical ideal which cannot be found in practice.

Military Patterns of Thought and Intelligence Analysis

Most intelligence organizations are either part of a larger military organization or include many members with military backgrounds. This unavoidably imbues intelligence organizations with a perspective that emphasizes such elements as military motives, capabilities, hierarchy, discipline and worst-case analysis. These traits are not always the most suitable for intelligence work, which deals as much with political as with military affairs, and in which 'freedom' of research and expression may be more important than rank and position.

The primacy of politics in strategic affairs can, as a result of the military perspective, be ignored in a more subtle way. Clausewitz's dictum that war must serve a political purpose is by now a cliché. Yet the extent of this logic merits further thought. Rational Western political and military leaders naturally assumed that war could be a political instrument *only* if, as Clausewitz said, we can compel our adversary to do our will, that is, defeat him on the battlefield. In Western tradition, it is usually (and often correctly) assumed that if it were impossible to win a war, starting one would be counterproductive and irrational. For the Chinese, the Vietnamese and the Arabs, for example, the Clausewitzian primacy of politics has been taken one step farther; in other words, it makes sense to resort to war even if victory is impossible, as long as one can win *politically*. This crucial point was repeatedly missed by Western analysts and policymakers in their experiences in Indochina, Algeria, and the Middle East. In 1973, Israeli intelligence, believing from its own experience that a military defeat was also, by definition, a political defeat and a direct threat to survival, did not understand that Egypt and Syria would even contemplate initiating a war with the full knowledge that they could not win militarily, but that they could triumph politically. Western rationality, national experience, and a military view of strategy caused Israeli intelligence to underestimate a weaker adversary's intention to resort to war. (This is another demonstration of the methodological difficulties hindering the rational assessment of risk across different cultures.)

It is therefore crucial to devote more attention to the corroboration and integration of military and political intelligence, especially at the highest levels of analysis. Focusing primarily on one or the other may give rise to serious analytical distortions, as evaluation of military situations cannot be made in a political vacuum, and vice versa. It is not desirable, then, that a preponderance of intelligence activity be controlled by the military, as was the case in Israel before 1973. This conclusion, though seemingly straightforward, has not been borne in mind by those who stand to profit from it the most. The majority of cases of strategic surprise evince a prior lack of coordination between political-diplomatic and military activities on the part of the victim, and grave errors in judgment are clearly shown to be biased in one direction. Observed military warning signals are completely dismissed or underestimated because of the absence of corresponding political-diplomatic activity. The attacker takes care to maintain a facade of routine diplomacy, lulling diplomats of the intended victim into suppressing the military warning signals through optimistic political interpretations. States planning an attack no longer present their victims with ultimatums or declarations of war, nor do they initiate hostile diplomatic campaigns. Contemporary conflicts are often begun against a quiet diplomatic-political backdrop. This leads to the paradox of *the sounds of silence. A quiescent international environment can act as background noise which, by conditioning observers to a peaceful routine, actually covers preparations for war.*[77] All meaningful changes in military warning signals should trigger an intensified probe into an apparently calm diplomatic-political environment. The reverse situation can be equally volatile; this occurs when an intensive diplomatic dialogue is deadlocked or abruptly terminated, yet is *not* accompanied by the observation of unusual military activity (e.g., the United States before Pearl Habor, Egypt prior to the Suez and Sinai Campaigns).

Another example of the damage that can result from the treatment of an intelligence problem as a purely military one concerns the head of Israeli military intelligence in 1973 – Eli Zeira – who felt that as a military officer, he should give the government an unequivocal yes or no reply regarding the likelihood of an Arab attack. Although the probability of war may have been 45 per cent 'yes' and 55 per cent 'no', he decided to take the responsibility and give the government a definite 'no' as his answer. A commander on the battlefield may indeed have no choice but to take clearcut action: an intelligence officer, however, must make his doubts known and let political and military leaders draw their own conclusions.[78]

Organizational Parochialism, Compartmentalization and Excessive Secrecy

The analytical quality and objectivity of intelligence is also distorted by parochial views arising out of the specialized functions of an organization. Of course, a naval or air force intelligence agency will have a narrower focus of attention than one that covers a broader area, such as the CIA. But even less specialized intelligence agencies often find it necessary to set an order of priorities. Specialization can produce a better analysis of specific problems, but this may also hamper the formation of a more general outlook and increases the difficulty of coordination within and between intelligence organizations. Such tradeoffs are, however, inevitable.

Before the Second World War, British naval intelligence focused on assessing German naval preparations for war. Far weaker than that of the British, the German navy was unprepared for war in 1939. From the vantage point of British naval intelligence, therefore, Germany was unlikely to launch a war because of the high risk involved. Considering Hitler's political intentions and the fact that Germany was a primarily continental power, Nazi intentions to go to war should not have been gauged by a naval estimate. '. . . The Admiralty remained untroubled by German activity in every other sphere – foreign policy, internal policy, the economy, the air force, and the army. Naval intelligence drew from too narrow a field of information conclusions which were too broad, if eminently rational.'[79]

It is worthwhile quoting at some length Basil Collier's analysis of the failure of British intelligence to warn of the German attack in Norway, as it was brought about by similar departmental biases or preconceptions.

> Each of the departments concerned had its own opinions about these questions, and inevitably these opinions coloured their attitudes to reports and predictions received from the intelligence agencies and from diplomatic sources. The Foreign Office was anxious that Britain should not imperil her relations with a friendly neutral power by putting troops ashore in Norway without at least the tacit consent of the Norwegian government. At the same time, it was not in a position to rebut the argument that Allied intervention was strategically desirable and that consequently any German move which gave the Allies good reason to intervene would be beneficial to the Allied cause. It tended, therefore, to view forecasts of imminent German intervention in Norway with scepticism because they seemed too good to be true. The War Office admitted that reports that the Germans were preparing for a seaborne expedition might have some substance, but it could trace only six divisions – about the normal peacetime strength – in the area in which troops were said to be assembling. This was the number of divisions eventually used by the Germans in Norway, but it was less than a quarter of the number the War Office thought they would need to tackle the Norwegians and the Swedes. Moreover, Military Intelligence could not exclude the possibility that the troops were intended not for an invasion of Norway but for some other purpose, such as a series of seaborne raids on the United Kingdom. The Admiralty was troubled by the fear that German surface raiders might break into the Atlantic, as had happened at the beginning of the war. It was determined, therefore, not to commit the Home Fleet to a wild goose chase on the strength of rumours. It was all the more disposed to assign reports about German intentions towards Norway to that category because the First Lord, Winston Churchill, believed that invasion of Norway was beyond Germany's powers. The Air Ministry was in some respects less sceptical about such reports than the other service departments. Even so, it tended to interpret them in the light of its

preoccupations with the danger of a major air offensive against the United Kingdom.

Examination of the evidence by a body of experts not wedded to the preconceptions of any particular department could scarcely have failed to lead to the conclusion that the second and third interpretations were too far-fetched to be accepted . . . But the evidence was not examined by independent experts. The Joint Intelligence Committee was not yet an effective body. It provided intermittent contact between Directors of Intelligence or their deputies, and between them and the Foreign Office; there was little or no contact between departments at the level at which reports were scrutinized by specialists. Inevitably, interpretations put upon reports by naval, army, or air intelligence officers were influenced to some extent by opinions current in the higher echelons of the departments they served. Also, there was a good deal of fragmentation within departments. Military intelligence officers concerned with Scandinavian affairs did not receive reports about events in Germany. In the Admiralty, the section of Naval Intelligence Division concerned with Scandinavian affairs did receive such reports, but some reports from MI6 or diplomatic sources were withheld from the Operational Intelligence Centre, which dealt with movements of German shipping and other day-to-day events. In both cases, provision was made for contributions from different sections to be co-ordinated at a higher level or by a section to which the task was delegated. But these arrangements did not work very well, because the co-ordinators lacked the detailed background knowledge needed to grasp the connections between two or more apparently unrelated sets of facts.[80]

Although the coordination between different intelligence organizations is crucial, it introduces a number of inevitable biases into the final intelligence product. Much depends on the number of organizations participating in the process, their character and above all their relative strength. The search for consensus may reduce the objective quality to truth of estimates in the sense that truth becomes a vector of the relative power and influence of each of the participating organizations – rather than the best and most professional judgment. Even the process of reaching a consensus may turn into a goal itself, often leaving intelligence estimates to smother different judgments with bland compromise. Hughes has, however, suggested that:

Unfortunately the drive for . . . consistency has become a felt necessity . . . Estimators now give it more than its due. In part the problem is a function of over-institutionalization in the intelligence community . . . the more coordination, probably, the more consistency.

But inconsistency is a virtue which should by no means be avoided at all costs. Consistency, after all, is not a goal of intelligence. There is little virtue in self-consciously adhering to a particular line of interpretation simply because a prior estimate on the subject took that line. Just because it was said last time is no reason to say it again. The intelligence community is not the Supreme Court. It need not strain over precedents or labor to extend the meaning of sanctified words. On the contrary, intelligence is supposed to provide current unimpeded judgments. As a vehicle for ventilating a variety of view-points, the intelligence process should be highly suspicious of con-sensus . . . The freedom to be inconsistent is a major argument bolstering the independence of the intelligence community.[81]

R.V. Jones has also some sharp comments on the consensus-seeking approach to intelligence work:

A single head in Intelligence is far better than a committee, however excellent the individual members of the committee may be. A com-mittee wastes too much time in arguing, and every action it under-takes merely goes as far as common agreement and compromise will allow. Common agreement and compromise, as every commander knows, generally do not go far enough. The head of an intelligence organization is really in the position of a commander planning a per-petual attack on the security of foreign powers, and he must be allowed all the privileges of a commander.[82]

A byproduct of the consensus-seeking process is not only the intro-duction of additional biases and the slowness of the process, but also its lack of clarity as a basis for action. McLachlan suggests that had there been no need to reconcile the views of five intelligence departments, the forecasts and reports of enemy strategy and intentions would have been worded in a 'firmer' way.[83]

Despite the aforementioned problems and imperfections of the coor-dination process, it must be kept in mind that coordination is absolutely essential for the production of high-quality intelligence estimates. In those countries in which the coordination between the different intelligence organizations was at times weak (such as in the US before Pearl Harbor) or never successfully achieved (such as in Germany or in Italy), the results were disastrous for the production of strategic intelligence.

Better coordination might correct somewhat the parochial biases of different intelligence organizations, but there is no perfect solution to the problem. Complicated and time-consuming, the coordination process itself can spur on competition for influence as well as a search for an acceptable compromise.[84]

Although each organization aspires to monopolistic control over its area of responsibility, *some* inter-organizational competition can be constructive. There are certainly considerable dangers in relegating all intelligence work to one agency. The need for diversity in intelligence estimates in order to provide leaders with a wider choice of interpretations is obvious, but there is also a price to be paid for competition. More organizations demand more resources, they duplicate efforts, and require coordination; like all other types of organizations, those in intelligence will fight for greater influence and larger budgets. Furthermore, the larger the number of organizations participating in the process, the longer the amount of *time* required for the process to take place. Under conditions of crisis or war, in which time and quick reactions are critical, the process of coordination will become sluggish and insufficiently responsive to the needs of decisionmakers in direct proportion to the number of participants.

The drawback of such competition is that it can encourage the politicization of the working process if the protection and expansion of parochial interests is enhanced by supplying the executive leader with the 'right' intelligence. These distortions are amplified if the executive or military leadership practices a policy of divide and rule. Since intelligence organizations do not function in a political vacuum, the biases occasioned by inter-agency competition are unavoidable; nevertheless, they should be minimized. The degree of objectivity achieved therefore depends largely upon the character of the leaders in the political, executive and military arenas, as well as upon the integrity of those responsible for the intelligence community. It is the political culture in the wider sense (e.g., freedom of expression, tolerance of different opinions, respect for professional skills, respect for the law), which makes the difference.

Finally, the need for coordination and the development of a political modus operandi *between* organizations also exists *within* each of them. It has been observed that individuals within groups feel compelled to develop a consensus, the maintenance of which may become a goal in its own right. 'Groupthink', like most of the aforementioned pathologies in organizational (and intelligence) work, can also fulfill positive functions. Individuals working together often share a similar educational and career background and common interests that need to be defended *vis-à-vis* other organizations. Moreover, any group that must achieve a common goal and implement a policy must also be able to arrive at an operational consensus that permits its members to work on a routine basis. No group can ever hope to implement the ideas of each of its members at the same time. Any collective action hence necessitates a political-social search for consensus.

The key question is, however, how was the group consensus arrived at? Was it reached through an open discussion based on the presentation of opposing opinions; was it enforced by a single person who discouraged debate; or was it brought about by submission to group pressure to conform? Agreement for its own sake will only prematurely stifle the expression of diverse, potentially valuable, opinions. The pitfalls of group-think as demonstrated by Janis of course exist in the intelligence evalua-tion process, in particular when under the strain of crisis conditions. Groupthink may have been one cause for the adoption of unrealistic images and concepts by US intelligence before Pearl Harbor and the Bay of Pigs fiasco, and during the war in Vietnam.[85]

Excessive secrecy in the handling of information poses a related problem. Perhaps the most obvious symptom of this approach is the exag-gerated compartmentalization that exists within and among intelligence organizations as well as between the intelligence community and other military or civilian agencies. Consequently, one organization often is not privy to the information held by another, an arrangement which may bring about failure to act, the duplication of efforts, or the inadvertent interfer-ence of one agency in the operations of another. Recent examples of such costly miscalculations are the Bay of Pigs operation and the ill-fated attempt to rescue the American hostages in Iran.

The overall vice of excessive secrecy may leave actors unaware of the pressing need to coordinate actions, or even of *which* new issues require coordination. Furthermore, valuable information may not be used to the fullest possible extent. Particularly in times of crisis, information should be passed more readily to lower and parallel echelons, for in all failures to antic-ipate sudden attacks, much data were misinterpreted or improperly corrob-orated with other information. In addition, information and the exchange of opinions should flow both upward and downward in the intelligence hier-archy and between it and its political counterpart, while better coordination between tactical intelligence and its headquarters must be ensured.[86]

Donald McLachlan had observed that 'Intelligence is indivisible. In its wartime practice, the divisions imposed by separate services and depart-ments broke down.'[87] The process of breaking down these artificial barri-ers may, however, take a prolonged time in the natural course of events, and should therefore be deliberately practiced to a greater extent in peacetime.

Some degree of tension will always exist between the desire to protect intelligence sources and the need to make the best and most profitable use of information. There is no formula by which to calculate the potential costs and benefits or missed opportunities in such circumstances. Almost miraculously, the Allies managed to protect the secret of 'Ultra' from the Germans, and in fact from the world, until the early 1970s. Yet, the deci-sion to attribute 'Ultra' information to spies or special operations in many cases discredited the information in the eyes of some senior field com-manders, who were not informed of the *actual* source. A wider distribu-tion of Ultra may have improved performance on the battlefield, reducing the number of opportunities missed. Nevertheless, Ultra and the double-cross system are unique events in the history of intelligence and may confuse the issues involved. It seems that in general, though, intelligence organizations tend to err in the direction of excessive caution and under-utilization of information. This may be an innate professional bias – yet information that is not used is ineffective and has repercussions beyond the mere wasting of the collection effort.[88]

The (Elusive) Quest for Effecting Organizational Reforms

Every major intelligence failure, especially if a traumatic error involving strategic surprise, is followed by a reexamination of the organizational structure of the intelligence community (or agency), including a detailed review of the decision-making process of each organization and its rela-tionship to others. A serious and earnest attempt is made to introduce reforms that will once and for all improve the performance of the intelli-gence/policy-making communities and provide better warning of the approach of the next crisis. These structural reforms are chiefly directed at developing inter- and intra-organizational mechanisms to improve the analytical objectivity of the intelligence process, as well as to reduce the negative consequences of inter-organizational politics and competition, or the negative political interference of either the political elite or that of senior military and intelligence professionals. In the final analysis, all of the newly introduced mechanisms are designed to encourage greater objec-tivity by increasing the variety of inputs (i.e., different and competing opin-ions of diverse individuals and organizations into the intelligence process).

The simplest way to attempt to achieve this goal is by increasing the number of participating organizations. As mentioned earlier, this creates new difficulties in coordination and cooperation and steps up political com-petition over scarce resources and for influence between the various agen-cies.[89] Another approach to improvement of the decision-making process starts *within* each organization. The two types of reform will usually be carried out simultaneously, and generally complement each other. In each case, an attempt is made to neutralize inter- and intra-organizational polit-ical competition, 'equalize' the roles and influence of the participants by providing each the opportunity to express his views without fear of suffering any negative consequences.

Since no two (or more) organizations are ever equal – in their functions, performance, *esprit de corps*, or leadership – they are never equal in influence. Furthermore, the creation of new organizations does not always achieve the desired outcome, since they often lack the vital support of a power base. (After the Yom Kippur War, the Agranat Commission in Israel recommended the establishment, in fact re-introduction, of the Israeli Foreign Ministry's intelligence unit. Unable to compete with the far more powerful position and resources of the Israeli military intelligence and the Mossad, this organization remains unimportant in the intelligence process in Israel.) On the positive side, new organizations can be provided with an extra amount of resources and powerful leadership in order to secure their productive survival.

While some of the reforms eventually succeed (e.g., the reform of the US intelligence community after the Second World War), many are difficult to put into practice and, while implemented *de jure*, cannot always take hold in a *de facto* sense. In any event, as has been observed by Richard Betts, most of these reforms involve some kind of trade-off, so none can be expected to solve completely the problem of avoiding strategic surprise.

Having warned the reader against putting too much hope in any reforms, we will proceed to discuss mechanisms designed to improve the objectivity and variety of input into the intelligence process. The first, multiple advocacy, is *primarily* intended to ensure each organization an equal opportunity to influence the intelligence decision-making process. The second, the Devil's Advocate, is supposed to guarantee diversity within each agency.

Multiple Advocacy[90]

Multiple advocacy entails the deliberate establishment of several independent intelligence agencies in order to foster increased competition and greater analytical variety, thereby affording policymakers access to a wider spectrum of views. Ideally, 'redundancy inhibits consensus, impedes the herd instinct in the decision process, and thus reduces the likelihood of failure due to unchallenged premises or cognitive errors'.[91] Yet multiple advocacy is more than the encouragement of free market competition. It requires strong, alert management if the competition is to have constructive direction and centralized coordination. For this system to function properly, three major conditions must be fulfilled. *One*, there should be an equal distribution of all types of intellectual, bureaucratic, and other assets (e.g., experts, adequate information, analytical support, equal political influence with the top executive, and equal bargaining skills). Alexander George emphasizes the need for a balanced distribution of assets and influence among the participants. 'The mere existence within the policy-making system of actors holding different points of view will not guarantee adequate multi-sided examination of a policy issue.'[92] *Two*, it requires the active participation of the top executive in monitoring and regulating the process. *Three*, time is required for adequate debate and give-and-take. Other requirements include the establishment of a special custodian-manager assistant to the top executive, if his own participation in the process is limited. The assistant would be expected to balance actor resources; introduce new advisors to argue for unpopular views; search for new channels of information or avoid dependence on a single channel of information; arrange for the independent evaluation of decisional premises when necessary; monitor the process and introduce appropriate corrective action. The process can be further strengthened by introducing 'adversary proceedings'; that is, a requirement that intelligence reports or policy recommendations 'run the gauntlet' of critical scrutiny by analysts other than those who produced them (or even by competing organizations).[93]

While the absence of competition and variety in intelligence is a recipe for failure, the institution of a multiple advocacy system does not guarantee success. To begin with, not every leader will possess the qualities needed for direct participation in the management of this type of system. 'Some executives find it extremely distasteful, disorienting, and enervating to be exposed directly in a face-to-face setting to the clash of opinion among their advisors . . . Such executives prefer a depersonalized presentation of the arguments.'[94] In other cases, the leader may lack a sense of balance or judgment, and can transform controlled competition into cut-throat competition. Or, if the chief executive does not have time to manage the multiple advocacy process, his advisor may lack sufficient prestige or leverage to maintain the desired level of competition.

The competition may also be corrupted from below, as it will always be beseiged by parochial, bureaucratic interests. Actors '. . . may decline to raise unpromising options even if they believe in them, for fear of ending up on the "losing side" too often, thereby losing "influence" or tarnishing their reputation or expending limited bargaining resources on fruitless or costly endeavors.'[95] In addition, 'competition within the advisory circle may occasionally get out of hand, strain the policy-making group's cohesion, and impose heavy human costs . . . Officials may be quicker to go outside the executive branch in search of allies for their internal policy disputes. This may encourage "leaks" and create difficulties for the executive.'[96]

Multiple advocacy at its best can lead to the presentation of a wide variety of opinions, but it cannot contribute to identification of the better choice; '. . . it may simply highlight ambiguity rather than resolve it.'[97] Variety does not prevent a leader from choosing the option or policy that he would have preferred anyway; it may merely serve as an objective facade for a subjective choice.[98] Another possible incorrect choice by the chief executive can stem from the temptation to '. . . accept the middle-of-the-road view, a compromise between advocates of opposing ideas, which may be indecisive . . .' Thus, the fundamental biases of neither the intelligence community nor the political executive are resolved by this system, while variety does not necessarily produce 'high quality policymaking. The content and quality of policy decisions is determined by many other variables – . . . the ideological values and cognitive beliefs of policymakers and others.'[99]

Multiple advocacy requires time for the give-and-take process among advocates, which may occasionally impose undue delays on decision-making. This prerequisite can seriously restrict its utility in times of crisis and war.

Despite its many imperfections, multiple advocacy makes sense. In reality, all other things are never held equal – neither resources nor the influence of different organizations or actors. Naturally, in a politically competitive environment some organizations (or one) will come to prevail over the others. Then in the aftermath of a major intelligence failure, multiple reforms will again provide corrective relief until one agency manages to build up its relative power to the point where the same cycle begins once more.

Other, and at times simpler, organizational mechanisms have been proposed as antidotes to the dangers of groupthink and conformity. In demonstrating his willingness to accept criticism, the executive (or other relevant leader) should encourage each member of a group to raise his objections and doubts. The executive leader 'should be impartial instead of stating preferences and expectations at the outset . . . [He should] limit his briefings to unbiased statements about the scope of the problem and the limitations of available resources without advocating specific proposals he would like to see adopted.' This allows the conferees the opportunity to develop an atmosphere of open inquiry and to explore impartially a wide range of policy alternatives:[100] to encourage multiple advocacy, to divide groups into new subgroups under new chairmen and then to come back together to discuss their differences again; whenever possible, individual group members should discuss the group's deliberations with trusted outside friends; to invite outside members to group discussions; after searching a preliminary consensus the group should hold a second chance meeting at which every member can express his residual doubts and rethink the entire issue before making a definitive choice.[101] Some of these suggestions are theoretically easy to implement and involve relatively little cost, while others, such as an initial neutral attitude on the part of the leader, would be much more challenging to bring about.

As stated earlier, organizational reforms cannot be expected to completely overcome the fundamental problems of inaccurate perception and insulate the intelligence policymaking process from political influences. Ultimately, the effectiveness of these mechanisms depends upon the general quality of the political culture and the character of the leaders who must make the final decisions. Yet even though the expected returns from organizational reforms can only be limited, all changes that increase diversity, criticism, and free discussion must be advocated.

The Devil's Advocate[102]
The institution of the devil's advocate is well known. The idea is to encourage an individual to freely express unpopular, dissenting opinions, which allows decisionmakers to consider alternative views while protecting those who present them. The role can be assigned on an *ad hoc* basis to individuals in a given discussion, or be institutionalized down to the smallest detail and assigned on a continuing basis to an individual or group. The problem with this mechanism is that it is an artificial method of introduc-

ing unpopular concepts. If the role is assigned to a typical member of an intelligence organization, for example, he cannot be expected to express the conviction and in-depth understanding of someone who genuinely believes in that position. In general, a true advocate of opposing views on an important issue would not be employed in an intelligence organization in the first place, unless he were to conceal his actual opinions in order to survive. If the dissenter is not expressing his personal viewpoint, he will end up playing the *role* of the opposition as perceived by the group to which he belongs. (This is akin to playing chess against oneself.) More misleading than helpful, such an arrangement would perpetuate the accepted image of the adversary instead of penetrating to the core of his (very different) perceptions. On the other hand, if the devil's advocate is presenting his real opinions, he will be singled out as hostile to the group's interest and will not be taken into its confidence. A genuine devil's advocate should come from outside the organizational system, but in practice he is usually part of it. In fact, the very obstacles that make it impossible to perceive the adversary correctly would also apply to him. Furthermore, the role of devil's advocate would soon become so routinized that no one would take it seriously.[103] An environment which can tolerate dissent would be far more constructive than the artificial tolerance of opposition.

Clearly, the majority of failures to anticipate strategic surprise can be correlated with conceptual rigidity and a high incidence of perceptual continuity. Therefore, analysts (and to a lesser extent, political or military leaders) should be encouraged to consider alternative interpretations of data and new evidence, and continuously to reevaluate their concept while avoiding dogmatic adherence to given concepts. The search for ways to promote more open-minded attitudes is basic to almost all proposals for the improvement of intelligence work; to this end, analysts must be encouraged to present their views openly, to be critical, to fight for their opinions if necessary, and to resist group and political pressures. This is perhaps the most rudimentary condition necessary for the upgrading of intelligence work – yet it is also an ideal demand that can never be fully attained within a human environment.

Inasmuch as the independent judgment of individual analysts at all levels cannot be guaranteed *within* each organization, the fostering of *inter*-organizational competition may enhance the diversity and freedom of the intelligence process in general.

Far-reaching advances in the technical means of gathering intelligence information, and the greater awareness of political, perceptual mechanisms undermining the intelligence process, have not yielded corresponding progress in the ability to anticipate strategic surprise.[104] On this account, understanding but not being able to avoid this phenomenon has led to a certain sense of futility. Napoleon once said, '. . . Uncertainty is the essence of war, surprise its rule.' If anything, history provides us with the consoling observation that there is no direct correlation between achieving the highest degree of surprise at the outbreak of a war and ultimately emerging victorious. The next best thing to avoiding the surprise, therefore, is to be able to cope with it once it has occurred, and this requires the judicious build-up of military strength in peacetime.

Post Surprise Measures (PSM)[105]

In light of the preceding observations, it is of the utmost importance to prepare an array of methods to deal with a sudden attack once it has taken place. Only a few of such measures will be mentioned in this context.

(a) Upgrade military plans and preparations for operations in the event of a surprise attack. This must include detailed contingency plans, staff exercises, and military field exercises.

(b) Special emphasis must be placed on the preparation and protection of headquarters, communications centers, military airfields,[106] mobilization centers, weapons, ammunition, and fuel depots, major bridges, tunnels, and other 'choke points'. All key bases and communication centers must be able to withstand a conventional first strike in order to provide a conventional second-strike capability, and communication networks should be designed with positive redundancy sufficient for post-attack survival.

(c) Special plans must be drawn up to carry out effectively and even accelerate mobilization procedures under attack conditions. Furthermore, they should be maintained and checked by exercises and updating at regular intervals.

(d) A variety of defensive counter-surprises, both technical and operational, should be prepared.[107]

(1) On the technological side, the defender can ready more effective anti-aircraft and/or anti-tank missiles to be operated in layered concentrations. New technologies can include dynamic mining, or the preparation of minefields that will channel the attacker into specific killing zones; electronic and other counter-measures to disrupt the attacker's communications (C^3I facilities); and neutralization of his major weapons systems.

(2) The initiation of counter-operations, and if possible interceptive attacks, against the attacker. A select number of units should always be available for counter-operations against the enemy's rear echelons, airfields, and communication and supply lines, to name a few. The defender's goal should be to throw the attacker off balance by resorting to aggressive, unexpected moves that concentrate on vulnerable points in the attacker's 'armor'. Most suitable for such operations is air power, the flexibility and nature of which allows for a short reaction time and the

ability to attack all echelons of the enemy forces. (For this reason, it is of great importance to develop the conventional second-strike capabilities of the Air Force, which includes protecting the aircraft, runways, ammunition and fuel depots from the enemy's first strike.) In addition to the air force, special operations units such as rangers, paratroopers, and SAS can react quickly and effectively to a sudden attack.

APPENDIX

Complex Man–Machine Accidents[108]

It is of great heuristic interest to compare accidents arising from the complex interaction of man and machine to the problems involved in trying to anticipate or prevent a strategic surprise. Complex man–machine accidents (such as the Three Mile Island nuclear reactor mishap) are in some ways simpler than a human conflict type of situation. Complex machines, unlike enemies, don't *deliberately* try to conceal aggressive intentions, nor do they resort to deception operations or tailor their strategies to 'attack' different operators. Furthermore, although the number of potential causes for an accident is very large, it is still finite and the possible structure or consequences of an accident *may* be better analyzed before it occurs (i.e., if a valve fails at point X, then the flow of water will be reduced by Y per cent which will increase the temperature in the reactor by a certain percentage, and so on). For this reason, it can also be expected that, in the future, the decision-making process in complex man–machine crisis situations could be left to computers, which would 'automatically' make better and faster decisions than any human being. Nevertheless, it has proven to be impossible either to predict or to avoid accidents (or man–machine 'surprises'). It is of course the human element in this situation which is the weakest, least predictable link.

Three types of accident are recognized in complex man–machine disasters: they are unique accidents, discrete accidents, and calculated risk accidents. To the first type of accident belongs, for example, the collapse of a dam in a powerful earthquate; or the simultaneous heart attack of a pilot and co-pilot in an airliner. 'No reasonable protection is possible against freak accidents or Acts of God.' Discrete accidents can involve equipment failure, a condition that can be corrected so that it will not happen again. Such mishaps frequently occur in all human–machine interactions and result from a limited design error, an operator's mistake, and the like. In a discrete accident, the system responds to that source of error without any significant synergistic developments, and backup systems and isolation devices come into play. The system as such is not abandoned, as it can be made 'safer' through modification.

Calculated risk types of accident are of a statistical nature (i.e., the probability of their occurrence could conceivably be calculated, and preventive or corrective measures can or will be taken according to a cost/benefit analysis and the probability involved). In reality, though, highly complex systems are susceptible to many unknown risks and, therefore, the actual risk of an accident occurring cannot be calculated.

These three types of accident can also be relevant to the analysis of strategic surprise. In many respects, particularly for each different country, strategic surprise in its magnitude has the characteristics of a unique accident. This is especially true of large-scale, out-of-the-blue surprise attacks. (The unprecedented launching of a nuclear surprise attack could fall under this category.)

Military and intelligence tend to treat strategic surprise as if it were a discrete accident which can be 'fixed'. History teaches us that no such failsafe corrective measures exist, and moreover, that strategic surprise *will* take place regardless of the improvements or modifications that have been made. Mistaking strategic surprise for a discrete accident can, in fact, be very misleading, for it creates illusions of safety leading to even more intense surprise in the future.

The calculated risk explanation for accidents is pertinent to strategic surprise in those situations where politicians or intelligence analysts assume that they know or can estimate the calculus of risk for an enemy attack with reasonable accuracy, whereas such calculations are rarely possible or reliable.

The student of strategic surprise is struck by the similarities between complex man–machine accidents and the latter phenomenon.

A. Complexity and inevitability. 'The accident at TMI was not a preventable one . . . They cannot be prevented. They are unanticipated. It is not feasible to train, design, or build in such a way as to anticipate all eventualities in complex systems where the parts are tightly coupled . . . the complexity of systems outruns all controls.' '. . . Normal accidents, whose origins lie fallow and simmer in the very complexity of the interactive system, waiting upon some failure of equipment, design, or operator action to give them brief, fierce life, cannot be eliminated. Indeed, they grow with the complexity of the system, *including the complexity added by the safety features.*'

B. Warning: signals and noise. The normal accident is characterized by 'signals which provide warnings *only* in retrospect, making prevention difficult'.

> Complex human-machine systems abound in warnings – signs in red letters, flashing lights, horns, sounding, italicized passages in training manuals and operating instructions, decals on equipment, analyses of faults in technical reports, and a light snowfall of circulars and

alerts . . . Warnings work; but not all the time. We should not be surprised; the very volume of warning devices testifies to this likelihood. If warnings were heeded, we would need only a few modest and tasteful ones rather than a steady drill of admonitions punctuated by alarms and lights.

. . . Why are warnings not always heeded? There are many reasons, and when we consider the overpopulation of complex, high-risk systems that someone has decided we cannot live without, they are disturbing.

Consider three categories of warnings. First, there are deviations, steady-state conditions that do not activate significant alarms. There was a rather long list of these at Three Mile Island . . . Each one individually is considered trivial or interpreted in a routine framework. Only hindsight discloses the meaning of these deviations. Second, there are alarms, such as flashing lights or circuit breaker trips or dials reading in the red zone. But operators are accustomed to interpreting these alarms as insignificant when they have a conception of the problem which triggered them. Or if the operators have no conception of the problem, the alarm may be attributed to faulty alarm equipment . . . Alarms, like deviations, always outnumber actual accidents: warnings are in greater supply than actual malfunctions.

Past accidents, mute predictors of future ones, form the third category of warnings. But history is no guide for highly infrequent events. They are not expected to occur again; generally they don't.

Following an accident, reforms, improvements, better procedures will be implemented . . . Operators will be flooded with new warnings. But it is normal for the systems to have accidents; warnings cannot affect the normal accident. Tight coupling encourages normal accidents, with their highly inter-dependent synergistic aspects, but loose coupling muffles warnings.

Whether systems are loosely or tightly coupled, they all face another problem with warnings – the signal-to-noise ratio. Only after the event, when we construct imaginative (and frequently dubious) explanations of what went wrong, does some of the noise reveal itself as a signal. The operators at TMI had literally to turn off alarms; so many of them were sounding and blinking that signals passed into noise.

The student of strategic surprise will be able to identify many additional similarities such as: problems of coordination and failures of communication when warnings are not made available to the proper people; the political dimensions in which top decisionmakers have other priorities and/or refuse to listen to warnings because they are reluctant to pay the *costs* of improvement and precautionary measures; problems of human perceptions where the possibility of unfamilar types of accidents and malfunctions is not taken seriously. '. . . The normal accident is unforeseeable; its "warnings" are *socially constructed.*'

There is still much more the strategic analysts can learn from man–machine accidents and disaster theory.

NOTES

1 On the inverse correlation between strength and the incentive to resort to surprise, stratagem and deception, see Michael I. Handel, 'Intelligence and Deception', *The Journal of Strategic Studies* 5 (March 1982), 122–54, 145.

2 This is perhaps the reason that in early Soviet military doctrine, surprise was seen as a 'transitory' but not a decisive factor. Primarily identified with Stalin's contribution to military science, these early views were still paid lip service after the German attack on the Soviet Union and even as late as the early 1950s and the nuclear age. The appearance of nuclear weapons rendered earlier Marxist–Leninist observations on the transitory (temporary) and permanent elements of war obsolete. Despite theoretical lip service to the secondary importance of strategic surprise, in pratice the Soviet military doctrine assigns it a great deal of importance in conventional as much as in nuclear war. See Raymond L. Garthoff, *The Soviet Image of Future War* (Washington DC: Public Affairs Press, 1959), Ch.3: 'The Role of Surprise and Blitzkrieg'.

By the 1970s, Colonel Savkin, a leading Soviet strategist, went one step further and referred to the principle of surprise as '. . . a most important principle of military art since olden times'. Col. V. Ye.Savkin, 'Surprise', *Military Review* (April 1974), 84–91; Col. Dr. L. Kuleszynski, 'Some Problems of Surprise in Warfare', and Maj. Mgr. Z. Poleski, 'Psychological Aspects of Surprise', in both Joseph D. Douglass and Amoretta M. Hoeber, eds, *Selected Readings From Military Thought 1963–1973* (Washington DC: GPO, 1983), vol. 5, Part II, US Air Force, and John M. Caravelli, 'The Role of Surprise and Preemption in Soviet Military Strategy', *International Security Review* 6 (Summer 1981), 209–36. See also Amnon Sella, 'Barbarossa: Surprise Attack and Communication', *The Journal of Contemporary History* 13 (July 1978), 555–83; John Francis O'Neil, 'German Counter-C³ and its Effects on Soviet Command Communications During Operation Barbarossa' (MA dissertation, Naval Post-graduate School, Monterey, CA, 1980); John Erickson, 'The Soviet Response to Surprise Attack; Three Directives, 22 June 1941', *Soviet Studies* 23 (April 1972), 519–59; Reuben Ainsytein, 'Stalin and June 22, 1941', *International Affairs* 42 (October 1966), 662–73; Vladimir Petrov, '*June 22, 1941*' *Soviet Historians and the German Invasion* (Columbia, SC: University of South Carolina Press, 1968).

3 All three quotations are from: Carl von Clausewitz, *On War*, ed. Michael Howard and Peter Paret (Princeton, NJ: Princeton University Press, 1976), pp. 198–9.

4 Ibid., p. 545.

5 For the impact of modern technology on warfare see: Michael Howard, *War in European History* (New York: Oxford University Press, 1979), in particular Chs. 5–7;

J.F.C. Fuller, *The Foundations of the Science of War* (London: Hutchinson, 1926), pp. 278–9; J.F.C. Fuller, *Armanents and History* (New York: Charles Scribner's Sons, 1945); J.F.C. Fuller, 'The Mechanization of War', in *What Would Be the Character of a New War*, The Inter-Parliamentary Union, Geneva (New York: Harrison Smith and Robert Haas, 1933), pp. 49–75; J.F.C. Fuller, *The Conduct of War 1789–1961; A Study of the Impact of the French, Industrial and Russian Revolutions on War and Its Conduct* (London: Eyre Methuen, 1972); Tom Wintringham, *Weapons and Tactics* (Harmondsworth: Penguin Books, 1973); Edwin A. Pratt, *The Rise of Rail-Power in War and Conquest 1833–1914* (Philadelphia: Lippincott, 1916); Brian Ranft (ed.) *Technological Change and British Naval Policy 1860–1839* (New York: Holmes & Meier, 1977).

6 This apt phrase was suggested by Thomas C. Schelling in *The Strategy of Conflict* (Cambridge, MA: Harvard University Press, 1960), pp. 207–30), and in *Arms and Influence* (New Haven: Yale University Press, 1966), p. 221. These two books have been neglected by the students of strategic surprise.

7 Clausewitz, p. 79. On strategic surprise in the nuclear age, see, for example, Richard K. Betts, *Surprise Attack: Lessons for Defense Planning* (Washington DC: The Brookings Institution, 1982), pp. 228–54; see also Paul Bracken, *The Command and Control of Nuclear Forces* (New Haven: Yale University Press, 1983), pp. 5–74.

8 Michael I. Handel, 'The Study of Intelligence', *Orbis* 26 (Winter 1978), 817–21.

9 These terms were first applied to the study of strategic surprise and intelligence analysis by Roberta Wohlstetter in *Pearl Harbor: Warning and Decision* (Stanford: Standford University Press, 1962), pp. 336–8. On the inevitability of surprise, see Michael I. Handel, 'The Yom Kippur War and the Inevitability of Surprise', *International Studies Quarterly* 21 (September 1977), 461–501. An expanded version is Michael I. Handel, *Perception, Deception and Surprise: The Case of the Yom Kippur War* (Jerusalem: The Leonard Davis Institute, 1976); and Richard K. Betts, 'Analysis, War and Decision: Why Intelligence Failures are Inevitable', *World Politics* 31 (October 1978), 61–89. Other interesting theoretical works on strategic surprise include (in addition to Roberta Wohlstetter's *Warning and Decision* and Richard Bett's *Surprise Attack*): Klaus Knorr and Patrick Morgan, eds, *Strategic Military Surprise* (New Brunswick, NJ: Transaction Books, 1983), pp. 147–71; Barton Whaley, *Stratagem, Deception and Surprise in War* (Cambridge, MA: MIT Center for International Studies, 1969, mimeo) (by now dated, this was unfortunately never published as a book); Alexander L. George and Richard Smoke, *Deterrence in American Foreign Policy: Theory and Practice* (New York: Columbia University Press, 1979), pp. 567–87; Ephraim Kam, *Failure to Anticipate War: The Why of Surprise Attack* (Ph.D. dissertation, Harvard University, 1983). Robert Jervis, 'Hypothesis on Misperception', *World Politics* 20 (April 1968), 454–79, is a pioneering study on the perceptual-psychological dimension of intelligence and decisionmaking in foreign affairs; earlier studies are Klaus Knorr, 'Failures in National Intelligence Estimates: The Case of the Cuban Missiles', *World Politics* 16 (April 1964), 455–67; Benno Wasserman, 'The Failure of Intelligence Prediction', *Political Studies* 8 (June 1960), 156–69; Abraham Ben-Zvi, 'Hindsight and Foresight: A Conceptual Framework for the Analysis of Surprise Attacks', *World Politics* 28 (April 1976), 381–95; Janice Gross Stein, '"Intelligence" and "Stupidity" Reconsidered: Estimation and Decision in Israel, 1973', *Journal of Strategic Studies* 3 (September 1980), 147–78; Avi Shlaim, 'Failures in National Security Estimates: The Case of the Yom Kippur War', *World Politics* 28 (April 1976), 348–80.

10 On deception, see for example: Barton Whaley, *Codeword Barbarossa* (Cambridge, MA: MIT Press, 1973); Whaley, *Stratagem*; Whaley, 'Covert Rearmament in

Germany 1919–1939; Deception and Misperception', *The Journal of Strategic Studies* 5 (March 1982), 3–39; Donald Daniel and Katherine Herbig, eds, *Strategic Military Deception* (New York: Pergamon, 1982).

Among the more interesting Second World War memoirs dealing with deception are: Ewen Montague, *Beyond Top Secret Ultra* (London: Corgi, 1979); R.V. Jones, *Most Secret War: British Scientific Intelligence in World War II 1939–1945* (London: Hamish Hamilton, 1978); R.V. Jones, 'Intelligence and Deception', in Robert Pfaltzgraff (ed.), *Intelligence Policy and National Security* (London: Macmillan, 1981), pp. 3–23; David Mure, *Practice to Deceive* (London: William Kimber, 1977); David Mure, *Master of Deception: Tangled Webs in London and the Middle East* (London: William Kimber, 1980); Charles Cruickshank, *Deception in World War II* (Oxford: Oxford University Press, 1979); J.C. Masterman, *The Double Cross System* (New Haven: Yale University Press, 1972); Richard J. Heuer, Jr., 'Strategic Deception: A Psychological Perspective', *International Studies Quarterly* 25 (June 1981), 294–327; *Thoughts on the Cost-Effectiveness of Deception and Related Tactics in the Air War 1939–1945* (Deception Research Program, Mathtech Inc., Princeton, NJ, and ORD/CIA Analytic, March 1979); *Covert Rearmament in Germany 1919–1939: Deception and Misperception* (Deception Research Program, Mathtech, Inc., Princeton, NJ, and ORD/CIA Analytic, March 1979).

11 See also Michael I. Handel, 'Intelligence and Deception', pp. 122–54.

12 For background and numerous alerts preceding the German attack in the west in May 1940, see Telford Taylor, *The March of Conquest* (New York: Simon & Schuster, 1958) Erich von Manstein, *Lost Victories* (London: Methuen, 1958); Hans Adolf Jacobsen, *Fall Gelb: Der Kampf über Den Deutschen Operationplan in Westoffensive 1940* (Wiesbaden: Franz Steiner, 1957); Major L.F. Ellis, *The War in France and Flanders 1939–1940* (London: HMSO, 1953); Basil Collier, *Hidden Weapons: Allied Secret or Undercover Services in World War II* (London: Hamish Hamilton, 1982), pp. 78–96; Betts, *Surprise Attack*, pp. 28–34; André Beaufre, *1940: The Fall of France* (London: Cassell, 1965); William L. Shirer, *The Collapse of the Third Republic* (New York: Simon & Schuster, 1969).

13 Handel, *Perception, Deception and Surprise*, p. 15.

14 Handel, 'Intelligence and Deception', p. 154n.

15 See Michael I. Handel, 'Crisis and Surprise in Three Arab-Israeli Wars', in Knorr and Morgan, eds, pp. 111–46.

16 Handel, *Perception, Deception and Surprise*, pp. 18–28.

17 For the difficulties involved in estimating Hitler's intentions and in predicting his style of operation, see Michael I. Handel, *The Diplomacy of Surprise* (Cambridge, MA: Harvard Center for International Affairs, 1981), Ch. 2, pp. 31–96. Under-estimating the capabilities of an adversary may lead to erroneous conclusions concerning his short-term intentions. Given the fact that capabilities are normally easier to assess than intentions, a competent intelligence organization is less likely to commit this type of error. Japanese intelligence in 1945 vastly underrated Soviet capabilities in Manchuria and therefore miscalculated Soviet intentions to launch a large-scale offensive in August 1945. For an interesting and detailed analysis, see Edward J. Drea, 'Missing Intentions: Japanese Intelligence and the Soviet Invasion of Manchuria, 1945', *Military Affairs* (April 1984), 66–73.

18 Handel, *Perception, Deception and Surprise*, p. 62.

19 Clausewitz, p. 190.

20 Handel, *Perception, Deception and Surprise*, pp. 15–16.

21 See Kam, p. 182. For the assessment of risks primarily on the tactical level, see Elias Carter Townsend, *Risks: The Key to Combat Intelligence* (Harrisburg, PA: Military Service Publishing Company, 1955).

22 Handel, *Perception, Deception and Surprise*, pp. 46ff.
23 Barry Leach, *German Strategy Against Russia 1939–1941* (Oxford: Oxford University Press, 1973), pp. 91–4 and Appendix 4, p. 270; Albert Seaton, *The Russo-German War 1941–1945* (London: Praeger Publishers, 1971); *German Military Intelligence* (Fredrick, MD: University Publications of America, 1984).
24 Waldemar Erfurth, *Surprise* (Harrisburg, PA: Military Service Publishing Company, 1943), pp. 6–7.
25 Handel, *Perception, Deception and Surprise*, p. 16.
26 The term is Schelling's. See *The Strategy of Conflict*, pp. 244–5.
27 For literature on this case, see note 12 above.
28 Both quotations are from: W.D. Howells, 'Intelligence in Crises', in Gregory R. Copley (ed.), *Defense '83* (Washington DC: D and F Conferences, Inc., 1983), pp. 351, 350.
29 Handel, *Perception, Deception and Surprise*, pp. 52–4; Betts, *Surprise Attack*, pp. 122–3.
30 Handel, *Perception, Deception and Surprise*, p. 54.
31 Ibid.
32 Howells, pp. 359–61; Betts, *Surprise Attack*, pp. 190–2; Kam, pp. 127–39.
33 For an interesting case, see Jones, *Most Secret War*, pp. 233–5.
34 Howells, 'Intelligence in Crises', p. 361.
35 Robert Jervis, *The Logic of Images in International Relations* (Princeton, NJ: Princeton University Press, 1970).
36 Betts, 'Analysis, War and Decision', pp. 73–5; Kam, pp. 461–2.
37 Ken Booth, *Strategy and Ethnocentrism* (New York: Holmes & Meier, 1979), pp. 123–4.
38 Luigi Albertini, *The Origins of the War of 1914*, vols. 2, 3 (Oxford: Oxford University Press, 1952); Ludwig Reiners, *The Lamps Went Out in Europe* (Cleveland, OH: World Publishing Co., 1966), pp. 134–9; Lawrence Lafore, *The Long Fuse* (Philadelphia: Lippincott, 1965), pp. 269–75; L.F.C. Turner, *The Origins of the First World War* (New York: W.W. Norton, 1970), pp. 91–112; Gerhard Ritter, *The Schlieffen Plan* (London: Oswald Wolf, 1958).
39 Paraphrased from an article by Charles Perrow, 'Normal Accident at Three Mile Island', *Transaction (Social Sciences and Modern Society)* 18 (July/August 1981), 17–26, 21.
40 See Jervis, 'Hypothesis on Misperception'; Robert Jervis, *The Logic of Images in International Relations*; and Robert Jervis, *Perception and Misperception in International Politics* (Princeton, NJ: Princeton University Press, 1976); Joseph de Rivera, *The Psychological Dimension of Foreign Policy* (Columbus, OH: Charles Merrill Pub., 1968); Jack S. Levy, 'Misperception and the Causes of War: Theoretical Linkages and Analytical Problems', *World Politics* 36 (October 1983), 76–100; Arthur S. Stein, 'When Misperception Matters', *World Politics* 34 (July 1982), 502–26; Herbert Goldhamer, *Reality and Belief in Military Affairs* (Santa Monica, CA: The Rand Corporation, Feb. 1979 R–2448–NA); *Misperception Literature Survey* (Mathtech Inc., Princeton, NJ and ORD/CIA Analytic, March 1979).
41 Handel, *The Diplomacy of Surprise*, pp. 97–176, 241–354.
42 For a detailed discussion, see Jervis, 'Hypothesis on Misperception'.
43 Booth. He refers to this phenomenon as the 'Hamlet syndrome'.
44 On problems of ethnocentrism, national character, and the difficulties of understanding other cultures, see the following sample: Washington Platt, *National Character in Action: Intelligence Factors in Foreign Relations* (New Brunswick, NJ: Rutgers University Press, 1961); Booth; A.J. Marder, *Old Friends, New Enemies: The Royal Navy and the Imperial Japanese Navy*, vol. 1: *Strategic Illusions*

1936–1941 (Oxford: Oxford University Press, 1981). The classic study of national character is still Salvador de Madariaga, *Englishmen, Frenchmen, Spaniards* (Oxford: Oxford University Press, 1927).

On the importance of familiarity with languages, see for example: Lev Navrozov, 'What the CIA Knows About Russia', *Commentary* 66 (September 1971), 51–9.

45 Zvi Lanir, *Fundamental Surprise: The National Intelligence Crisis* (In Hebrew) (Tel Aviv: HaKibbutz HaMeuchad, 1983).

46 Handel, *Perception, Deception and Surprise*, pp. 40–42.

47 Lanir. By basic or fundamental surprise, Lanir means the lack of 'correct' understanding by a given society of its *own* problems, situation, capabilities, direction of development, the gap between its goals and means, the absence of understanding how its neighbors perceive it and the like. This new concept does not add any constructive dimension to the study of intelligence for reasons mentioned in the preceding text, and may be methodologically more confusing than helpful.

48 Samuel P. Huntington, *The Soldier and the State* (New York: Vintage Books, 1964).

49 Ibid., p. 49.

50 For an excellent discussion of this point, see Richard K. Betts, *Soldiers, Statesmen, and Cold War Crisis* (Cambridge, MA: Harvard University Press, 1977), Ch.10, pp. 183–209.

51 Donald McLachlan, *Room 39: A Study in Naval Intelligence* (New York: Atheneum, 1968), p. 365.

52 See Thomas L. Hughes, *The Fate of Facts in the World of Men: Foreign Policy and Intelligence Making* (New York: Headline Series, Foreign Policy Association, December 1976, n. 233), p. 15. This is one of the best essays on the use and misuse of intelligence by political leaders, and on the problems of cooperation between the intelligence community and political decisionmakers.

Despite its importance, little has been written on politics and intelligence, or the politics of intelligence. Most of the existing observations are scattered throughout memoirs, histories of specific intelligence operations, and the like. An excellent chapter on this subject can be found in McLachlan, Ch. 15, pp. 338–66, as well as in the rest of the book. Some material concerning the bureaucratic politics of intelligence can be found in Mark M. Lowenthal, *U.S. Intelligence: Evolution and Anatomy*, The Washington Papers, 105, vol. 12 (1984).

An interesting case study in the politics of intelligence concerns the process used to estimate the North Vietnamese-Vietcong order of battle. See Sam Adams, 'Vietnam Cover-Up: Playing War with Numbers', *Harper's Magazine* (May 1975), pp. 41–4, 62–73; also Patrick J. McGarvey, *CIA: The Myth and the Madness* (Baltimore: Penguin Books, 1974), Ch. 7, 'Intelligence to Please', pp. 148–60. A brief discussion can also be found in Richard K. Betts, *Soldiers, Statesmen and Cold War Crises*, Ch. 10, 'Careerism, Intelligence and Misperception', pp. 183–208.

Similar to those of Howells, are the observations of Yehoshafat Harkabi in 'The Intelligence Policymaker Tangle', *Jerusalem Quarterly* 30 (Winter 1984), 125–31. For a different angle on intelligence and policymaking, focusing on the influence of intelligence estimates on US–USSR relations, see Raymond L. Garthoff, *Intelligence Assessment and Policymaking: A Decision Point in the Kennedy Administration* (Washington DC: The Brookings Institution, 1984).

53 Handel, *The Diplomacy of Surprise*, pp. 1–31, 241–53; or Michael I. Handel, 'Surprise and Change in International Politics', *International Security* 4 (Spring 1980), 57–85. On the failure of Japanese intelligence, see Ashman, *Intelligence and Foreign Policy: A Functional Analysis* (Ph.D dissertation, University of Utah,

1973), pp. 99–119. See also Christopher Andrew and David Dilks, eds, *The Missing Dimension: Governments and Intelligence Communities in the 20th Century* (Urbana, IL: University of Illinois Press, 1985).

54 Ashman, p. 53.

55 Ibid., p. 61. On Hitler as a decisionmaker, see Walter Warlimont, *Inside Hitler's Headquarters* (London: Weidenfeld & Nicolson, 1964); Percy Ernst Schramm, *Hitler: The Man and the Military Leader* (Chicago: Quadrangle Books, 1971); Franz Halder, *Hitler as a Warlord* (London: Putnam, 1950); Andreas Hillgruber, *Hitler's Strategie: Politik und Kriegsfuhrung 1940–1941* (Munich: Bernard Greife, 1982).

On Ribbentrop's attitude, see D.C. Watt's introduction in David Irving, *Breach of Security* (London: William Kimber, 1968) in particular pp. 39–40. Also David Irving, *The War Path* (New York: Viking Press, 1978), pp. 243–4.

56 McLachlan, *Room 39*, p. 135.

57 Handel, *The Diplomacy of Surprise*, pp. 241–355.

58 Howells, p. 352 (my emphasis).

59 A well-known example is Walter Langer's psychoanalytical study of Hitler for the OSS during the Second World War. Walter Langer, *The Mind of Adolf Hitler* (New York: Basic Books, 1972); also James David Barber, *The Presidential Character: Predicting Performance in the White House*, 2nd ed. (Englewood Cliffs, NJ: Prentice Hall, 1977).

60 Gerhard L. Weinberg, 'Hitler's Image of the United States', *American Historical Review* 69 (July 1964), 1004–21.

61 See John Erickson, *The Road to Stalingrad: Stalin's War with Germany*, vol. 1 (New York: Harper & Row, 1975); John Erickson, *The Soviet High Command* (London: Macmillan, 1962). See also Seweryn Bialer (ed.), *Stalin and His Generals* (New York: Pegasus, 1969).

62 Ronald Lewin, *Churchill as a Warlord* (New York: Stein & Day, 1982). For a different viewpoint, see A.J.P. Taylor *et al.*, *Churchill Revisited: A Critical Assessment* (New York: Dial Press, 1969). More sympathetic is Martin Gilbert's *Winston S. Churchill*, vol. 5, *The Prophet of Truth* (Boston: Houghton Mifflin, 1977) and vol. 6, *Finest Hour 1939–1941* (Boston: Houghton Mifflin, 1983). R.W. Thompson, *Generalissimo Churchill* (New York: Charles Scribner's Sons, 1973).

63 Gaddis Smith, 'How the British Held the Fort', *The New York Times Book Review* (25 December 1983), pp. 1–2. This is a review of Martin Gilbert's *Winston S. Churchill, vol. 6, Finest Hour*.

64 Lewin, p. 75.

65 See McLachlan, *Room 39*, Ch. 6, pp. 124–43, and Ch. 15, pp. 338–67. Many leaders cannot resist the temptation to become their own intelligence officers. This practice is dangerous for the following reasons: (a) Leaders have only a limited amount of time to devote to the in-depth analysis of almost any subject. (b) Most often they are not experts or have only limited knowledge of the problems they intend to analyze. (c) Above all, they will be unable to be objective on exactly those subjects that interest them the most. (d) They tend to focus on pressing issues but ignore other important issues. This danger is best demonstrated by the statement attributed to Kissinger, 'I don't know what kind of intelligence I want, what I know is when I get it.'

66 Major Sir Desmond Morton, quoted in R.W. Thompson, *Churchill and Morton* (London: Hodder & Stoughton, 1976), p. 45.

67 Lewin, p. 21.

68 Ibid., pp. 30–31.

69 Ibid., p. 20.

70 Howells, p. 364. On supplying US Presidents with the 'right information' or the

56   PARADOXES OF STRATEGIC INTELLIGENCE

information they like to hear, see, among others: Thomas Powers, *The Man Who Kept Secrets: Richard Helms and the CIA* (New York: Alfred A. Knopf, 1979), in particular Chs.10–12; David Halberstam, *The Best and the Brightest* (New York, Random House); and Morton H. Halperin, *Bureaucratic Politics and Foreign Policy* (Washington, DC: The Brookings Institution, 1974).

71 McLachlan, *Room 39*, p. 366.
72 See Nigel West, *MI6; British Secret Intelligence Service Operations 1909–1945* (London: Weidenfeld & Nicolson, 1983), pp. 137–9.
73 Alouph Hareven, 'Disturbed Hierarchy: Israeli Intelligence in 1954 and in 1973', *The Jerusalem Quarterly* 9 (Fall 1978), 3–19; and Janice Gross Stein, 'The 1973 Intelligence Failure: A Reconsideration', *The Jerusalem Quarterly* 24 (Summer 1982), 41–54.
74 Perrow, p. 21.
75 Howells, p. 362.
76 A recently published article by a former senior Israeli intelligence officer (apparently the former head of collection of Israeli military intelligence) tries to demonstrate that the 'purely rational' decision-making process in intelligence analysis as well as in intelligence relations with policymakers can exist. The author recommends that the collected facts be allowed to speak for themselves. In light of his experience, this is a startlingly naive recommendation (yet a persistent one) because (a) the intelligence process cannot be totally isolated from the effect of politics; and (b) facts *don't* and cannot speak for themselves. See Brigadier General (ret.) Yoel Ben-Porat, 'The role of the Political Level in Estimates', *Haaretz* (in Hebrew) (20 March 1984), p. 3; see also Yoel Ben-Porat, 'Estimates – Why They Collapse', in *Ma'arachot* (in Hebrew) (October 1983), pp. 29–39.
77 Handel, *Perception, Deception and Surprise*, p. 17.
78 On the military personality and intelligence see: Alouph Hareven, 'Disturbed Hierarchy', 5–19.
   For the reasons outlined in the preceeding text – and primarily, for the low interest in, and regard for, intelligence work by military people (according to McLachlan), McLachlan suggests that this work is better performed by civilians. See McLachlan, *Room 39*, Ch. 15. In his conclusion he recommends that '. . . intelligence for the fighting services should be directed as far as possible by civilians', pp. 365, 342–5. He makes a powerful case, but seems to carry it a bit too far. See also Handel, 'Intelligence and Deception', p. 140.
79 Quoted from Wesley K. Wark, 'Baltic Submarine Bogeys: British Naval Intelligence and Nazi Germany 1933–1939', *The Journal of Strategic Studies* 6 (March 1983), 60–81, 78.
80 Quoted from Collier, pp. 64–5, 70. For the problems of, and measures taken to improve, the coordination of British intelligence operations during the Second World War, see: McLachlan, *Room 39*, p. 298, Ch. 11. 'Three Heads are Better . . .'. Includes an excellent discussion of British intelligence coordination at the highest level during the Second World War. See also McLachlan, 'Naval Intelligence in World War II', p. 222. See also F.H. Hinsley *et al., British Intelligence in the Second World War*, vol. 1 (London: HMSO, 1979), Ch. 9: 'Reorganizations and Reassessment During the Winter of 1940–1941', pp. 267–314, in particular pp. 291–314; and vol. 2 (New York: Cambridge University Press, 1981), Ch. 15, 'Development and Organization of Intelligence', pp. 3–41.
81 Hughes, pp. 49–50.
82 R.V. Jones, *Most Secret War* (London: Hamish Hamilton, 1978), p. 157.
83 McLachlan, *Room 39*, Ch.11, 'Three Heads are Better . . .', p. 298.
84 Graham T. Allison, *Essence of Decision* (Boston: Little Brown, 1971); Morton Halpern, *Bureaucratic Politics and Foreign Policy* (Washington DC: Brookings

Institution, 1974); and Patrick McGarvey, 'CIA: Intelligence to Please', in Morton Halpern and Arnold Kanter, eds, *Readings in American Foreign Policy: A Bureaucratic Perspective* (Boston: Little Brown, 1973), pp. 318–28.

85 Irving Janis, *Victims of Groupthink* (Boston: Houghton Mifflin, 1972).

86 Michael I. Handel, 'Avoiding Political and Technological Surprise in the 1980s', in Roy Godson (ed.), *Intelligence Requirements for the 1980s: Analysis and Estimates* (New Brunswick, NJ: Transaction Books, 1980), pp. 85–112, 105.

87 On the problems of parochialism, over-secrecy, compartmentalization, coordination, and the 'indivisible nature' of intelligence work, see also McLachlan, *Room 39*, pp. 360, 362–3; also Lowenthal.

88 McLachlan, *Room 39*, p. 366.

89 See Lowenthal.

90 Alexander L. George, *Presidential Decision Making in Foreign Policy: The Effective Use of Information and Advice* (Boulder, CO: Westview Press, 1980), in particular, pp. 145–69; and Alexander L. George, 'The Case for Multiple Advocacy in Making Foreign Policy', *American Political Science Review* (September 1972), 751–95.

91 Betts, 'Analysis, War and Decision', pp. 77–8.

92 George, *Presidential Decision Making*.

93 Ibid., pp. 195–6, 207.

94 Ibid., p. 203.

95 Ibid., p. 204.

96 Ibid. Betts, 'Analysis, War and Decision', p. 77.

97 Betts, 'Analysis, War and Decision', p. 76.

98 Ibid.

99 George, *Presidential Decision Making*, p. 204.

100 Janis, pp. 210–11.

101 Ibid., pp. 207–24.

102 See George, *Presidential Decision Making*, pp. 169–74; Jervis, *Perception and Misperception in International Politics*, pp. 415–18; Betts, 'Analysis, War and Decision', pp. 80–81; Janis, pp. 215–16.

103 Betts, 'Analysis, War and Decision', p. 80.

104 In the acquisition of information, a balance must also be struck between technological and human intelligence. The trend during the last two decades has been to invest more heavily in the technical collection of information and relatively to weaken the human effort. This is not an unexpected development in view of the fantastic progress in technology in recent years, yet it will inevitably result in a search for 'the coin not where it fell but under the lamp'. The emphasis on technical collection through such methods as satellite reconnaissance and electronic monitoring will naturally focus on the military and not the political-diplomatic dimension, and on military capabilities rather than on intentions. Nevertheless, there is no substitute for the human collection effort when it comes to the political dimension. Normally, only the agent on the spot may be able to give timely warning of a plan for a coup d'état in Saudi Arabia. No satellite could report a last-minute decision by Galtieri and the Argentinian military junta to launch an attack on the Falkland Islands half a year ahead of earlier plans, nor could it warn against a car bomb or terrorist attack by a radical Iranian group in Lebanon. See also Patrick J. McGarvey, *CIA: The Myth and the Madness* (Baltimore: Penguin 1972), Ch. 5, 'Technology: The Tail Wagging the Dog?', pp. 93–116.

105 See Handel, *Perception, Deception and Surprise*; Betts, *Surprise Attack*, pp. 285–312.

106 On protecting air fields against surprise attacks, see P. Korobkov, 'Dispersed Basing of Aviation Under Conditions of Waging a Modern War', in Douglass and Hoeber, eds, pp. 216–25.

107 One weapons system that was considered to have great potential to halt a surprise attack (with the central front in Europe being the particular consideration) was the neutron bomb – a low-yield intense radiation nuclear bomb which presumably could be used instantaneously with less fear of the conflict deteriorating into nuclear escalation. See Col. Daniel Gans, 'Neutron Weapons: Solution to a Surprise Attack?', *Military Review* (January 1982), 19–37 (Part I) and (February 1982), 55–72 (Part II).

108 This discussion is primarily based on Perrow; all quotations are from this excellent article. See also Daniel F. Ford, *Three Mile Island: Thirty Minutes to Meltdown* (Harmondsworth: Penguin Books, 1982), and Barry A. Turner, 'The Organizational and Interorganizational Development of Disasters', *Administrative Science Quarterly* 21 (Sep. 1976), 378–96.

2

Politicization of Intelligence: Costs and Benefits

Richard K. Betts

Everyone knows that 'politicization' is bad.[1] It is assumed to damage the credibility of intelligence. Some are unconcerned because they believe it seldom happens, or matters little when it does. Virtually no one, however, believes that it is a *good* thing. For the most part this is true – especially when we think only in terms of the popular understanding of the concept. Depending on the definition of the term, however, politicization is to some degree inevitable, and, in some forms, necessary.

The notion that there could be anything less than evil about politicization is never admitted by anyone on either side of debates on the subject, but is nonetheless true. The strict definition of 'politicize' is not *ipso facto* pejorative, but is 'to give a political tone or character' or 'to bring within the realm of politics'[2] – which is, after all, the realm with which intelligence is concerned. In foreign policy, only simple facts or explanations of minor matters about which policymakers know or care little are uncontroversial. *Assessments* of facts on matters of much importance are always controversial. Most of what is seen as illegitimate politicization is only the reflection of what, in other arenas, is considered normal controversy. It is seen as evil because of the universal norm that intelligence judgments be more objective, non-partisan, and scientific than other judgments. The paradox, however, is that the real world of policy makes politicization in one form the worst thing that can happen to intelligence, but, in another form, the best. The pejorative presumption obscures this, and makes it harder to navigate away from the worst and toward the best forms.

The prevalent conception behind the pejorative connotation is that politicization fabricates or distorts information to serve policy preferences or vested interests.[3] This view covers a multitude of sins, some blatant and crude, some subtle and artful. But in any degree this sort of politicization is a malign choice, a simple act of corruption – although it is one usually motivated by the best of intentions to serve what is seen as a good higher than intellectual probity.

The more forgiving concept sees the problem not as a choice but as a condition. For issues of high import and controversy, any relevant analysis is perforce politically charged, because it points to a policy conclusion. Various disputes – about which elements of information are correct, ambiguous, or false; which of them are important, incidental, or irrelevant; in which context they should be understood; and against which varieties of information pointing in a different direction they should be assessed – are in effect, if not in intent, disputes about which policy conclusion stands or falls. The latter view of the problem is more realistic in its approach to making intelligence serve policy, but entails much greater risks in keeping straight the boundaries between the two realms. In one sense, intelligence cannot live with politicization, but policy cannot live without it. Grappling with the problem is frustrated by the unwillingness of any, on any side of the debate, to see their own approach as politicized.

Before proceeding further, let us stipulate one simple standard to which intelligence analysis must adhere, and let none of what follows confuse the absolute sanctity of the standard. The irrevocable norm must be that policy interests, preferences, or decisions must never determine intelligence judgments. As I will argue, there is a difference between such corruption and another form of bringing intelligence 'within the realm of politics' – the presentation and packaging of assessments in ways that effectively engage policymakers' concerns. Keeping the difference straight may be difficult, and skeptics will think that it is so difficult that it should not be attempted, lest the attempt slide down the slippery slope to corruption. Nothing in what follows, however, should be read as challenging the principle that intelligence cannot serve policy if it panders to it.

Types of Politicization and Intelligence–Policy Interaction

The prevalent concept of politicization as the unforgivable top-down dictation of analytical conclusions to support existing policy dominates discussion of the problem, but this is seldom seen in stark form. The second, more forgiving concept of politicization as subtle contamination of analysis by policy predispositions is manifested far more frequently, but there is no consensus about whether it should be considered politicization, whether it can be avoided, or what should be done to cope with it. Politicization in either sense exists in the eye of the beholder, and more specifically, the beholder whose political frame of reference differs from the implications of the analysis beheld. Much confusion and rancor about what constitutes politicization flows from different models of how the intelligence process should relate to policymaking. These might be considered the 'Kent' and 'Gates' models.[4]

The Kent model derives from the legendary Yale historian Sherman Kent, who wrote the first major postwar treatise on intelligence and headed the Office of National Estimates in its formative years. Kent warned against the danger of letting intelligence personnel get too close to policymaking circles, lest their objectivity and integrity be compromised by involvement.[5] This view that objectivity takes precedence over everything dominated the culture of the Central Intelligence Agency (although not of all other intelligence organizations in the line operating departments) for at least its first three decades.

The Gates model – after Robert Gates, Deputy Director for Intelligence at the Central Intelligence Agency (CIA) in the Reagan Administration, and Director of Central Intelligence (DCI) in the administration of Bush the Elder – arose from critiques of ineffective intelligence contributions to policymaking, and the view that utility is the *sine qua non*. To be useful, intelligence analysis must engage policymakers' concerns. Policymakers who utilize analysis need studies that *relate* to the objectives they are trying to achieve. Thus analysis must be sensitive to the policy context, and the range of options available, to be of any use in making policy. (As Robert Jervis says, 'intelligence is also easier to keep pure when it is irrelevant'.[6]) This view emerged in the 1980s and has been ascendant ever since.[7] Partisans of the Gates model see the earlier orthodoxy as a prescription for irrelevance, and see their own approach not as politicization, but as contextualization, or as realistic management of policymakers' cluttered radar screens. Adherents of the Kent model see the Gates approach as a prescription for politicization in the prevalent pejorative sense, and indeed made a public issue of this in Gates' 1991 confirmation hearings.

Full disclosure: I have always leaned, with some ambivalence, toward the Gates model.[8] Every analysis on any matter of great policy importance inevitably has implications for the success or failure of any given policy option. Packaging intelligence to be productive makes it harder to draw sharp lines between what is relevant and what supports a particular policy choice. How this may be done has implications for how to preserve honesty and utility at the same time. Whether it *can* be done is a question that underlines competing models of the role of analysis in policy.

The dimensions of the problem are better appreciated if we recognize that disputes are not just about whether or not intelligence is politically contaminated, but often involve contending forms of politicization. The form that evokes the most direct protests is the top-down variety, whereby policymakers are seen to dictate intelligence conclusions. A second form, however, is the reverse – a bottom-up coloration of products by the unconscious biases of the working analysts who produce intelligence analyses. Since the founding of the modern US intelligence community, liberal policymakers have suspected analysts in the intelligence agencies of the military services and the Defense Intelligence Agency (DIA) of hawkish predispositions, and conservative policymakers have suspected analysts in CIA and the State Department's Bureau of Intelligence and Research

(INR) of dovish inclinations. These images suggest a problem for the Kent model, because unacknowledged prejudices allow analysts' autonomy to foster politicization in the name of objectivity, and enable analysts 'to pass off opinions as facts'.[9]

A third form operates in both directions, mediating between contrasting mind-sets of policymakers and analysts. This involves the shaping of intelligence products by analysts' managers, acting in their capacity as editors or institutional brokers, in ways that original drafters consider to be inconsistent with evidence and motivated by policy concerns. Accusations of politicization often flow from a crash between the latter tendencies, unconscious bottom-up bias, and bias in editorial management.

Contrasting Functions and Thin Lines

In principle, no one can be against maximizing either credibility or utility in intelligence analysis. Why, then, must a choice ever be made between them? The main reasons lie in the contrasting responsibilities for analysis and action, and resulting trade-offs between accuracy and impact; thin lines between packaging that is sensitive to policy context and political pandering, and between editorial management and distortion; and competition between the managerial need to render consensus judgments and the intellectual need to highlight disagreements.

Pure professional analysts optimize the analysis and let the chips fall where they may – even if they fall into a hole and are never noticed by anyone who could use them. As Uri Bar-Joseph puts it, 'the quality of the intelligence product is more important than its marketing'.[10] Indifference to the reception that analysis gets, however, is a form of goal displacement, and as irresponsible as any other parochial bureaucratic tendency to let means become ends. Taxpayers hire intelligence analysts to inform policymakers, to produce useful rather than useless truth, not to produce truth for its own sake. If analysts or managers compromise quality in order to improve receptivity, however, they vitiate the purpose too, since informed judgment depends on accurate knowledge. These points are only truisms, but controversies about politicization reflect unresolved notions about how to navigate between the pitfalls.

Often the main issue in compromising quality is the danger of haste or oversimplification. Avoiding those problems leads analysts to take longer to produce, and to produce longer papers. As Arthur Hulnick's surveys indicated, 'policymakers value research work . . . on the basis of brevity, timeliness and relevance *in that order*. Intelligence producers tend to reverse those priorities.'[11] Analysis that undermines a policy option is most useful if it arrives before a decision to choose that option is made. It may be discomfiting or unwelcome even then, but it has more of a chance of

affecting choice. Once policymakers move from decision to implementation, however, their interests become vested. Revisiting policy choice is not
impossible, but is likely only in the face of outright failure. 'We've fallen into
the same pattern of mistakes as the French', George Allen told Sam Adams,
during the controversy over estimating the number of Communist forces in
Vietnam. 'They didn't begin by faking intelligence; they merely assumed
success in the absence of clear proof of failure.'[12] Negative analysis has a
higher hurdle to surmount if it is to figure in the implementation phase.[13]

Analysts' awareness of the complexity of the issues they deal with
makes them sensitive to the reasons that policies will not work. Analysts
who complicate and equivocate do not compete as effectively for the limited
attention of consumers as those who simplify and advocate – but the latter
politicize their product more egregiously. 'Advocacy is always not only
more simple', Harold Ford writes, 'but more fun than intelligence assessment. The latter has to be all-seeing, responsible, free from any taint of
being "cooked." The former can pick, choose, and skew its facts and arguments. This is not a fair fight: advocacy will always look more attractive to
a harassed policymaker than will the usually more sober facts of life.'[14]

Outright pandering to policymakers is clearly recognizable as politicization. But what about a decision simply not to poke a policymaker in
the eye, to avoid confrontation, to get a better hearing for a negative view
by softening its presentation, when a no-compromise argument would be
certain to provoke anger and rejection? Here is the fine line between corruption and counter-productive honesty. Intelligence managers who
operate at high levels get to know that there are times and issues when it
serves no purpose to fall on their swords, and when it is more sensible to
live to fight another day – even if it means caving in on a hopeless issue.
'We live out our lives with families, friends, bosses, allies, and opponents
(who may become allies)', Loch Johnson observes. 'How we deal with
them at time t_a will influence how they deal with us at t_b, as every legisla-
tor who practices logrolling and compromise understands.'[15] On the other
hand, Kent warns, 'When intelligence producers realize that there is no
sense in forwarding to a consumer knowledge which does not correspond
to preconceptions, then intelligence is through. At this point there is no
intelligence and the consumer is out on his own with no more to guide him
than the indications of the tea leaf and the crystal ball.'[16]

Straddling these pitfalls takes us to the thin line between managerial
responsibility and manipulation of analysis to suit policy. Intelligence
products are supposed to represent the best judgments of whole organizations, not single authors. Thus, as managers point out, 'There is an inherent tension between the intellectual autonomy of the analyst and the
institutional responsibility for the product',[17] and 'If you are a manager,
you are responsible for the product. You have to satisfy yourself that you
can stand behind those judgments.'[18] As Robert Gates himself put it in a

message to analysts after his bruising confirmation battle and the report of a task force on politicization that he established:

> unwarranted concerns about politicization can arise when analysts themselves fail to understand their role in the process. We do produce a corporate product. If the policymaker wants the opinion of a single individual, he can (and frequently does) consult any one of a dozen outside experts on any given issue. Your work, on the other hand, counts because it represents the well-considered view of an entire directorate and, in the case of National Estimates, the entire intelligence community. Analysts . . . must discard the academic mindset that says their work is their own.[19]

These are responses to the frequent complaints of working-level analysts that their work is massaged and distorted by higher-ups before it is disseminated.

The next sections suggest ways in which policy interests can affect intelligence analysis, with illustrative cases that involved allegations of politicization. Each also involved policy issues of the highest priority – those on which it is more realistic than in most instances to argue that a process that focuses on careful organization of alternative interpretations, rather than a single best estimate, should be the solution to concerns about politicization. How such a comparison of alternative interpretations should be organized, however, can be a matter of controversy in itself.

Conscious Politicization: The Vietnam Order of Battle Estimate

The most blatant forms of politicization are deliberate suppression of information that undermines policy or fabrication of information to fortify policy. This is the common image of politicization, but it rarely happens unambiguously. The long war in Vietnam, however, provided many instances of stark dishonesty motivated by the need of those waging the war to convince audiences (and to believe themselves) that they were winning.[20] The most discussed major case was the 1967 dispute over the estimate of Communist military strength in South Vietnam. CIA was arguing for higher numbers in the order of battle (O/B) estimate and the Military Assistance Command, Vietnam (MACV) for lower numbers. CIA wanted to count a wider range of irregular forces (including organizations with marginal roles in supporting military operations) and to attribute higher numbers than the military to those forces. Most public accounts of the dispute come from those who sided with CIA, and who saw MACV's behavior as intellectually corrupt.

Even this case is more ambiguous than the common conception of politicization implies. There are some grounds on which to argue that MACV's overall judgments turned out to be better than CIA's. For example, the number of Communist forces used in the Tet Offensive was substantially lower than even MACV's strength estimate.[21] The dispute over the proper numbers was also not hidden from top policymakers at cabinet level and in the White House. The official published Special National Intelligence Estimate (SNIE 14.3-67), which settled more or less on the military's lower numbers as the best estimate, also included discussion of the disputed categories of forces and higher estimated figures. That made the exercise technically honest, but did not neutralize the impact of the lower figures. Unlike academics, policymakers are not attuned to careful scrutiny of qualifications and footnotes: 'Prose caveats buried deep in the SNIE . . . could not compete among senior readers with the impression created by the tabulation of ostensibly hard numbers up front in the Conclusions section.'[22]

Holding in abeyance the question of which methods of estimation were correct in their ultimate implications, we find instances of raw politicization, especially in connection with the conference between CIA and MACV to thrash out the figures before the SNIE. For example, the military applied methodological double standards in counting. All casualties from Communist irregular forces, marginal in combat roles or not, were included in the 'body count' that was then compared with the aggregate strength figures that did not include those forces from the beginning, thus inflating the apparent progress in attrition. In one conference, military representatives insisted that a CIA estimate was invalid because it was based on too small a sample of districts – 28 – but defended an estimate of their own that was based on a single district.[23]

Military personnel involved in the negotiations confessed privately that the O/B figure should be higher, but that there had been a command decision to keep the number below 300,000.[24] This was implicitly confirmed in an Eyes Only cable from General Creighton Abrams (then Westmoreland's deputy) to the Chairman of the Joint Chiefs of Staff, Earle Wheeler, three weeks before the conference. Abrams suggested dropping two categories of Viet Cong irregular organizations to keep the number at the previous level, because 'We have been projecting an image of success over the recent months', and the press would draw 'an erroneous and gloomy conclusion. . . . All those who have an incorrect view of the war will be reinforced.'[25] At the time of the O/B conference, Robert Komer, the highest civilian in MACV, lobbied against coming up with a higher number for similar reasons: 'Komer concluded that there must not be any quantifying of the enemy's irregular forces, on the grounds that so doing "would produce a politically unacceptable total over 400,000." '[26] George Allen quoted Komer as saying 'You guys [CIA] simply have to back off. Whatever the true O/B figure is, is beside the point.'[27]

The honest answer would have been to acknowledge that the categories of analysis had been changed, and to note that therefore earlier estimates were too low in the new terms of reference, and thus current estimates that were higher than the old ones could be consistent with the position that Communist strength had declined. Political and military leaders naturally feared that such an explanation, even if true, would either be overlooked, misunderstood, or seen as disingenuous, leading the press to ignore the methodological issue and trumpet the upward change in the estimated number, creating a false impression that would undermine policy.[28] When MACV gave a press briefing in November the new O/B figures were lowered further to 242,000, but, in line with advice from Ambassador Ellsworth Bunker, no mention was made that the figures were the result of dropping categories of units from the count. The announced estimate thus was not simply questionable in terms of overall accuracy; it purveyed incommensurate data in order to manipulate impressions of military progress not supported by commensurate comparisons with earlier data.[29] The change in categories counted was admitted later, but after the press had moved on.

There were three linked problems in this imbroglio. First, the subject of the estimate bore directly on the issue of single greatest priority in US foreign policy: the success of US strategy in the Vietnam War. There was no way that the conclusions could be insulated from political passions. Second, because of this, the conclusions had to be made public in a press conference. Sensitivity about misinterpretation or leaps to the wrong conclusions by opinion makers could not be assuaged by the comfort of secrecy. Policy leadership that could have afforded a thoroughly honest analysis if it was to remain classified could not possibly accept one that would be seen as striking at the heart of the policy.[30] Third, policymakers were no longer interested in using intelligence to make basic choices about strategy. The die had been cast, implementation was well under way, and reevaluation of alternatives would subvert the effort. These points do not excuse the politicization, but they explain it.

The main problem, however, was that the intelligence dispute could not be depoliticized because it could not be kept secret – a prime example of the view that politicization flows from the opening of intelligence to democratic debate.[31] If the O/B controversy could have remained hidden from public view, the political dynamite latent in the analytical problem might have been handled by turning the estimate into a carefully refereed *debate*, where contention makes clear what assertions are known for sure to be true, which are deduced, and which are simply assumed. All points of view can hold each others' feet to the fire and highlight the reasons for differing judgments, rather than trying to provide 'the answer' when the answer had to carry so much political freight. Biases may not be purged by making the exercise a debate, but the biases can compete on a level playing field. This solution is intellectually attractive, and is sometimes necessary in practice, although mostly for mid-level consumers or other readers in the intelligence community. Policymakers, however, will most often consider such exercises academic and unhelpful to them. Harried authorities at the top lack the time to digest and ponder long and complicated studies.

In most instances, policymakers want analysis that gives them the consensus, or best single estimate, of the intelligence community. The way to keep a single best estimate depoliticized, however, is to split differences and reduce judgments to lowest common denominators – which transmutes analysis into mush. This renders the product useless, and is a form of distortion in its own right – just one that is politically neutral. If there is to be a single best estimate, and it is not to be soporific and spineless, there will be competition to dominate the choice of what is to represent the institutional view.[32] That maneuvering, and the victory of one group over another, can politicize the result in effect. That is what happened in the O/B controversy.

The one adjustment that could and should have been made to minimize manipulation would have been to highlight the disagreement in the 'Conclusions' section of the estimate that everyone reads, rather than relegating the discussion to the main text, which high-level consumers ignore. This would have made the exercise more of a competitive analysis, rather than a single best estimate. But on a matter of such priority, so fraught with high political stakes, it is an illusion to believe a single best estimate is meaningful when there is not actual consensus among analysts, and equally illusory to believe that a completely depoliticized estimate was realistically possible.

Balanced Politicization? Team B and NIE 11-3/8

In 1976, at the behest of the President's Foreign Intelligence Advisory Board (PFIAB), the Director of Central Intelligence undertook an explicit exercise in competitive analysis, doing something closer to what should have been done in the 1967 Vietnam O/B dispute. Two separate estimates reflecting different assumptions were to be arrayed together. Like the O/B controversy, this case too concerned the issue that was the highest priority in US foreign policy at the time – in this case, assessment of Soviet strategic capabilities and objectives. In addition to the regular drafting of the National Intelligence Estimate (NIE) 11-3/8 on Soviet nuclear capabilities, three parallel studies were commissioned to be done by a prestigious panel of outsiders – 'Team B' – under the leadership of Harvard historian Richard Pipes. Team B was deliberately selected from among those known to have views on the subject more hawkish than what the PFIAB considered the general orientation of the regular NIE. In effect, this turned out to be a sort of open and balanced politicization – giving two fundamental attitudes toward the nature and extent of the Soviet threat a chance to make their best case.

The emphasis here is on 'in effect'. The regular estimators (Team A) did not initially consider the exercise to be adversarial, nor did they realize the extent to which it had been consciously organized to criticize and counter past NIEs. In the end, the Team B report presented a sharp contrast in tone and content to the NIEs of the previous decade, and the whole exercise involved reciprocal charges of bad judgment and unsupported assertion. Defenders of the regular NIEs charged Team B with setting out to support preconceived conclusions and use the study to undermine detente.[33] The leader of Team B charged that the problem with earlier NIE 11-3/8s was that 'politicized scientists and uncritical devotees of arms control had misconstrued the Soviet strategic threat'.[34]

In the initial stage of the exercise some objected to including the non-technical subject of Soviet objectives.[35] (The latter is what dominated public reports and controversy about the Team B report, although much of the entire project consisted of technical panels on Soviet programs such as air defense.) Pipes refuted objections by arguing that 'it is not possible completely to divorce an assessment of capabilities from the judgment of intention: the significance of a person's purchasing a knife is different if he is a professional chef or the leader of a street gang, although the technical "capability" which the knife provides is the same in each case'.[36]

After the Team B report, the drafters of NIE 11-3/8 revised the final estimate in a manner that made statements about Soviet intentions more consistent with Team B's views. The changes were mainly deletions of statements not based on hard evidence.[37] The Team B report on Soviet objectives, however, focused primarily on criticism of 'mirror imaging' and underestimation of offensive aims, rather than adducing evidence to justify its own assumptions about Soviet motives. Team B's interpretation was essentially an essay asserting the difference in Soviet worldview and the quest for military superiority as the driving force in Soviet programs and diplomacy.[38]

In a public article that was in effect an unclassified version of Team B's report on Soviet objectives, Pipes did cite a number of sources for his interpretation, including articles in the classified Soviet journal, *Soviet Military Thought*.[39] Soon thereafter, Raymond Garthoff published an article drawing on the same sorts of Soviet sources – but citing different passages – which refuted the view propounded by Pipes. Garthoff's article was implicitly a defense of the record of estimates attacked by Team B.[40]

Part of the problem was a confusion about which level of analysis was at issue – an implicit elision of Soviet *policy* and *strategy*. At the level of what might be called *strategic* intent (how to approach war *if* it came), Soviet military doctrine was indeed clearly offensive and aimed at securing maximum military advantage. Hardly anyone challenged this point. Team

B and Pipes focused on this, but did not distinguish the orientation clearly from *political* intent (objectives to be achieved), on which there were many more indications of Soviet orientation to avoiding nuclear war at nearly all costs. Team A and Garthoff focused on the latter point. Pipes compared apples and oranges – US policy intent with Soviet strategic intent.[41] Neither side clarified sufficiently that apples and oranges were being intermingled in the estimates and the dispute between the two camps.

The confrontation of interpretations in Teams A and B only reflected the essential debate of the 1970s between hawks and moderates over the nature and extent of the Soviet threat. (Doves were not represented in the exercise; that would have required a Team C staffed by Soviet apologists.) The real driving force was the question of Soviet policy intent – whether Moscow aimed for peaceful coexistence or military aggression – a question of high politics (and, for most in the policy world, articles of faith) on which it would have been utterly futile to attempt a single best intelligence estimate. Once the issue for assessment was cast in terms of Soviet capabilities and objectives, and arms-control negotiations had energized hawks, moderates, and doves to focus on indices of power and policy that would support their views, there was no way to keep such assessments free of policy predispositions. Complexity of data meant that any selectivity in presentation of evidence, any emphasis, could be seen as manipulation to support policy preferences. Data could not help but be political ammunition, and attitudes toward data analysis naturally paralleled attitudes on the high politics of US-Soviet relations. Indeed, as Jim Klurfield concluded, when Ronald Reagan defeated Jimmy Carter, 'Team B, in essence, became Team A.'[42]

Unconscious Politicization? The Gates Revolution and Reaction

Allegations of politicization come up periodically, but they grew especially prominent in the Reagan and elder Bush administrations. At the end of the Cold War, grumblings inside the intelligence community burst into public view in the confirmation hearings for the nomination of Robert Gates to be Director of Central Intelligence (DCI). One major long-serving analyst charged that as head of the Directorate of Intelligence (DI) under DCI William Casey, Gates had politicized intelligence to support the extreme anti-Soviet policies of the administration, by:

> the imposition of intelligence judgments, often over the protests of the consensus in the Directorate of Intelligence to slant intelligence . . . suppression of intelligence that didn't support the Casey agenda . . . use of the Directorate of Operations to slant intelligence of the Directorate of Intelligence . . . manipulation of the intelligence

process that existed for forty years to protect dissent, to protect difference of opinion . . . manipulation of personnel or what I call judge-shopping in the courthouse, finding someone to do your bidding . . . to reach your conclusions.[43]

Other junior and senior analysts testified in a similar vein. Views of this sort made some conclude that 'never before in the history of the CIA was the intelligence process so systematically corrupted' as in the Reagan–Casey–Gates era.[44] Allegations against Gates were countered by testimony that denied the charges and interpreted acts in dispute differently. The differences in view depended to some extent on whose ox was being gored ideologically. As Mark Lowenthal notes, some who charge politicization are simply the ' "losers" in the bureaucratic battles'.[45]

Where analysts saw corruption of the process, Gates and other leaders of the intelligence bureaucracy in the 1980s believed they were using managerial discretion to improve the rigor and relevance of analytical products. Their concern was not just about their responsibility for the corporate imprimatur, but also with the biases of analysts themselves. Politicization, as noted earlier, is not just a top-down phenomenon; it can operate unconsciously from the bottom-up, if analysts let their own policy biases contaminate their writing. Indeed, the fear of some policymakers that professional analysts share a common bias and politicize their conclusions to undermine alternative policies had been the reason behind the Team B exercise. When National Intelligence Officer (NIO) Graham Fuller defended Gates in the 1991 confirmation hearings he raised counter-charges, in effect, of unconscious politicization or simple naivete among the analysts attacking Gates, analysts who came primarily from the Office of Soviet Affairs (SOVA) in the Directorate of Intelligence (DI):

> Because of the strongly felt Casey position, I am afraid a counter-culture seems to have sprung up among SOVA analysts . . . SOVA seemed to bend over backwards to compensate . . . in my own personal observation [SOVA] seemed inclined towards, yes, a highly benign view of Soviet intentions and goals . . . SOVA analysts may perhaps have been expert on the Third World . . . but few of them had gotten their feet dirty, so to speak, in the dust of the Third World, and had not watched Soviet embassies work abroad.[46]

How does one know where the line lies between editing and distortion, when both original analysis and revision by editors involves decisions about proper scope, emphasis, and selection of relevant data? When evidence is mixed, as it always is on difficult issues, choices about emphasis are political choices – whether made by dovish analysts or hawkish managers. One charge against Gates was that in 1981 he and NIO Jeremy

Azrael rewrote the Key Judgments (the summary of conclusions at the beginning) of a study 'to suggest greater Soviet support for terrorism, and the text was altered by pulling up from the annex reports that overstated Soviet involvement'.[47] Who should decide what information should go in main text or annex, or which data overstate or understate evidence?

Initial versions of the latter study concluded that there was scant support for the view that Moscow was a major instigator of terrorism. In a subsequent redraft by a member of the DCI's Senior Review Panel, Lincoln Gordon, the scope of the study was broadened to include revolutionary war, which led to more evidence of Soviet support. One of the analysts involved considered this politicization because it allowed the paper to 'avoid definitions of terrorism', and to suggest 'that the Soviet Union, by providing support for revolutionary violence, supported international terrorism'.[48] This exemplifies the problem that the very terms of reference for an analysis can be heavily freighted with political bias. There has never been a consensus on how to define terrorism, primarily because it is a highly pejorative and politically loaded term. Narrow definitions are favored by those who wish to exclude actions by groups whose cause they approve, and broad definitions by those who wish to tar groups whose cause they abhor.[49]

Another example of difficulty in disentangling editing from politicization was an estimate on Mexico produced in the mid-1980s. The NIO for Latin America, John Horton, believed that the Reagan administration was exerting pressure to produce an estimate emphasizing instability in the country. His superior, Herbert Meyer, maintained that Horton revised the draft done by a CIA Mexico expert, and Meyer in turn revised Horton's revisions to reinstate the other analyst's conclusions. Horton charged that the estimate that emerged from Meyer's action 'was full of unsubstantiated allegations. What Meyer was doing was putting in what Casey wanted.'[50] When a higher manager supports an analyst against a lower manager, who is winning – autonomous analysts or coercive management? Did this episode demonstrate editorial disagreements or dueling politicization?

Navigating the Thin Lines

The challenge remains to make intelligence relevant without making it dishonest by pulling punches in a way that lets policymakers believe what they want. In practical terms, if intelligence is to be useful, politicization will be a continuum from more to less, with the least being the aim for which intelligence professionals strive, but zero being unattainable without denuding analysis of all connection with political reality. Minimal political contamination, or open and balanced competition between analysis from different predispositions, must be the norm, but enforcing the norm may generate as many charges of politicization as it averts. Much depends on artful straddling of thin lines by intelligence managers – something not easily done – or signals sent in the choice of managers.[51]

There was less concern that intelligence was politicized in the first half of the Cold War, mostly because of the greater policy consensus among the players, but also because of the care given to symbolic protections such as the appointment of professionals unassociated with political parties to the top positions in the intelligence community. Until the post-Watergate era and the Congressional investigations of the 1970s, eight of ten DCIs were military officers (Sidney Souers, Hoyt Vandenberg, Roscoe Hillenkoetter, Walter Bedell Smith, William Raborn), career intelligence officers (Richard Helms, William Colby), or a member of the opposition party (Republican John McCone under Democrats Kennedy and Johnson). Only Allen Dulles and James Schlesinger were political appointees in the mold of cabinet members. In the period in which there have been more public controversies about politicization, however, leadership has been more typically political. Since Colby, only two of eight DCIs have been ostensibly non-political (Stansfield Turner, William Webster). Two were as visibly partisan as one could possibly imagine (George Bush the elder, who had been Chairman of the Republican National Committee, and William Casey, Ronald Reagan's campaign manager). The others were a former career intelligence officer (Gates) who made his reputation serving near the top of the White House and who had earlier been accused of trying to coopt the DI for the Reaganite worldview, and three standard cabinet-like political appointees from the President's own party (James Woolsey, John Deutch, George Tenet).[52] Two other nominees who had to withdraw from confirmation battles were visible partisans of the President's party (Theodore Sorensen, Anthony Lake).

There is something to be said for the idea that it would be desirable for DCIs to be from the opposition party (or non-political career profession-als from the military or intelligence community itself), and also that DCI be a terminal office for elder statesmen who are not suspected of ambition for further advancement in the military or the policy world. At the least, these symbolic criteria would dull suspicions of politicization when intel-ligence seemed to support administration policy by providing prima facie reasons to believe that the DCI has no vested interest in pandering. This would complicate the process of choosing an effective DCI, however, because the most important criterion is to have rapport with the President. Otherwise, all the good intelligence in the world will have less entrée to the decision than it could. More to the point, there is yet no constituency of any consequence for the norm of avoiding political appointment to the position of DCI.

Despite complaints from some analysts and intellectuals, moreover, the Gates model has continued to dominate in the management of intelligence analysis. Policymakers are scarcely bothered by the danger of politicization, and many in the foreign policy establishment genuflect to the danger of politicization yet endorse closer connections between intelligence and policy.[53] Indeed, George Tenet was called on at several junctures to function as a diplomat, brokering delicate elements of negotiation in the Israeli–Palestinian peace process.

Some bad effects of the accentuated politicization that has come with increased publicity may be ameliorated by the natural dynamics of constitutional pluralism, which fosters dueling politicization and hence some rough balance. The institutionalization of oversight in Congress contributes to this. After the Team B exercise, for example, the Senate Select Committee on Intelligence issued a staff report examining and criticizing it, essentially from the point of view of Team A. A Republican PFIAB countered alleged CIA bias with Team B, and Senate Democrats countered alleged Team B bias with their own assessment. In turning intelligence disputes into public controversies, intelligence may be damaged, but policy may be served by forcing fundamental issues on to the table. Protracted battles between intelligence and policy, as in the history of bleak estimates on the Vietnam War, are probably no longer possible, because congressional oversight would bring them 'quickly to the surface and thus cause them to be resolved'.[54]

Within the executive branch where the rubber meets road on a day-to-day basis, however, no formula has been found to square the circle. There is still a tension between objectivity and influence. As Lawrence Freedman puts the paradox, 'there is a direct relationship between the potential importance of the estimates in critical policy debates, and the difficulty faced within the community in forging an agreed consensus and in preventing estimates being misused by the political masters'.[55] In no small part, however, this is because of the struggle to produce *a single best estimate* on the most fundamentally controversial disputes – indeed, they are in effect theological – about threats to national security. Single best estimates can be useful, and often uncontroversial, on secondary matters, or ones in which leaders do not have well-formed views of their own already, and in which their convictions are not already invested. On matters of high politics, however, producing a consensus estimate is likely to be meaningless, because it rests on negotiated mush, or else it will be bloodily contested. In the latter instance, politicization in some measure is virtually inevitable.

In those cases, futile attempts to combine quality and consensus make less sense than a conscious process for careful presentation of contrasting views. The organizational pluralism of the intelligence community is the best defense against deceptive and damaging politicization, and that defense may best be provided by unmasking and setting up a competition of predispositions rather than letting biases sneak into products striving for ideal objectivity. SNIE 14.3-67 could have done this better on the O/B controversy, by giving equal time in the summary conclusions to the analyses that yielded higher strength figures for Communist forces. The Team B exercise was a more explicit step in the direction suggested, but an incomplete one – and the incompleteness severely marred the result.

The best way to tell which cases warrant a single best estimate and which require casting the estimate as a debate is to find out whether a single best estimate can be obtained without splitting differences. If undiluted Key Judgments that are not obvious can be agreed with, say, no more than one major agency represented on the National Foreign Intelligence Board dissenting (or perhaps two of the minor ones), such a consensus can be useful. Otherwise, a lengthier product that lays out the alternatives may be unwelcome to policymakers, but it is better to make clear the limits of intelligence than to obscure them. This puts the ball in the consumers' court. It puts them on notice that intelligence cannot solve their problem, that they must either make the effort to look harder at the bases for disagreement among the experts, or forthrightly accept that they are operating on the basis of their own preferences or articles of faith rather than a complex reading of divided expert opinion.

If politicization includes all contamination of analysis by policy predispositions, it will never be fully purged from the process, because every analyst's ideas and assumptions, and those of managers or competing analysts, will be politicizing forces, however muted or constrained professional standards of rigor may make them. Analysis that remains trenchant, rather than descending into negotiated mush, will never be free of political agendas. Bias can be minimized, however, by enforcement of rigorous standards of evidence and comparison, and the effects of bias can be mitigated or made productive by organizing the confrontation of views in as systematic a manner as possible. All of this involves artful management, and walking dangerous lines. Robert Gates may have strayed too far and too energetically from the Kent model, but his message to analysts after the chastening of his confirmation hearings – a message that he composed by drawing on competing drafts supplied by a variety of analysts – charts the right course among pitfalls:

> a manager challenging assumptions should not be seen as a threat by analysts . . . We must draw a line:
> - Between producing a corporate product and suppressing different views.
> - Between adjusting stylistic presentation to anticipate consumers' predilections, and changing the analysis to pander to them . . .
> - Between viewing reporting critically and using evidence selectively . . .[56]

Gates' message also noted that the main entrance to CIA headquarters is dominated by the chiseled inscription from the Bible, 'And ye shall know the truth and the truth shall make you free.'[57] To many cynical observers, especially those lay critics whose image of CIA derives from Hollywood or the history of dirty tricks by the Directorate of Operations, that inscription is ironic, paradoxical, or disingenuous. But for working analysts, intelligence managers, and policymakers who place any value on knowledge as a basis for making and implementing decisions, there can be no other rationale to give the enterprise meaning.

NOTES

1 'The term "politicization" is nearly always applied to actions of which one disapproves.' David A. Baldwin, *Economic Statecraft* (Princeton, NJ: Princeton University Press, 1985), p. 209n.

2 *Webster's Third New International Dictionary* (Springfield, MA: Merriam-Webster, 1986), p. 1755.

3 For other definitions see Harry Howe Ransom, 'The Politicization of Intelligence', in Stephen J. Cimbala, ed., *Intelligence and Intelligence Policy in a Democratic Society* (Dobbs Ferry, NY: Transnational, 1987), p. 26.

4 See the discussion of these approaches, and the various other terms used to characterize them, in H. Bradford Westerfield, 'Inside Ivory Bunkers: CIA Analysts Resist Managers' "Pandering" – Part I', *International Journal of Intelligence and Counterintelligence*, vol. 9, no. 4 (Winter 1996/97), p. 409 and *passim*.

5 Sherman Kent, *Strategic Intelligence for American World Policy* (Princeton, NJ: Princeton University Press, 1949), pp. 195–201.

6 Robert Jervis, 'What's Wrong with the Intelligence Process?', *International Journal of Intelligence and Counterintelligence*, vol. 1, no. 1 (1986), p. 39.

7 See, for example, L. Keith Gardiner, 'Dealing with Intelligence-Policy Disconnects', *Studies in Intelligence*, vol. 33, no. 2 (Summer 1989), and David D. Gries, 'New Links Between Intelligence and Policy', *Studies in Intelligence*, vol. 34, no. 2 (Summer 1990), both reprinted in H. Bradford Westerfield, ed., *Inside CIA's Private World: Declassified Articles from the Agency's Internal Journal, 1955–1992* (New Haven, CT: Yale University Press, 1995), pp. 346–7. See also Richard K. Betts, 'Policy-Makers and Intelligence Analysts: Love, Hate or Indifference?', *Intelligence and National Security*, vol. 3, no. 1 (January 1988). For a detailed account of the shift, and the organizational changes that facilitated it, from the perspective of the aggrieved, see John A. Gentry, 'Intelligence Analyst/Manager Relations at the CIA', in David A. Charters, Stuart Farson, and Glenn P. Hastedt, eds, *Intelligence Analysis and Assessment* (London: Frank Cass, 1996).

8 As academics often forget, models are more distinct in theory than in practice. For example, while Kent warned of the danger of corruption from too close a relationship between intelligence and policy, he also warned, 'of the two dangers – that of intelligence being too far from the users and that of being too close – the greatest danger is the one of being too far'. Kent, *Strategic Intelligence*, p. 195. Uri Bar-Joseph uses the terms 'professional' and 'realist' for what I call the Kent and Gates models. He identifies Michael Handel as one of the main proponents of the 'professional approach', and cites me as a member of the realist school (*Intelligence Intervention in the Politics of Democratic States: The United States, Israel, and Britain* (University Park, PA: Pennsylvania State University Press, 1995), pp. 25–8). The fact that Handel and I were close friends and agreed more than we disagreed is a reminder that the models are only indications of tendency and emphasis.

9 Bruce D. Berkowitz and Allan E. Goodman, *Best Truth: Intelligence in the Information Age* (New Haven, CT: Yale University Press, 2000), p. 97.
10 Bar-Joseph, *Intelligence Intervention in the Politics of Democratic States*, p. 28.
11 Arthur S. Hulnick, 'The Intelligence Producer-Policy Consumer Linkage: A Theoretical Approach', *Intelligence and National Security*, vol. 1, no. 2 (May 1986), p. 227 (emphasis in original).
12 Quoted in Sam Adams, *War of Numbers: An Intelligence Memoir* (South Royalton, VT: Steerforth Press, 1994), p. 80.
13 See Yehoshafat Harkabi, 'The Intelligence-Policymaker Tangle', *Jerusalem Quarterly*, no. 30 (Winter 1984), pp. 126, 128.
14 Harold P. Ford, *Estimative Intelligence*, revised edn (Lanham, MD: University Press of America, 1993), p. 177.
15 Loch K. Johnson, 'Decision Costs in the Intelligence Cycle', in Alfred C. Maurer, Marion D. Tunstall, and James M. Keagle, eds, *Intelligence: Policy and Process* (Boulder, CO: Westview Press, 1985), p. 186.
16 Kent, *Strategic Intelligence*, p. 205.
17 Kay Oliver testimony in Gates hearings, quoted in Westerfield, 'Inside Ivory Bunkers: CIA Analysts Resist Managers' "Pandering" – Part II', *International Journal of Intelligence and Counterintelligence*, vol. 10, no. 1 (Spring 1997), p. 19.
18 Douglas MacEachin's testimony in Gates hearings, quoted in Westerfield, 'Part II', p. 24.
19 'A Message to Analysts on "Politicization" by Robert M. Gates', 16 March 1992 (manuscript), p. 7.
20 See the many examples cited in George W. Allen, *None So Blind: A Personal Account of the Intelligence Failure in Vietnam* (Chicago, IL: Ivan Dee, 2001), especially the charge against Walt Rostow on pp. 236–7.
21 Lt Gen. Phillip B. Davidson, USA (Ret.), *Secrets of the Vietnam War* (Novato, CA: Presidio Press, 1990), pp. 64–5; Harold P. Ford, *CIA and the Vietnam Policymakers: Three Episodes, 1962–1968* (n.p.: Central Intelligence Agency, Center for the Study of Intelligence, 1998), p. 100; James J. Wirtz, *The Tet Offensive: Intelligence Failure in War* (Ithaca, NY: Cornell University Press, 1991), pp. 158–62; T.L. Cubbage II, 'Westmoreland vs. CBS: Was Intelligence Corrupted by Policy Demands?', in Michael I. Handel, ed., *Leaders and Intelligence* (London: Frank Cass, 1989), p. 133; see also p. 165. See also Renata Adler, *Reckless Disregard: Westmoreland v. CBS et al.; Sharon v. Time* (New York: Alfred A. Knopf, 1986).
22 Ford, *CIA and the Vietnam Policymakers*, p. 102.
23 Adams, *War of Numbers*, pp. 105, 114–15. This is the lengthiest account of the dispute by the CIA analyst most involved in challenging MACV estimates. For the main points behind his position see especially chs 4–5.
24 Colonel Gains Hawkins, George Allen, and George Carver cited in Ford, *CIA and the Vietnam Policymakers*, pp. 91, 93–4.
25 Cable quoted by Samuel Adams in testimony in US House of Representatives, Select Committee on Intelligence (the Pike Committee), *Hearings: US Intelligence Agencies and Activities: The Performance of the Intelligence Community*, Part 2, 94th Cong., 1st sess., September–October 1975, pp. 684–5.
26 Ford, *CIA and the Vietnam Policymakers*, p. 94.
27 Cable from Saigon, and Allen, quoted in Ford, *CIA and the Vietnam Policymakers*, pp. 92, 97.
28 Davidson, *Secrets of the Vietnam War*, pp. 34, 44, 66–7. Davidson's is the only published insider's account I have found that defends MACV's performance on the O/B estimate.
29 Adams testimony in Pike Committee Hearings, Part 2, pp. 685–6.
30 In other cases, policymakers can use secrecy to politicize intelligence by manipu-

lating its dissemination. Analysis may retain integrity, but be kept out of channels that could cause trouble. This can occur on behalf of policy views anywhere along the spectrum of hawks and doves or conservatives and liberals. For example, in mid-1980, when Congress required that aid to Nicaragua 'be contingent on a presidential certification that Nicaragua was not "aiding, abetting, or supporting acts of violence"', the Carter administration refused routine Congressional staff requests to speak with the relevant CIA analyst. The embargo was lifted only two days before certification was announced. The committee staff reviewed the intelligence and found that it did not support the administration position. US House of Representatives, Permanent Select Committee on Intelligence, *Staff Report: US Intelligence Performance on Central America: Achievements and Selected Instances of Concern*, 97th Cong., 2d sess., September 1982, pp. 5–7.

31 Glenn P. Hastedt, 'The New Context of Intelligence Estimating', in Cimbala, ed., *Intelligence and Intelligence Policy in a Democratic Society*, pp. 49–50, 56, 59–60, 64.
32 'We frequently fall into what I call the institutional view syndrome. For a long time in my career, we did not in actual practice foster a tradition of careful treatment of alternatives ... Rather than trying to lay out the threatening situation to the reader ... we routinely got bogged down in an internal contest as to whose views would win the institutional place.' Douglas MacEachin testimony, in US Senate, Select Committee on Intelligence, *Hearings: Nomination of Robert M. Gates*, 102d Cong., 1st sess., September–October 1991 (hereafter cited as 'Gates Hearings'), vol. II, p. 271.
33 US Senate Select Committee on Intelligence, Subcommittee on Collection, Production, and Quality, *Staff Report: The National Intelligence Estimates A–B Team Episode Concerning Soviet Strategic Capability and Objectives*, February 1978; Anne Hessing Cahn, *Killing Detente: The Right Attacks the CIA* (University Park, PA: Pennsylvania State University Press, 1998), *passim*.
34 Richard Pipes, 'Team B: The Reality Behind the Myth', *Commentary* (October 1986), p. 40.
35 Cahn, *Killing Detente*, p. 127.
36 Pipes, 'Team B', p. 29. Although Pipes' application of this insight was in many respects questionable, he is right in principle. Intelligence officers sometimes fail 'to realize that facts and theory are not separable'. Captain Robert Bovey, USN, 'The Quality of Intelligence Analysis', *American Intelligence Journal*, vol. 3, no. 3 (Winter 1980–81), p. 4 of repaginated Pentagon 'Current News' reprint. Or, as E.H. Carr made the point: 'The facts speak only when the historian calls on them: it is he who decides which facts to give the floor, and in what context . . . It is the historian who has decided for his own reasons that Caesar's crossing of that petty stream, the Rubicon, is a fact of history, whereas the crossing of the Rubicon by millions of other people before or since interests nobody at all.' *What Is History?* (New York: Vintage Books, 1961), p. 9.
37 Howard Stoertz, cited in Cahn, *Killing Detente*, p. 174.
38 The report itself is *Intelligence Community Experiment in Competitive Analysis: Soviet Strategic Objectives, an Alternate View: Report of Team B*, December 1976 (sanitized declassified copy from the National Security Archive); see especially pp. 9–16, 41–8.
39 Richard Pipes, 'Why the Soviet Union Thinks It Could Fight and Win a Nuclear War', *Commentary*, vol. 64, no. 1 (July 1977).
40 Raymond L. Garthoff, 'Mutual Deterrence and Strategic Arms Limitation in Soviet Policy', *International Security*, vol. 3, no. 1 (Summer 1978). For the later and definitive version of Garthoff's research and interpretation see his *Deterrence and the Revolution in Soviet Military Doctrine* (Washington, DC: Brookings Institution, 1990).

41 The salience of the difference between policy intent and strategic intent is my own
    view, not one emphasized explicitly by partisans in the debates of the Cold War.
    Pipes criticized US acceptance of assumptions about mutual deterrence, which
    were articulated at the policy level, but failed to note that in operational planning
    at the strategic level, the US military engaged in counterforce targeting and devel-
    oped options for pre-emptive launch of offensive forces. He mistook the evolu-
    tionary change in PD-59 (President Carter's 1980 directive to emphasize planning
    for counter-force targeting, prolonged nuclear war, and attacks on command and
    control structures) for a revolutionary shift.
42 Quoted in Pipes, 'Team B', p. 40n.
43 Melvin Goodman, testimony in Gates Hearings, vol. II, p. 143. See also testimony
    against Gates by Jennifer Glaudemans and Harold Ford.
44 Bar-Joseph, *Intelligence Intervention in the Politics of Democratic States*, p. 33.
45 Mark M. Lowenthal, *Intelligence: From Secrets to Policy* (Washington, DC:
    Congressional Quarterly Press, 2000), p. 91.
46 Graham Fuller, testimony in Gates Hearings, vol. II, p. 161. See also testimony in
    support of Gates by Charles Allen, Douglas MacEachin, Lawrence Gershwin, and
    Kay Oliver. Earlier, Jimmy Carter's DCI, Admiral Turner, recounted instances of
    analysts who considered his editorial revisions of their work to be politicization,
    while he believed he was simply correcting misleading methods in comparison on
    a subject about which he was more expert than the analysts – naval capabilities.
    Turner also dealt with the case of David Sullivan, an analyst who leaked his own
    work to anti-Soviet Senate staff because he feared that it would be suppressed by
    detentist leadership at CIA. Stansfield Turner, *Secrecy and Democracy: The CIA in
    Transition* (Boston, MA: Houghton Mifflin, 1985), pp. 122–3.
47 Memorandum by Carolyn Ekedahl, reprinted in Gates Hearings, vol. III, p. 84.
48 Ekedahl memorandum, in Gates Hearings, Part III, p. 186. This study has been
    the subject of another story about policy contamination of intelligence, via blow-
    back from covert action. The story I have heard verbally several times is that
    Casey was energized to prove that the Soviets supported terrorism because of
    claims to that effect in Claire Sterling's book, *The Terror Network: The Secret War
    of International Terrorism* (New York: Holt, Rhinehart & Winston, 1981), and
    that he discovered only later that Sterling's information had come from a disin-
    formation operation by the CIA's own Directorate of Operations. The only
    account of this that I have seen in print says that according to Lincoln Gordon 'a
    small part' of the Sterling information had come from such blowback. Bob
    Woodward, *Veil: The Secret Wars of the CIA 1981–1987* (New York: Simon &
    Schuster, 1987), pp. 124–9.
49 Richard K. Betts, 'The Soft Underbelly of American Primacy: Tactical Advantages
    of Terror', *Political Science Quarterly*, vol. 117, no. 1 (Spring 2002), pp. 19–20.
50 Quoted in David C. Morrison, 'Tilting With Intelligence', *National Journal*, 9 May,
    1987, p. 1115. See also John Horton, 'Mexico, the Way of Iran?', *International
    Journal of Intelligence and Counterintelligence*, vol. 1, no. 2 (1986), and Horton,
    'The Real Intelligence Failure', *Foreign Service Journal*, vol. 62, no. 2 (February
    1985).
51 Some of the points below echo Ransom, 'The Politicization of Intelligence', and
    Hastedt, 'The New Context of Intelligence Estimating', which I discovered just
    before making final revisions to my initial draft.
52 Tenet's continuation in office under Bush the younger might be seen as a latter-day
    equivalent of McCone's service.
53 For example, see *Making Intelligence Smarter: The Future of US Intelligence*,
    Report of an Independent Task Force (New York: Council on Foreign Relations,
    1996), pp. 18–19, and *In From the Cold: The Report of the Twentieth Century Fund*

Task Force on the Future of US Intelligence (New York: Twentieth Century Fund Press, 1996), pp. 10–12.
54 Hans Heymann, 'Intelligence/Policy Relationships', in Maurer, Tunstall, and Keagle, eds, *Intelligence: Policy and Process*, p. 63.
55 Lawrence Freedman, *US Intelligence and the Soviet Strategic Threat*, 2nd edn (Princeton, NJ: Princeton University Press, 1986), pp. xi–xii.
56 'A Message to Analysts on "Politicization" ', pp. 9, 13.
57 Ibid., p. 1.

3

Intelligence Failures: Forecasting and the Lessons of Epistemology

Woodrow J. Kuhns

The study of intelligence failures is perhaps the most academically advanced field in the study of intelligence.[1] This is particularly true of strategic surprise, that most dramatic and consequential of intelligence failures. Michael Handel, who made a major contribution to the study of this issue, once listed the various disciplines that had made contributions to its study:

> It is related to, and dependent on, earlier research in psychology (problems of perception); communication and information theory (the problems of signal-to-noise ratio, information bottlenecks, improved processing procedures of information, etc.); theories of organizational and bureaucratic behavior (for example, problems of overlapping and duplicate intelligence work by a number of different intelligence agencies, ways to improve interagency coordination); statistics; disaster theory; mathematical theories (the study of cryptanalysis, the optimal timing of surprise, etc.); anthropology (the study of the influence of different cultures and their impact on mutual perceptions and misperceptions, different attitudes toward risk acceptance); and history (the basic information needed for detailed case studies).[2]

Much of the attention that surprise has received in academia is due to Roberta Wohlstetter's seminal work on Pearl Harbor.[3] Wohlstetter's thesis, that the surprise attack was possible not because the United States lacked information about Japanese designs, but rather because the available intelligence was misperceived or was hidden in a larger universe of irrelevant information, established the paradigm for most succeeding works on surprise. Indeed, many academic specialists have come to believe that the obstacles to conducting adequate intelligence analysis are so formidable that strategic surprise, and therefore intelligence failures in general, are inevitable.[4]

Christopher Brady summarized the majority view of surprise this way:

> It is commonly accepted that intelligence failures are rarely a problem of collection but generally one of interpretation – 'intelligence as knowledge' – and that the route from collection to decision is punctuated by a series of 'barriers' between that competent collection and the incompetent utilization of the information. These barriers can be structural, psychological, organizational, or cultural and can exist either in the nature of the information or as a result of the process performed by analysts who are themselves merely cogs in a complex machine.[5]

Richard Betts adds detail to the paradigm:

> While many sources of surprise lie in the attacker's skill in deception or operational innovation, orthodox studies emphasize the victim's mistakes – how interactions of organizations, psychology, and inherent ambiguity of information create pathologies in the process of absorbing and reacting to indicators. For example, hierarchical and fragmented bureaucracies retard communication and block dissemination and coordination; individuals along the line misunderstand or transmute the implications of messages; ambient 'noise' from irrelevant data obscures the significance of revealing signals; or false alarms feed a 'cry wolf' syndrome.[6]

Studies of strategic surprise focus on the most difficult and controversial task that intelligence analysts face, that of prediction, more commonly referred to within the intelligence community as estimating or, when threat of attack is involved, as warning. This chapter also will focus on the role of prediction in intelligence failures, but, rather than following the orthodox approach as outlined above, it will examine the potential contribution of philosophy, especially its subfield of epistemology.[7] Intelligence is really little more than useful knowledge – useful to the policymaker – and epistemology is the study of knowledge.

This chapter, then, will address the following questions: What is the evidentiary base we start from? In particular, what is the error rate in intelligence forecasting? Is it true that most errors are attributable to analysis instead of collection? Is intelligence analysis closer to science or pseudoscience? If it is closer to science, why do its forecasts fail in crucial instances? Is there an epistemological or methodological reason that these failures occur? Is there a better way for intelligence analysts to attempt predictions? And how much does estimating matter to policymakers anyway?

It seems prudent to begin with a discussion of the extent of the forecasting problem in analysis.

Just How Bad Is It Out There?

The short answer is, no one knows. Abbot Smith, former chief of the Board of National Estimates, once noted that, 'It would seem reasonable to suppose that one could get a truly objective, statistical verdict on the accuracy of estimates. Go through the papers, tick off the right judgments and the wrong ones, and figure the batting average. I once thought that this could be done, and I tried it, and it proved to be impossible. The reasons are various.'[8]

One important obstacle that Smith identified was the huge quantity of data a researcher would have to sift through to reach an accurate count. Each National Intelligence Estimate (NIE) actually contains a multitude of judgments, and Smith guessed that to judge the track record of just 20 years' worth of NIEs a researcher would need to check the accuracy of no fewer than 25,000 judgments.

> Common sense tells us that a box score of estimates must be selective if it is to mean much; it must take account only of the *important* judgments. In saying this, however we have left behind the wholly objective approach. Doubtless there are many estimates which everyone would agree to be important, but there are many others on which opinions would differ. The hard fact of life is that the high-level consumer of NIEs – the only person whose opinion really matters – is apt to judge the whole output on the basis of two or three estimates which strike home to him. If they prove correct, NIE's are good; if incorrect, they are bad.[9]

An equally difficult obstacle to overcome in establishing the estimative track record, according to Smith, is the fact that estimates must be judged by the impact of the document as a whole, including 'the choice of facts which are cited, the distribution of emphasis, the cogency of argument, even the literary quality. I think that such a paper could be basically correct even though it had a great many statements which proved incorrect, and basically wrong even though many statements were accurate.'[10]

The community and its individual agencies have episodically – some would say spasmodically – made attempts to review the accuracy of the analytical products, but these efforts have always been passing fads, often sparked by a major failure, and involving little more than examination of a handful of case studies. The first effort of this sort came between 1973 and 1975, when the Product Review Division of the Intelligence Community Staff produced seven post-mortem reports at the behest of the Director of Central Intelligence and the United States Intelligence Board.[11] The project met its end when it became a casualty of the political confrontation between the Pike Committee and the Executive Branch.

To many in the intelligence community, it appeared that the House committee cynically was trying to use the post-mortems as ammunition to attack the community, and the project was cancelled.[12]

Another effort, made a decade later, involved the preparation of 12 case studies by the Senior Review Panel.[13] The cases studied by the Panel were either nominated by DCI and DDCI for review or were chosen because of their consequences to US national interests. Only well-known failures were examined; no effort was made to look at the longer-term 'batting average' of either the Agency or the community.

These examples are illustrative of the types of performance review that have been undertaken. The bottom line is that no one inside the intelligence community – or outside of it, for that matter – knows what the 'batting average' is when it comes to analysts' forecasts. A number of highly visible failures have created the impression in the media, in academia, and among some in Congress, that the failures greatly outnumber successes. This may be true, but we do not *know* that it is.

One writer characterized the problem with existing studies of strategic surprise this way:

> Insensitivity to sample size can lead to unwarranted inferences about population parameters . . . This insensitivity produces the view that strategic surprise is pervasive, when in fact this view is based on a very small portion of the universe of potential instances of surprise. More important, it cannot be empirically tested. The null hypothesis (i.e., success in strategic warning outnumber failures) cannot be tested because instances of success are extremely difficult to ascertain and the universe of these instances is essentially unknowable. Tendencies such as this one lead to unwarranted inferences about the ease of initiating surprise and over-pessimistic expectations about the feasibility of guarding against it.[14]

Still, it does seem fair to conclude that there are enough examples of important failures to adequately warn the policymaking community of impending danger, such as with the Chinese Communist intervention in the Korean War or the Cuban Missile Crisis, to conclude that there is some sort of problem with the intelligence product. But is the problem one of analysis or collection?

Who's to Blame?

Academics who focus on the role of the intelligence community in intelligence failures, as compared with the role of the policymaking community, tend to believe that the analysts are to blame for intelligence failures, while within the US intelligence community itself, blame for failures has more often been laid at the door of poor collection. Indeed, major intelligence failures ordinarily have resulted in calls from the bureaucracy, and often from the Congress, for greater monetary investment in collection efforts.

The cause of failure is not so easily characterized, however. The evidence is clear that at various times faulty analysis has been to blame, while at other times, poor collection has made it extraordinarily difficult for the analysts to reach the correct conclusion. Whether it is one or the other is contingent on the specific crisis. In the Yom Kippur War, for example, it does seem that sufficient evidence was available for US analysts to warn Washington of the approaching Arab attack on Israel.[15] In other cases, such as with the famous pre-Cuban Missile Crisis Estimate of 19 September 1962, a fair judgment would be that there was insufficient intelligence available to the drafters, at the time of publication, to permit them to reasonably conclude that the Soviets were placing offensive nuclear missiles in Cuba.[16]

The point is, we do not *know* what percentage of failures is due to analytical errors versus what percentage is due to collection deficiencies. Until a more empirical investigation is done, the most sensible way to look at the issue may be to use a typology Sherman Kent once developed to categorize the statements that typically appear in National Intelligence Estimates. He listed three types: (1) statements of indisputable fact; (2) statements about things that are knowable but are not known by us; (3) statements about things that are not known to anyone at all.[17]

It is with the second category – for example, the number of missiles in an adversary's arsenal, the flight parameters of certain type of aircraft, the secret decisions taken in a government ministers' meeting – that collection can make an important difference in the quality of analytical judgments. But even this can be far more difficult than it sounds, as Handel once pointed out: 'Even the enemy's military and political elite is uncertain about its own goals; more than one set of military, national, and political aims may, in fact, coexist. For example, until September 1941, the Japanese had not decided whether to attack Russia or to turn south toward Southeast Asia.'[18]

With the third category, however, which deals with factors beyond individual human control – Will a given regime, or its economy, collapse? What threats will the United States face five or ten years hence? How will the democratic transformation of a given country or region progress? – there is relatively little collection can do to make the analyst's life easier. These issues involve trends and forces that may be, and in many cases are, beyond the control of even the key individuals involved in them.

In this regard, the so-called 'Schlesinger Report' of 1971 was unusual for a government report in that, although it recognized the role that poor collection played in contributing to intelligence failures, it expressed doubt that collection could be improved sufficiently to justify the expenditure of ever greater sums of money on it.[19] Instead, the report suggested that more attention be given to improving analysis.

> It has become commonplace to translate product criticism into demands for enlarged collection efforts. Seldom does anyone ask if a further reduction in uncertainty, however small, is worth its cost . . . Despite the richness of the data made available by modern methods of collection and the rising costs of their acquisition, it is not at all clear that our hypotheses about foreign intentions, capabilities, and activities have improved commensurately in scope and quality.[20]

But is it in fact possible to improve the quality of analysis, particularly the accuracy of forecasts, with improving the quality of the information available to the analysts through collection mechanisms? The following two sections address this question.

Science or Pseudo-Science?

First, it is worth determining whether the forecasts made by intelligence analysts are based more closely on the principles of science or are really only the prophecies of pseudo-scientists. If it is the latter, forecasting failures are easily explained, as are forecasting successes: they are the products of pure chance. But if it is the former, explaining the epistemological or methodological causes of prediction failures becomes both more interesting and more important.

Like natural science, social science, and pseudo-science, intelligence aims at performing three principal functions: description, explanation, and prediction.[21] In other words, they try to answer questions that begin with the interrogatives *who, how, what, where, when, whence,* and *why*.[22] But if both astronomy and astrology seek to answer these questions, what makes one a science capable of making predictions that help us understand the universe, and the other a pseudo-science whose prophecies are the equivalent of flipping a coin?

The classical answer is that, 'Science is distinguished from pseudo-science . . . by its empirical method, which is essentially inductive, proceeding from observations or experiment.'[23] Some contemporary philosophers continue to hold to that definition, such as David Papineau: 'What distinguishes successful scientific theories from non-science is that the observational evidence gives us inductive reason to regard scientific theories as true.'[24] Ideally, an intelligence forecast, like one made in science, should be a 'rational prediction that is based on grounds whose merits are discernible prior to the event . . . Predictions whose merits are discernible only after the fact are useless.'[25]

I will have more to say about induction below; here it is enough to say that intelligence analysis usually does proceed on the basis of inductive inference, working from observations of past or present experience. Thus, according to the classical definition of science, intelligence forecasts would seem to be closer to science than pseudo-science.

Karl Popper, however, was dissatisfied with this classical definition because he believed that what he considered pseudo-sciences, such as Marxism or Freudian analysis, could equally claim to be based on observation. Popper was troubled by the constant stream of observations that Marxists and Freudians used to 'verify' their theories.[26] It soon dawned on Popper that he could not think of any human behavior that could not be interpreted to confirm, in one way or another, the theories of Marx and Freud. To rectify this perceived shortcoming, Popper developed his now famous and influential method of *conjecture and refutation*.

His inspiration was Einstein's theory of relativity, which could be proven wrong in any number of ways, and it was this aspect that Popper seized upon as the determining characteristic of a scientific theory: 'A theory which is not refutable by any conceivable event is non-scientific . . . One can sum up all this by saying that the criterion of the scientific status of a theory is its falsifiability, or refutability, or testability.'[27]

Are intelligence predictions falsifiable? The answer must be 'yes', for if they were not, we would not have the large body of literature that exists on intelligence failures and strategic surprises! By this definition as well, then, intelligence estimating seems closer to science than pseudo-science.

But there is another argument to consider, the view that human affairs are essentially chaotic, ungoverned by laws (meaning regular patterns of observable behavior of the kind found in astronomy, for example) and determined only by the capriciousness of free will. Many philosophers would argue that free will – some would say instead the imperfect rationality of man – creates an essential difference between the causal laws of nature and the predisposition of individuals to act in certain ways. 'Causal laws necessitate events and hence will support deductive predictions about them. The dispositions of individuals are simply patterns of behavior that are characteristic of them, but this does not mean individuals may not occasionally act in an entirely different way in the same sort of situation.'[28]

This understanding has not stopped some from trying to find a rational order in the affairs of man similar to that found in nature, as exemplified in the following passage by the Scottish philosopher David Hume: 'Ambition, avarice, self-love, vanity, friendship, generosity, public spirit: these passions, mixed in various degrees, and distributed through society, have been, from the beginning of the world, and still are, the source of all the actions among mankind . . . Mankind are so much the same, in all times and places, that history informs us of nothing new or strange in this particular.'[29]

There are other considerations that make the problem of free will less daunting in practice than in theory as well. Sherman Kent once summarized why this is so:

> Within certain limits there is nothing very difficult or esoteric about estimating how the other man will probably behave in a given situation. In hundreds of cases formal estimates . . . have quite correctly – and many times boldly and almost unequivocally – called the turn . . . The other man will act as diagnosed because (1) he is in his right mind or at least he is not demonstrably unhinged; (2) he cannot capriciously make the decision by himself – at a minimum it will have to be discussed with advisers, and in nondictatorial governments it will have to stand the test of governmental and popular scrutiny; (3) he is aware of the power of traditional forces in his country, the generally accepted notions of its broad national interests and objectives, and the broad lines of policy which are calculated to protect the one and forward the other; (4) he is well informed . . . These and other phenomena very considerably narrow the area of a foreign statesman's choice, and once thus narrowed it is susceptible to fairly sure-footed analysis by studious intelligence types.[30]

If free will was the disruptive influence in studying human affairs that it is sometimes thought to be, then 'social scientists and historians could aspire to nothing but a more or less artistic chronicling of separate, unintelligible, hence useless facts'.[31] But patterns of behavior, similarities that exist in events that are widely separated by time and distance, do make it possible for us to generalize about important human endeavors. Warfare is an example. Although no two wars are exactly alike, it is possible to study the tactics and strategies that belligerents have used in the past in order to develop general principles that will be applicable in similar situations in the future. Indeed, the curricula of our war colleges are based on this idea.[32]

The Problem of Induction and the Consequences for Analysis

It seems that, across the board, there is a strong case for considering intelligence forecasts as a scientific activity. But do we not have a contradiction here, then? How can estimating be essentially scientific and yet be wrong in important instances?

Part of the problem is that we, especially those of us who work outside the natural sciences, tend to have an exaggerated sense of the certainty associated with science. And at least part of the reason we seem to attach such respect to science is the uniformity of procedures, the reference to laws or rules from which explanations and predictions can be deduced, and, of course, the principle of empiricism, which dictates that only observation and experiment can decide the acceptance or rejection of scientific statements. Yet there are obstacles to prediction in science as well as social science: 'In nature we have volatility and chance (stochastic phenomena); in human affairs innovation and chance (free will). Chaos is a phenomenon that straddles both domains.'[33]

Popper put it this way:

> One should be careful not to confuse the problem of the reasonableness of the scientific procedure ... with ... *the belief that this procedure will succeed.* In practice, in practical scientific research, this belief is no doubt unavoidable and reasonable, there being no better alternative. But the belief is certainly unjustifiable in a theoretical sense ... Moreover, if we could show, on logical grounds, that the scientific quest is likely to succeed, one could not understand why anything like success has been so rare in the long history of human endeavours to know more about the world.[34]

Even if we accept the point that science is not nearly so certain as is often believed, we must still show why predictions are so difficult to make. The central problem is that the method by which analysts make their forecasts has traditionally been one of *induction*. There are two common forms of inductive reasoning: moving from the particular to the general, and moving from the past to the future. Suppose, for example, that intelligence analysts see, from imagery, indications A, B, C, and D at country X's nuclear test range. In the past, whenever those same indications at country X's test range have appeared, a nuclear test soon followed. The analysts may infer, inductively, that country X is again about to test a nuclear weapon and so warn the policymakers. Or, suppose that divisions 1, 2, 3, and 4 of country X's army have been observed to possess a new artillery piece. The analysts may well infer, inductively, that the remaining divisions of country X's army, or at least those sharing the same front with divisions 1, 2, 3, and 4, will also possess the new artillery piece.

It was Francis Bacon who in the sixteenth century first drew attention to the possibilities induction offered as a means for scientific advancement.[35] Prior to Bacon, science had been thought to depend mainly on the use of deduction. Two hundred years later, the Scottish philosopher David Hume created one of the enduring problems of epistemology when he demonstrated that induction was logically indefensible. Hume began his argument by dividing subjects of inquiry into two types: 'relations of ideas, and matters of fact'. The first category, relations of ideas, did not interest Hume because they concerned matters of geometry, algebra, and arithmetic, 'in short, every affirmation which is either intuitively or demonstratively certain'.[36]

Instead, Hume's interest was captured by what he termed 'matters of fact'. Here, he took the view that 'all reasonings concerning matter of fact seem to be founded on the relation of *cause and effect*', and that all knowledge arises entirely out of experience and cannot come from a priori reasoning.[37]

Hume then asked himself, 'What is the foundation of all conclusions from experience?' His answer has disconcerted philosophers for centuries: 'All our experimental conclusions proceed upon the supposition that the future will be conformable to the past.' He then demonstrated that there was no logical reason for us to believe this. Past experience can only provide certain information about those same experiences of the past, but 'why this experience should be extended to future times, and to other objects, which for aught we know, may be only in appearance similar; this is the main question on which I would insist . . .'.[38]

From Hume's analysis came a number of troubling conclusions: (1) Inductive inferences – using the past to forecast the future – can only be made on the basis of probabilities. They cannot be made certain.[39] (2) This is because inductive inferences presuppose that the future will resemble the past, and, 'If there be any suspicion that the course of nature may change, and that the past may be no rule for the future, all experience becomes useless, and can give rise to no inference or conclusion.'[40] (3) Inductive inference is simply a matter of custom: 'All inferences from experience, therefore are effects of custom, not of reasoning . . . Custom, then, is the great guide of human life. It is that principle alone which renders our experience useful to us, and makes us expect, for the future a similar train of events with those which have appeared in the past. Without the influence of custom, we should be entirely ignorant of every matter of fact beyond what is immediately present to memory and senses.'[41]

A simple syllogism based on an inductive inference will serve to illustrate Hume's points:

Major premise: What is true of Crow 1, Crow 2, Crow 3, etc., is true of all crows.
Minor premise: Crow 1, Crow 2, Crow 3, etc., are black.
Conclusion: All crows are black.

Hume demonstrated that the best we can do in such an argument is suggest that all crows are *probably* black. There is no way to verify the statement. No matter how many crows we examine and find to be black, there is always the possibility that the next crow we see will not be black, and, therefore, that not all crows are black.[42]

Hume's work on induction appeared to pose a threat to science in general because it suggested that there was no rational basis for its discoveries, and much of the writing that has been done on the epistemology of science since Hume has consisted of efforts to either prove him wrong or to propose substitutes to induction. Of course, Hume's conclusions are no less troubling for the intelligence analyst, for if induction can only lead to solutions that are more or less probable, then estimating failures are, indeed, inevitable, although no particular forecast need necessarily be wrong.

What types of event are most likely to trip up analysts who reason inductively? A report made in 1983 by a group of senior advisors to the Director of Central Intelligence provides the answer. The group was charged with the responsibility of considering the quality of intelligence judgments preceding significant historical failures. Their conclusion was, in essence, an essay on the weakness of induction:

> In the estimates that failed, there were a number of recurrent common factors which, in retrospect, seem critical to the quality of the analysis. The most distinguishing characteristic of the failed esti- mates – the Sino-Soviet split, the development of the ALFA subma- rine, the Qadhafi takeover in Libya, the OPEC price increase, the revolutionary transformation of Ethiopia, the Soviet invasion of Afghanistan, or the destruction of the Shah's Iran – *was that each involved historical discontinuity and, in the early stages, apparently unlikely outcomes. The basic problem in each was to recognize qualita- tive change and to deal with situations in which trend continuity and precedent were of marginal, if not counterproductive, value.* Analysts of the period clearly lacked a doctrine or a model for coping with improbable outcomes.[43]

For a more specific example, Sherman Kent once gave a one-paragraph summary of how, with little direct evidence of Soviet designs, inductive inference helped the CIA to misjudge the Cuban Missile Crisis:

> When we reviewed once again how cautiously the Soviet leadership had threaded its way through other dangerous passages of the Cold War; when we took stock of the sense of outrage and resolve evinced by the American people and government since the establishment of a Communist regime in Cuba; when we estimated that the Soviets must be aware of these American attitudes; and when we then asked ourselves would the Soviets undertake the great risks at the high odds – and in Cuba of all places – *the indicator, the pattern of Soviet foreign policy, shouted out its negative.*[44]

If induction is unable by its nature to guarantee certainty, are there any viable alternatives to the inductive method? Specifically, can any other method more reliably forecast events that are historical discontinuities?

Alternatives to Induction

In the world of science, much faith is placed in the method of conjecture and refutation championed by Karl Popper. In the course of the twentieth century, it became the dominant procedure through which most scientists and philosophers of science *believed* science should proceed. But is it appropriate for intelligence analysis?

Popper took the position that science does not actually advance through induction, since scientists do not just collect observations in the hope that they will fall into some recognizable pattern or generalization. Rather, says Popper, the scientist begins with a hypothesis, from which he deduces certain consequences. He then employs observation and experimentation in order to see if the predicted consequences actually occur. If they do not, then the hypothesis has been proven false; if they do appear, the hypothesis has not been verified but only corroborated to a certain extent. The scientist must then deduce additional consequences and continue to test them, but at no point can the hypothesis be considered verified, although naturally we can have greater confidence in those hypotheses that we have tried hard to falsify and failed.[45]

Popper's approach is appealing to many, not least because it features the use of deduction, which has the cachet of being more 'scientific' than induction. Not everyone agrees with that view, however. Bertrand Russell, for example, makes the claim that, 'All the important inferences outside logic and pure mathematics are inductive, not deductive; the only exceptions are law and theology, each of which derives its first principles from an unquestionable text, viz. the statute books or the scriptures.'[46] Similarly, the philosopher Nicholas Rescher holds that, 'Every rational prediction is an induction – a projection of some sort from past experience, though it need not, of course, be a simple linear projection . . .'[47]

Russell points out that the premises of deductive arguments are very often simply inductive inferences in disguise. To take a famous syllogism as an example,

> All men are mortal.
> Socrates is a man.
> Therefore: Socrates is mortal.

The first premise, 'All men are mortal', is an inductive inference. Moreover, entirely valid deductive arguments can still be false if one or more of the premises of the argument are false.[48]

But it is for another reason that Popper's approach seems a poor choice with which to conduct intelligence analysis: he has no basis for discriminating among different hypotheses that are each consistent with all the known data. Because Popper rejects induction, he cannot believe that evidence ever provides positive proof for any hypothesis.[49] Therefore, all hypotheses that have not been falsified are equally plausible. 'In insisting that scientific theories are just conjectures, and that therefore we have no rational basis for believing their predictions, Popper is simply denying that we can make rational judgments about the future.'[50]

There is merit in reminding the policymaker of all the various hypotheses about a given situation that cannot be ruled out by the evidence, and it is here that Popper's approach could make a useful contribution. To adopt a pure Popperian approach, however, where evidence *for* any given hypothesis is considered trivial or largely irrelevant, would not help the decisionmaker. As we shall see below, what the policymaker values above all else are the facts upon which he can base a decision.

Living With Uncertainty

In the end, induction may resemble the remark Winston Churchill once made about democracy: 'No one pretends that democracy is perfect or all-wise. Indeed, it has been said that democracy is the worst form of Government except all those other forms that have been tried from time to time.'[51] Indeed, Hume himself was more concerned with the theoretical validity of induction than he was with its practical usefulness: 'None but a fool or a madman will ever pretend to dispute the authority of experience, or to reject that great guide of human life . . .'.[52]

Some philosophers have decided that Hume's theoretical challenge of induction is less important than it seems, especially if one avoids the trap of trying to justify our ability to make predictions *in general*. Max Black, for example, gave the following answer to the inductive skeptic's question, What reason is there to suppose that if a number of observed As are all B, all As are therefore B? 'The answer, so far as I can see, is that in general there is no reason. It all depends upon the As, the Bs, and what we already know about them.'[53]

Nelson Goodman, author of the most influential book about induction since Hume, took the position that, 'If the problem is to explain how we know that certain predictions will turn out to be correct, the sufficient answer is that we don't know any such thing. If the problem is to find some way of distinguishing antecedently between true and false predictions, we are asking for prevision rather than for philosophical explanation.'[54] Goodman instead took the position that an inductive inference should be justified in the same manner as a deductive conclusion: by showing that it conforms to sound rules of inductive inference. Thus, a deductive argument is considered valid, even if its conclusion is false, if it conforms to the general rules of deductive inference, and for Goodman, 'Predictions are justified if they conform to valid canons of induction; and the canons are valid if they accurately codify accepted inductive practice.'[55]

The lesson of epistemology is thus a harsh one: there is no obvious way in which predictions can be known in advance to be true or false, and therefore, there is no obvious way in which intelligence failures can be prevented. They are a function of the uncertain manner in which knowledge is gained. It is perhaps of some small consolation that the acquisition of knowledge in the natural sciences is only somewhat less difficult.

In fact, the ability of intelligence analysts to accurately forewarn of a potential surprise resembles in some ways the manner by which discoveries are made in the natural science. The philosopher Max Black paints it this way:

> There is something lawless in the creative process itself, and the scientists whom scientists have most wished to honor have made their discoveries by means as mysterious to themselves as to their contemporaries. But if their results are to be useful they must be communicable to those who are not themselves geniuses. Thus what begins as a brilliant discovery, as incoherent as it is dazzling, is eventually converted into a routine which the mere artisan of science can master and apply . . . In some ways the progress of science . . . smacks too much of the marvelous and the unpredictable for comfort; and the hope has never been abandoned of reducing the process of discovery itself to a routine that can be communicated and taught. This hope has inspired investigators of scientific method from Aristotle to Descartes and from Bacon to Eddington . . . We can write off such a project as illusory and no more likely to succeed than the quest of the Grail itself . . .[56]

This view is very much in the tradition of the distinguished nineteenth-century British scientist William Whewell, who argued that, 'logic could not bring certainty to science because discovery depended ultimately on personal genius and not on impersonal correctness of method'.[57] This is particularly true of induction, which 'depends on the ability and application of the person doing the work. From a given set of observations, I may induce one general statement, you may induce quite another. The problem is that, unlike the conclusion in a deductive argument (which is, so to speak, "contained" in the original premise), that in an inductive argument is not, and could in theory be anything at all.'[58]

If Black and Whewell are right, perhaps the way to reduce the number and importance of intelligence failures is not through such things as devil's advocacy, bureaucratic reform, or any of the other changes that are regularly suggested after major failures. Perhaps it can best be done through the identification and recruitment into the analyst corps of those well-established students of foreign affairs who have a track record of being ahead of their peers when it comes to insights, rather than the untried and unproven graduates who are typically recruited into the analytical ranks.

This by itself would be a monumental task, not least because it would require a 'cultural revolution' within the intelligence bureaucracies. There, the analytical slots are, for the most part, the entry-level positions, the thing young analysts do until they can break into management or administration, which is where most of the higher salaries and perquisites can be found. Moreover, it would be difficult to recruit large numbers of accomplished specialists into the community. Some smaller, critical mass of senior people, such as the old Board of National Estimates, however, might be sufficient to accomplish the task of creatively questioning the conclusions drawn by more junior analysts and advancing to the policy level their own interpretations international events.

As we shall see in the next section, it would take such people of significant reputation and accomplishment to have their estimates heard and acted upon by the policymakers, for the latter group has traditionally preferred to act as their own intelligence analysts.

Policymaker Attitudes

Finally, perhaps the key questions of this chapter: How much does estimating matter to the policymakers? How concerned are policymakers about the necessarily uncertain nature of forecasting? The answers may surprise the reader.

Roger Hilsman, writing nearly 50 years ago, gave us an answer that still pertains today:

> Most popular writers on the subject of intelligence assume that the warning function is a basic role of intelligence; an efficient intelligence service, they seem to believe, would have warned us of the Pearl Harbor attack, the Berlin blockade, the victory of the Chinese Communists, the attack on South Korea, the Chinese intervention in Korea, and of each of the long list of events that have surprised and dismayed us through the years. If one is talking about the kind of warning a secret agent would give, spying out some dramatic bit of information that has obvious and immediate significance, the operators [Hilsman's archaic term for policymakers] would almost unanimously agree. But if one is talking about the kind of warning that comes from estimating trends, analyzing capabilities, and deducing intentions, their opinions would tend to vary.[59]

Hilsman's conclusion came as a result of a number of interviews he conducted with policymakers of the day, and he found that, far more than forecasts and warnings of impending trouble, what policymakers really wanted were all the facts. Indeed, Hilsman found that most policymakers were opposed either entirely or in part to having intelligence analysts responsible for estimating and warning. Intelligence was to provide the facts, and the policymakers were to interpret them.[60] Hilsman explained that policymakers felt this way because the analysts could rarely offer greater expertise than that possessed by the policymakers. In particular, the personal contacts of policymakers with foreign leaders made it difficult for the analyst to provide insights that had not already occurred to the policymaker.[61]

For the reader who is surprised by these views, it is worth remembering President Truman's concerns when he created first the Central Intelligence Group and then the Central Intelligence Agency. It is well known that the surprise at Pearl Harbor was what motivated Truman in general, but it is worth looking more carefully at the President's reasons. In creating CIG/CIA, Truman in fact did not hope to develop superior forecasting or estimating skills; rather, he wanted to be certain that all the facts he needed to make intelligent decisions were reaching him:

> I have often thought that if there had been something like co-ordination of information in the government it would have been more difficult, if not impossible, for the Japanese to succeed in the sneak attack at Pearl Harbor. In those days the military did not know everything the State Department knew, and the diplomats did not have access to all the Army and Navy knew . . . The war taught us this lesson – that we had to collect intelligence in a manner that would make it available where it was needed and when it was wanted, in an intelligent and understandable form.[62]

Perhaps the most interesting part of Truman's conception of centralized intelligence was the role he would play as his own analyst:

> Therefore, I decided to set up a special organization charged with the collection of all intelligence reports from every available source, and to have those reports reach me as President without departmental 'treatment' or interpretations. I wanted and needed the information in its 'natural raw' state and in as comprehensive a volume as it was practical for me to make full use of it. But the most important thing about this move was to guard against the chance of intelligence being used to influence or to lead the President into unwise decisions – and I thought it was necessary that the President do his own thinking and evaluating.[63]

Policymaker attitudes toward estimating and forecasting apparently have changed surprisingly little since Truman founded the CIA and Hilsman did his research. While there are no publicly available surveys of contemporary policymaker attitudes toward this issue, recent public remarks by General Brent Scowcroft, National Security Advisor to two Presidents and Deputy National Security Advisor to a third, would seem to suggest considerable agreement with the views summarized above.

Much like Sherman Kent, Scowcroft divides intelligence statements into three categories: facts, facts plus interpretation, and predictions:

> The confidence of the decisionmaker in the intelligence goes down with each one of the categories. He trusts the experts so that the facts are taken pretty much wholesale. Interpretation, a little less so, but since they're so intimately related to the facts, and the expert is going to know more about the surrounding circumstances, yes. But when you get to the predictions, there's a lot of skepticism on the part of the decisionmaker, again, depending on his personality, but frequently to the point that they're considered just one opinion of another . . . What intelligence estimates do for the policymaker is to remind him what forces are at work, what the trends are, and what are some possibilities he has to consider.[64]

This conclusion may be disappointing to the intelligence professional and disconcerting to the student of intelligence issues, but it is not irrational. Policymakers intuitively understand the uncertainty associated with estimating, and they understand that the skill of the individual forecaster accounts for a great deal. Many simply have more confidence in their own abilities and insights than they do in the skills of the intelligence officers who work for them. Whatever the headlines may blare when the media reveal another 'intelligence' failure, the estimates of future trends, developments, and dangers that matter most are made within policymaking circles.

Conclusions

The following points seem to me to be a reasonable summary of the current state of play:

- We don't know precisely what the track record for estimates or warning judgments is, although we do know there have been a number of significant failures in the past.
- We don't know precisely what percentage of failures is due to problems in collection versus analysis, although we can identify a number of important failures where the problem appears to have been principally analytical.
- It seems that intelligence forecasts are closer to science than pseudo-science.
- We know that this fact, however, does not guarantee certainty; on the

contrary, it does seem that analytical failures, in general, are inevitable, although this does not mean that any given forecast need be erroneous.
- We know that estimates are less important to the policymaker than other forms of intelligence, and that policymakers tend to trust their own judgment more than that of the analysts.

What do these conclusions mean for the intelligence analysts, particularly those engaged in some aspect of estimating? Abbot Smith gave the answer 30 years ago:

> Sophisticated estimating ... ought always to be something more than bald prediction. A good paper on a complicated subject should describe the trends and forces at work, identify the contingent factors or variables which might affect developments, and present a few alternative possibilities for the future, usually with some judgment as to the relative likelihood of one or another outcome.[65]

This type of estimative analysis would be welcomed by all policymakers, for while it leaves the final judgment to them, it would help them in a significant way to make the best possible decisions. Estimates done in this fashion would be hard to characterize in the traditional terms of failure or success. A successful estimate would then be one that had adequately and in a timely fashion prepared the policymaker to make an intelligent choice, even if that choice ultimately turned out to be incorrect. It would have considered all major trends and issues, and it would have delineated all major possible outcomes. A failed estimate would be just the opposite – one that had failed adequately to prepare the decisionmaker by neglecting to review some important possibilities or trends, or by appearing too late for him to include in his calculations, for example. An estimate that contained a single outcome forecast would be considered unsuccessful by these criteria.

The foregoing discussion suggests four topics for additional research:

1 We need to undertake an empirical assessment of the track record of estimates. Enough National Intelligence Estimates have been declassified to make a systematic effort in this regard worthwhile.
2 We need to arrive at a similarly empirical judgment on the number of failed estimates that are due to collection failures as opposed to analytical errors.
3 We should try to understand why, if policymakers have always been more interested in facts than forecasts, the estimative process has developed in the manner it has.
4 We should seek to identify other epistemologically based causes of errors in forecasting, for the evidence suggests that not all miscues can be blamed on induction.

NOTES

1 This material has been reviewed by the CIA. That review neither constitutes CIA authentication of the information nor implies CIA endorsement of the author's views.

2 Michael Handel, 'Intelligence and Crisis Forecasting', *Orbis* (Winter 1983), p. 819.

3 Roberta Wohlstetter, *Pearl Harbor: Warning and Decision* (Stanford, CA: Stanford University Press, 1962).

4 See, for example, Michael Handel, 'The Yom Kippur War and the Inevitability of Surprise', *International Studies Quarterly*, vol. 21, no. 3 (September 1977), pp. 461–502; Richard Betts, 'Analysis, War and Decision: Why Intelligence Failures are Inevitable', *World Politics*, vol. 31 (Spring 1978), pp. 61–89.

5 Christopher Brady, 'Intelligence Failures: Plus ça Change . . .', *Intelligence and National Security*, vol. 4, no. 8 (October 1993), p. 86.

6 Richard Betts, 'Surprise, Scholasticism, and Strategy: A Review of Ariel Levite's *Intelligence and Strategic Surprises* (New York: Columbia University Press, 1987)', *International Studies Quarterly*, vol. 33 (1989), p. 330. Levite's work is one of the few that challenge the conventional wisdom. He argues that the fault lies with poor collection. David Kahn takes the same tack in Ernest May's *Knowing One's Enemy* (Princeton, NJ: Princeton University Press, 1986), p. 500. Kahn, in his chapter, 'United States Views of Germany and Japan in 1941', puts it directly: 'Not one intercept, not one datum of intelligence ever said anything about an attack on Pearl Harbor or on any other possession.' Abraham Ben-Zvi has put his own twist on the problem of strategic surprise, arguing that the surprise is not the enemy's intention to attack, but rather his capabilities once the attack has been launched. See, for example, 'The Dynamics of Surprise: The Defender's Perspective', *Intelligence and National Security*, vol. 12, no. 4 (October 1997), pp. 113–44; 'Between Warning and Response, The Case of the Yom Kippur War', *International Journal of Intelligence and Counterintelligence*, vol. 4, no. 2 (Summer 1990), pp. 227–42.

7 Isaac Ben-Israel has made a start in this direction by making a case for the adoption of a modified Popperian approach to the production of intelligence estimates in order to reduce the likelihood of failure. Isaac Ben-Israel, 'Philosophy and Methodology of Intelligence: The Logic of Estimate Process', *Intelligence and National Security*, vol. 4, no. 4 (October 1989), pp. 660–718.

8 Abbot E. Smith, 'On the Accuracy of National Intelligence Estimates', *Studies in Intelligence*, vol. 13, no. 3 (Fall 1969), p. 25.

9 Ibid., pp. 25, 26.

10 Ibid., pp. 29–30.

11 Richard W. Shryock, 'The Intelligence Community Post-Mortem Program, 1973–1975', *Studies in Intelligence* (Fall 1977), pp. 15–28.

12 Ibid., p. 27.

13 Willis C. Armstrong, William Leonhart, William J. McCaffrey, and Herbert C. Rothenberg, 'The Hazards of Single-Outcome Forecasting', in H. Bradford Westerfield, ed., *Inside CIA's Private World* (New Haven, CT: Yale University Press, 1995), p. 241.

14 Steve Chan, 'The Intelligence of Stupidity: Understanding Failures in Strategic Warning', *American Political Science Review*, vol. 73, no. 1 (March 1979), p. 174.

15 See Shryock, 'The Intelligence Community Post-Mortem Program', pp. 16–17.

16 See Sherman Kent, 'A Crucial Estimate Relived', *Studies in Intelligence*, vol. 35, no. 4 (Winter 1991), p. 65. This article was originally published in *Studies in Intelligence*, vol. 8, no. 2 (Spring 1964), pp. 1–18.

17 Ibid., p. 65.

18 See Handel, 'The Yom Kippur War', p. 464.

19 The report was the product of President Nixon's unhappiness with the intelligence community, especially its convoluted organization. It was conducted by Assistant Director of the Office of Management and Budget James R. Schlesinger, and followed on the heels of a similar review of the organization of the Department of Defense by a Blue Ribbon Panel. The report was notable for its reliance on the views of intelligence consumers, rather than intelligence producers, to form the basis of its conclusions.

20 James R. Schlesinger, 'A Review of the Intelligence Community', March 10, 1971, pp. 10A–12.

21 The difference between explanation and prediction is outlined by Carl Hempel, a leading theorist of scientific explanation: 'In the case of an explanation, the final event is known to have happened, and its determining conditions have to be sought; the situation is reversed in the case of a prediction: here, the initial conditions are given, and their "effect" – which, in the typical case, has not yet taken place – is to be determined.' See Carl G. Hempel, 'The Function of General Laws in History', in Herbert Feigl and Wilfrid Sellers, eds, *Readings in Philosophical Analysis* (New York: Appleton-Century-Crofts, 1949), p. 462.

22 Mario Bunge, *Causality and Modern Science* (New York: Dover Publications, 1979), p. 248.

23 Karl R. Popper, *Conjectures and Refutations: The Growth of Scientific Knowledge* (New York: Harper & Row, 1963), p. 33.

24 David Papineau, 'Philosophy of Science', in Nicholas Bunnin and E.P. Tsui-James, eds, *The Blackwell Companion to Philosophy* (Oxford: Blackwell, 1996), p. 304.

25 Nicholas Rescher, 'Prediction', in T. Hondereich, ed., *The Oxford Companion to Philosophy*, (Oxford: Oxford University Press, 1995), www.xrefer.com/entry.jsp?xrefid=553248&secid=.-, 1995.

26 See Popper, *Conjectures and Refutations*, p. 35.

27 Ibid., pp. 36, 37.

28 Leon Pompa, 'Philosophy of History', in Bunnin and Tsui-James, eds, *The Blackwell Companion to Philosophy*, p. 422.

29 David Hume, 'An Enquiry Concerning Human Understanding', Section VIII, 'Of Liberty and Necessity, Part I,' in D.C. Yalden-Thomson, ed., *Hume: Theory of Knowledge* (Austin, TX: University of Texas Press, 1953), p. 85.

30 See Kent, 'A Crucial Estimate Relived', p. 70.

31 See Bunge, *Causality and Modern Science,* p. 268.

32 Ibid., p. 271.

33 See Rescher, 'Prediction'.

34 Popper, *Conjectures and Refutations*, p. 57. Emphasis in original.

35 Bertrand Russell, *A History of Western Philosophy* (New York: Simon & Schuster, 1945), p. 543.

36 Hume, Section IV, 'Sceptical Doubts Concerning the Operations of Understanding, Part I', in *Hume: Theory of Knowledge*, p. 24.

37 Ibid., p. 25.

38 Ibid., pp. 33, 34.

39 Ibid., p. 35.

40 Ibid., p. 37.

41 Hume, Section V, 'Sceptical Solution of These Doubts, Part I', pp. 43–5.

42 The example above is taken from William H. Halverson, *A Concise Introduction to Philosophy* (New York: Random House, 1967), p. 291.

43 See Armstrong, Leonhart, McCaffrey, and Rothenberg, 'The Hazards of Single-Outcome Forecasting', p. 241. Emphasis added.

44 See Kent, 'A Crucial Estimate Relived', p. 67. Emphasis added.

45 A quick summary of Popper's method is found in Chris Horner and Emrys

Westacott, *Thinking through Philosophy* (Cambridge: Cambridge University Press, 2000), p. 106.

46 See Russell, *A History of Western Philosophy*, p. 199.

47 Rescher, 'Prediction'.

48 See Russell, *A History of Western Philosophy*, pp. 196, 199.

49 A number of authors have pointed to this problem with Popper's approach, including Horner and Westacott, *Thinking through Philosophy*, p. 112.

50 Papineau, 'Philosophy of Science', p. 293.

51 Cited in *The Oxford Dictionary of Quotations* (Oxford: Oxford University Press, 1996, revised 4th edn), p. 202.

52 Hume, Section IV, 'Sceptical Doubts Concerning the Operations of Understanding, Part II', in *Hume: Theory of Knowledge*, p. 35.

53 Max Black, *Problems of Analysis* (Ithaca, NY: Cornell University Press, 1954), p. 188.

54 Nelson Goodman, *Fact, Fiction, and Forecast* (Cambridge, MA: Harvard University Press, 1979), p. 63.

55 Ibid., p. 64.

56 Black, *Problems of Analysis*, p. 7.

57 Shirley Robin Letwin, 'Certainty Since the Seventeenth Century', in Philip P. Wiener, ed., *Dictionary of the History of Ideas*, vol. I (New York: Charles Scribner's Sons, 1973), p. 318.

58 Kenneth McLeish, 'Scientific Method', in idem, ed., *The Bloomsbury Guide to Human Thought*, www.xrefer.com/entry.jsp?xrefid=344724&secid=.

59 Roger Hilsman, *Strategic Intelligence and National Decisions* (Glenco, IL: The Free Press, 1956), p. 46.

60 Ibid., p. 49.

61 Ibid., p. 50.

62 Harry S. Truman, *Memoirs*, vol. II, *Years of Trial and Hope* (Garden City, NY: Doubleday, 1956), p. 56.

63 Harry S. Truman, 'Limit CIA Role to Intelligence', *The Washington Post*, 22 December 1963, p. A11.

64 General Brent Scowcroft, remarks given at the conference on 'US Intelligence and the End of the Cold War', Panel V, 'The Use of Intelligence by Policymakers', 20 November 1999, Texas A&M University.

65 Smith, 'On the Accuracy of National Intelligence Estimates', pp. 29–30.

4

Theory of Surprise

James J. Wirtz

Why do states, non-state actors or individuals attempt to surprise their opponents? Why do they often succeed? How does surprise affect strategic interactions, competitions in which the behavior of both sides determines the outcome? Why do some surprise initiatives succeed spectacularly, only to end in disaster for the side that initially benefited from surprise? If we can explain surprise, can we prevent it from occurring?

To answer these questions, one would have to develop a theory of surprise – a unifying explanation of why states, for example, attempt to surprise their opponents with diplomatic or military initiatives, why they succeed, and how surprise helps them achieve their objectives. Some might protest, however, that such a powerful (in the sense that it would apply to people, businesses, bureaucracies, and states) and parsimonious (thrifty in the number of causal factors it highlights) explanation would be impossible to construct because of the many challenges that often bedevil those wishing to avoid surprise.[1] At the heart of the problem are the limits to human cognition that constrain our ability to anticipate the unexpected or novel, especially if the future fails to match our existing analytical concepts, beliefs, or assumptions.[2] Idiosyncratic factors – the 'Ultra syndrome', the 'cry-wolf syndrome', denial and deception or an unfavorable signal-to-noise ratio – complicate institutional efforts at intelligence analysis and the production of finished estimates.[3] Compartmentalization, hierarchy, 'group think', a deference to organizational preferences, or an organizational culture that creates 'intelligence to please', in other words, bureaucracy itself, can impede efforts to avoid surprise.[4] Historians also might note that each instance of surprise is wedded to a unique set of circumstances, institutions, and personalities. They would suggest that efforts to surprise an opponent have been present throughout history, but attaining and benefitting from surprise really is embedded in a specific technical, political, or military context.

Given this Pandora's box of cognitive weaknesses, intelligence pathologies, and bureaucratic nightmares, it is impossible to say exactly which combination of shortcomings will conspire to assist cunning opponents in surprising their victims. But it is possible to predict when and why that Pandora's box will be opened and why its consequences can be devastating for the victim. It also is possible to explain why the side that achieved surprise can suffer a devastating setback when the box snaps shut. Additionally, they key role played by surprise in asymmetric attacks and special operations can be identified. There are discernible patterns in the history of surprise in warfare and diplomacy, suggesting that surprise is a general phenomenon that can be explained with a general theory.[5]

To the best of my knowledge, the theory of surprise has never been fully articulated elsewhere. The theory is derived largely from Michael Handel's writings, especially his early philosophical musings about the nature of intelligence and surprise. It is no coincidence, therefore, that the theory of surprise is based on Clausewitz's concept of strategy and war. The theory relies on this Clausewitzian vision of war to explain why surprise is attractive to a specific party in a conflict, although it diverges sharply from the great Prussian philosopher's judgment that surprise was overrated as a strategic instrument in war. It then turns to Handel's insights about actors' incentives to base their strategy on the element of surprise and how this inherently risky enterprise increases the likelihood that efforts to achieve surprise will succeed. These insights, what I call 'Handel's risk paradox', provide an important link between the structure of conflict and the psychology of surprise. The theory, then, explains why those who rely on surprise might win a battle, but rarely achieve overall victory in war. The theory also identifies a way at least to mitigate the threat of being victimized by surprise in the future.

War as Administration

Surprise often is described as a force multiplier, something that increases the effectiveness of one's forces in combat. Across cultures and history, military doctrines have encouraged soldiers to incorporate surprise, along with other force multipliers such as the use of cover or maneuver, into their military operations because they increase the prospects for success and reduce casualties. In 1984, Handel summarized the battlefield advantages derived from surprise:

> A successful unanticipated attack will facilitate the destruction of a sizable portion of the enemy's forces at a lower cost to the attacker by throwing the inherently stronger defense psychologically off balance, and hence temporarily reducing his resistance . . . the numerically inferior side is able to take the initiative by concentrating superior forces at the time and place of its choosing, thereby vastly improving the likelihood of achieving a decisive victory.[6]

Clearly, surprise serves as a force multiplier or, as Handel notes, it allows one side to achieve the temporary numerical superiority needed to launch offensive operations. But Handel only alludes to how surprise produces this force-multiplier effect. Surprise temporarily suspends the dialectical nature of warfare (or any other strategic contest) by eliminating an active opponent from the battlefield. Surprise turns war into a stochastic exercise in which the probability of some event can be determined with a degree of certainty or, more rarely, an event in which the outcome can be not only known in advance, but determined by one side in the conflict.

Surprise literally transforms war from a strategic interaction into a matter of accounting and logistics. Probability and chance still influence administrative matters and friction still can bedevil any evolution, whether it is conducted in peacetime or in war. But surprise eliminates war's dialectic: achieving a military objective is no longer impeded by an opponent who can be expected to do everything in their power to make one's life miserable. This has a profound effect on military operations.[7] For example, the amount of time it might take to arrive and seize a destination can be derived from simple calculations about how fast a unit can drive down some autobahn (of course, those gifted in mathematics might use more elegant algorithms to determine the effects of equipment breakdowns, road conditions, or crew fatigue to estimate probabilities of likely arrival times). No account need be made for delays caused by roadblocks, blown bridges, pre-registered artillery, or major enemy units astride one's path. 'Without a reacting enemy', according to Edward Luttwak, 'or rather to the extent and degree that surprise is achieved, the conduct of war becomes mere administration.'[8]

Doctrine and planning guides universally encourage officers to incorporate surprise and other force multipliers into military operations. Even when surprise is virtually non-existent, military planners appear compelled to explain that they have attained a degree of surprise. US planners, for example, prior to the start of air strikes against Iraq in 1991 and Afghanistan in 2001, claimed they surprised their opponents, even though the attacks were proceeded by very public force deployments and diplomacy.[9] But all the lip service paid to the desirability of utilizing force multipliers hides the fact that surprise really offers a 'silver bullet' in war. Whether it occurs at the tactical, theater, or strategic level of operations, surprise allows weak adversaries to contemplate operations that are simply beyond their capability in wartime.[10] Although usually a matter of degree,[11] when it approximates to its ideal-type, surprise literally makes war go away.

Since the theory is avowedly based on Clausewitz's work, it might at first appear a bit odd to reach a conclusion about the potential utility of surprise that diverges completely from the judgment of the great philosopher of war.[12] From a dialectical perspective, there is a cost to everything in war: operational security can prevent proper planning and briefing; diversionary attacks and deception operations can take on a life of their own or draw resources away from the main battle. Even spectacular successes like the 11 September attacks operate on the narrowest margins of success. For instance, there simply were too few al-Qaida operatives aboard hijacked aircraft to maintain control in the face of determined opposition from the passengers and crew. But inserting more operatives into the United States only would have increased the chances of detection and overall failure of the terrorist attacks.[13] Clausewitz estimated that the costs of obtaining surprise generally outweighed the benefits surprise provided. Clausewitz, however, was more concerned with explaining war's dialectic and the way it shaped the nature, course, and outcome of battle. What the theory of surprise posits is that under ideal circumstances that occasionally can be achieved in practice, war's dialectic can be eliminated. In other words, it identifies a way to eliminate one's opposition by preempting the 'duel' that is war.

Surprise makes extraordinary kinds of military activity in warfare possible because it eliminates an active opponent from the battlefield. Special operations or commando raids, for instance, are a good example of a type of activity that is made possible by the element of surprise. Despite their cultivated reputation for ferocity, combat skill, and daring, commandos and other types of special forces are lightly armed, poorly supplied, and generally outnumbered by their adversaries. In a pitched battle against competent conventional units, they would be quickly surrounded and outgunned. To achieve their objectives, they have become experts in unconventional modes of transportation and operations to enable them to appear and disappear in unexpected ways and at unanticipated times and places. Surprise is the key enabler of all types of unconventional operations, because it allows commandos to achieve some objective or attack some target without significant opposition or with no opposition at all. Surprise also creates the opportunity for special operations to produce strategic effects. A dozen or so operatives appearing at a crucial command center deep behind enemy lines can affect the course of some battle. But the same commandos would have no discernible impact on the course of a conflict if they joined a divisional engagement on the front line.[14]

Unless it produces complete victory, the ability of surprise to transform conflict is fleeting. Enjoying the benefits of complete surprise, the first wave of Japanese aircraft that attacked Pearl Harbor on 7 December 1941 apparently suffered few casualties. But by the time the second wave left the airspace over Oahu about two hours later, 29 aircraft had been lost, even though the island's defenses had been damaged by the first wave of attacks.[15] When the Japanese returned in June 1942 to ambush the US Navy in the waters around Midway, it had become extremely difficult to surprise Americans with a carrier air strike in the waters around Hawaii.

After all, the concept was no longer novel after the attack on Pearl Harbor. An outstanding US intelligence effort denied Japan the element of surprise that was crucial to their success in the engagement. The US Navy then delivered a stunning defeat to the Japanese, making Midway the beginning of the end for Imperial Japan. Similarly, surprise was the crucial element in the 11 September 2001 terrorist attacks against the World Trade Center and the Pentagon. When passengers aboard a fourth hijacked airliner learned of their probable fate in cellphone conversations with loved ones, they stopped the terrorists from completing their mission. Without the surprise needed to prevent the passengers from realizing that they were engaged in a conflict, the terrorists lacked the forces necessary to maintain control of the aircraft.

Surprise is extraordinarily attractive because it allows actors to achieve objectives that would normally be well beyond their reach if they faced an alert and determined opponent. Surprise allows one side to operate with virtually no opposition. Relying on the element of surprise, however, is extraordinarily risky. It is impossible *ex ante* to guarantee that surprise will occur, or for that matter, exactly when the effects of surprise will begin to wear off, and the inability to achieve surprise will doom the operation to failure. Stronger adversaries always can rely on more predictable attrition strategies to wear down weaker opponents.[16] In fact, stronger adversaries generally do not want to surprise their opponents. They prefer to intimidate them into surrender by announcing clearly their intention to fight if the adversary does not comply with their demands. US officials, for example, made clear their intention to attack Afghanistan if the Taliban did not hand over the al-Qaida ringleaders responsible for the 11 September attacks. The Taliban might have been surprised by the way the US campaign unfolded and by the speed with which their forces collapsed, but they were not really surprised by the war itself.

The Risk Paradox and Surprise

Surprise is attractive to the weaker party in a conflict because it allows it to contemplate decisive actions against a stronger adversary.[17] But because achieving surprise is a risky proposition and because it allows actors to consider initiatives that are beyond their capabilities, the victim of surprise often will dismiss potential surprise scenarios as harebrained. In other words, even if the victims of surprise detect the beginnings of an initiative, they will have to overcome their existing assumption that the unfolding initiative is beyond the capability of their adversary or will prove to be suicidal. This asymmetry in the perception of what is prudent and what is reckless creates a paradox, identified by Handel, which lies at the heart of the theory of surprise: 'The greater the risk, the less likely it seems, and the less risky it becomes. In fact, the greater the risk, the smaller it becomes.'[18] Handel is suggesting that there is a direct link between the weaker party's incentive to use surprise and the stronger party's propensity actually to be surprised by the initiative. He offered this insight, however, without fully outlining the causal linkages he was suggesting. Elsewhere, for example, he wrote 'The powerful stronger side conversely lacks the incentive to resort to surprise and thus not only sacrifices an important military advantage but also plays into his enemy's hands.'[19] From this passage it would appear that Handel believes that weakness is a necessary condition for one side to gamble an entire operation on surprise. In this sense, he is probably correct; stronger parties lack the incentive to risk everything on an effort to gain surprise. Stronger parties, however, often hope to achieve and benefit from surprise. US officials thought that the technological surprise suffered by Japan over Hiroshima and Nagasaki would shock the Japanese into surrender, but they did not stop their preparations to launch a bloody attritional invasion of the home islands to force a surrender. They did not risk everything on gaining and benefitting from surprise. In other words, the causal claims made by Handel required some refinement (for example, the weaker party in a conflict is more likely than the stronger side to attempt operations or strategies that *require* the element of surprise to succeed). Similarly, Handel never really explains how victims of surprise contribute to their own demise. In this sense, he missed an opportunity to offer an important advance in the theory of surprise.

From a political scientist's perspective, what is especially elegant about Handel's risk paradox is that it provides a link between explanatory levels of analysis.[20] The incentives to seek surprise are located at a systemic level of analysis, or in the very structure of the situation we find ourselves in. Without parties in competition, without surprise becoming a priority for the weaker party in its quest for victory, there would be no deliberate efforts to risk everything on strategies that require surprise for success. But surprise is not a systemic or a structural phenomenon; it exists in the mind of the victim. Surprise is about human cognition, perception, and psychology. In other words, the different perceptions of risk between the stronger and weaker opponent link the structural setting, which creates the incentive for surprise, with the cognitive setting, which creates the opportunity to surprise an opponent. The weaker party has a stronger interest in basing its plans on the element of surprise, while the more powerful side has reason to overlook the danger of enemy attack.

The *ex ante* divergence in perceptions of risk and opportunity sets the stage for human cognition and psychology to create the phenomenon of surprise. The weaker side becomes mesmerized by the potential opportunity created by surprise (that is, suspending the dialectic of war), while the stronger side fails to consider possible courses of enemy action based on stochastic estimates, because it becomes focused on estimates of the enemy's *wartime* capabilities. This cognitive divergence, for example, sets the stage for the use of denial and deception. It is relatively easy for the weaker side to hide (deny) information from opponents who are not looking for it, or to mislead opponents by feeding them information that confirms their more realistic expectations of what is possible in war. A leading student of denial and deception has even gone so far as to claim that 'deception operations usually have substantial payoffs and never backfire'.[21] Moreover, if accurate information reaches the victim concerning what is about to transpire, it is likely to be dismissed as fantastic or implausible based on the real facts of the situation. In planning surprise, the weaker side, out of desperation, is likely to grasp at straws and to believe that it has opportunities that really do not exist with or without the element of surprise. Prior to the Tet Offensive, most US analysts dismissed information that the North Vietnamese and their Viet Cong allies were planning to instigate a revolt among the South Vietnamese population, because they accurately perceived that southerners would not rebel against the regime in Saigon.[22] Opponents who are desperate enough to gamble everything on surprise can be expected to ignore data that complicates their planning or calls into question their predictions about how their victims will respond to surprise.[23] Nikita Khrushchev was warned repeatedly by various advisors that even if he surprised the Americans with his plan to deploy nuclear weapons and associated delivery vehicles to Cuba, the US reaction to the deployment would erase any gains the Soviets might obtain from the gambit. (The Central Intelligence Agency's Special National Intelligence Estimate [SNIE] 85–3–62 that was published in September 1962 also predicted that the Soviets would not place missiles in Cuba because it would be too risky.[24]) The side planning surprise is prone to make mistakes, because it walks an extraordinarily fine line between success and failure. This fact creates a real challenge for intelligence analysts: they often have to convince their chain of command that the opponent is about to launch an operation that appears *ex ante* to suffer from a fundamental flaw, a perception that is likely to undermine the plausibility of their warning.

To prevent surprise, the victim must overcome several challenges. It must overcome efforts at denial and deception. It must anticipate how weaker opponents might expect to achieve wildly ambitious objectives aided by surprise. It must anticipate that its opponent's strategy might be riddled with errors of omission or commission, or at least an over-optimistic view of its prospects of success. All of this must occur, however, as analysts and policymakers are blinded by their own assumptions and theories about how the conflict should unfold, perceptions colored by their conservative, attritional view of the battlefield. The possibility that the opponent will launch asymmetrical attacks is hard to imagine because of the inherent difficulty in discovering weaknesses in one's own forces or strategies. In the absence of compelling data, mirror imaging – or the use of one's own preferences, culture, and strategy to explain an opponent's behavior – is likely to occur. This tendency to understand the opponent's behavior in light of one's own perception of the situation really constitutes the heart of the surprise problem from the victim's perspective. This is the point at which a host of cognitive biases, intelligence pathologies, or bureaucratic weaknesses will conspire to hide the possibilities for surprise from potential victims.[25] Even more troubling is the fact that evidence of what is about to transpire, or an eerily prophetic analysis, generally can be identified somewhere in the intelligence pipeline in the aftermath of surprise.[26] What is missing from the victim's perspective is the analytical context necessary to use accurate data to generate a useful and timely warning.

The fundamental divergence in the perception of what is possible and what is foolish creates a paradox that leaves open the possibility for surprise to occur. Extraordinarily ambitious initiatives are not only planned, but are often brilliantly executed against opponents who fail to recognize what is happening before it is too late. They succeed because extraordinarily risky operations that require an acquiescent opponent to succeed appear implausible *ex ante* to the victim. This plausibility assumption will lead the victim to place impending signals of an opponent's unfolding initiative in an analytic context that is likely to be flawed.

The Failure of Surprise

Much is written about intelligence failure, but little is written about the failure of surprise. Scholars have focused on successful surprise at the operational level of war, not on the effect of surprise in achieving overall victory. Surprise attacks often produce spectacular results temporarily or locally, but surprise rarely wins wars. Successful operational surprise may even hasten defeat by mobilizing the victim (e.g., the US response to the Japanese attack on Pearl Harbor) or by expending scarce assets without achieving a decisive victory (for example, the fate of the Nazi offensive through the Ardennes forest in the winter of 1944). Even when surprise produces positive strategic consequences, the price can be extraordinarily high. The shock of the Tet attacks or the Egyptian surprise attack at the outset of the 1973 Yom Kippur war can be said to have produced victory in the important sense that they altered the political balance between the combatants; but, from the North Vietnamese or Egyptian perspective, events on the battlefield did not unfold according to plan. In that sense, the shock of surprise itself, not the temporary suspension of war's dialectic, helped deliver victory. But this political shock effect is rare and in the previously mentioned cases it was an unanticipated, albeit not unwelcome, positive effect produced by a failed military attack. Because they can alter the political balance in a conflict, the consequences of surprise are often unanticipated and unintended by the side launching the initiative. If surprise is an *immediate force multiplier*, then over time it can act as a *resistance multiplier*.[27] The side that achieves surprise may reach the culminating point of attack, thereby achieving some fantastic local victory, without ever reaching the culminating point of victory, thereby hastening its defeat in war.

Surprise attacks often fail disastrously because the side undertaking the initiative miscalculates in several ways. Those contemplating surprise might correctly estimate that surprise is needed to achieve their military objectives, only to find that a successful surprise attack undermines the political or moral basis of their campaign. The Japanese attack on Pearl Harbor was a military tour de force, a feat of professional skill that will be remembered for a thousand years. But the successful surprise attack was a political disaster for Japan, because it eliminated the basis of its grand strategy in the Pacific: a 'casualty-averse' American public that would negotiate rather than fight over relatively unknown and unwanted territory. The Japanese failed to understand that the military force multiplier they needed to succeed – surprise – would destroy the political basis of their quest for empire. Those launching an attack often fail to understand that surprise can maximize the impact of a specific blow, but that even the most successful surprise attack needs to be integrated into an overall strategy to win the war. Surprise can worsen the weaker side's position once the dialectic of war is re-established because it can elicit a heightened response from the stronger victim. Successful surprise can make it impossible for the attacker to reach the culminating point of victory in war, because it causes the more powerful victim to engage fully in battle.

Failures also occur because of a mismatch between the weaker side's objectives and the degree, duration, or scope of the paralysis induced in the stronger opponent. The attacker might achieve surprise, but not across a large enough front or for a sufficient enough time, allowing the opponent to muster its superior forces to crush the attack. Indeed, when the effects of surprise begin to dissipate, the weaker side risks being caught overextended without the combat power needed to manage even a decent fighting withdrawal. This is what happened to the Nazi counterattack through the Ardennes forest. Nazi forces achieved surprise and punched through the Allied line, but the Allies had sufficient forces to absorb the attack and launch their own counterattack against the exposed Nazi flanks and lines of communication. If surprise is not linked to some sort of knockout blow or an overall strategy to win the conflict, it often worsens the weaker party's position and accelerates its loss of the war.[28]

The failure of surprise is related to Handel's risk paradox in the sense that it vindicates the stronger side's judgment that a possible operation is extraordinarily risky or simply irrational. It made no sense for the

Japanese to attack Pearl Harbor because they lacked the resources to defeat the United States; the sneak attack on 7 December simply guaranteed that superior American resources would be brought to bear against them. Even aided by the element of surprise, operations that appear harebrained *ex ante* can actually turn out to be harebrained. The analysts who predicted in SNIE 85–3–62 that the Soviets would not place missiles in Cuba because it would be too dangerous stated in the aftermath of the Cuban Missile Crisis that their analysis was at least partially vindicated by events. In other words, the Soviets should not have placed missiles in Cuba because the gambit risked superpower war for what were at best marginal benefits. CIA analysts were not alone in this judgment. When Secretary of State Dean Rusk called on Soviet Ambassador Anatoly Dobrynin to inform him that the United States had detected missiles in Cuba, he surprised the Soviet official with the news. (Dobrynin had not been privy to the decisions made in Moscow.) Rusk stated informally that it was incomprehensible to him how leaders in Moscow could make such a gross error of judgment about what was acceptable to the United States.[29] Years later, he noted that Dobrynin was so shaken by the news that he aged ten years right before his eyes.[30]

Surprise fails because it leads the weaker side in the conflict to reach for goals that are truly beyond its grasp or to forget that when the effects of surprise dissipate, the dialectic of war returns with a vengeance. Indeed, the ultimate paradox of surprise is that it often amounts to a 'lose–lose' proposition: it creates a disastrous initial loss for the victim and a painful loss of the war for the attacker. The outcome of the war actually confirms both sides' estimate of the pre-war balance of power as the stronger power defeats the weaker side in the conflict. The theory of surprise thus offers an important caveat to Geoffrey Blainey's argument that war is more likely as states near parity.[31] Even though the leaders of the weaker side in a conflict might recognize the disparity in power between them and their opponent, the prospect of surprise can prompt them to believe that they can nullify that disparity and achieve their objectives.

The Future of Surprise

In the aftermath of 11 September 2001, the idea that the United States, its allies, military forces, or interests are likely targets of surprise attacks or initiatives would not stir much controversy. But this prediction is not based solely on recent events. Instead, the theory of surprise suggests that the United States' opponents must somehow circumvent its diplomatic, economic, or military might to achieve goals that Washington opposes. Its relative strength creates incentives for its opponents to launch surprise initiatives or asymmetric attacks to achieve their objectives before the

United States and its allies can bring their full power to bear. Americans' relative strength also creates an attritional mind-set that blinds them to the possibility that enemies will use surprise to attempt to achieve objectives that in war would be beyond their reach.

Evidence exists to support the idea that the problem of surprise is especially acute for the United States. Thomas Christensen, for example, notes that the American academic and policy debate about the potential threat created by the emergence of China as a peer competitor (that is, a state capable of challenging the United States in a battle of attrition) ignores a more likely road to war. Chinese leaders' perceptions of their own weakness have led them to a search for methods to distract, deter, or bloody the United States.[32] What is particularly chilling is that the thinking emerging in China is eerily similar to Japanese strategy on the eve of Pearl Harbor: a casualty-averse United States will seek a negotiated settlement following some military setback. The fact that many American observers fail to realize that China might gamble on surprise rather than work for decades to match US military capabilities is also disturbing. Additionally, al-Qaida's recent success in the skies over New York and Washington demonstrates that terrorists, fanatics, or syndicates might find the element of surprise attractive because it affords them a way to attack an infinitely more powerful United States. As the information and communication revolution continues to empower individuals, the US intelligence community now has to worry that non-state actors will attempt to capitalize on surprise to achieve their objectives. The stage is set for surprise to occur.

Michael Handel was a pessimist when it came to the future of surprise, agreeing with his colleague Richard Betts that intelligence failures are inevitable.[33] Handel came to this conclusion in his early writings, and the advent of advanced data-processing and reconnaissance capabilities did little to alter his judgment. Indeed, what is especially vexing to Handel, Betts, and a host of other scholars is that victims of surprise often had a chance to avert disaster, but cognitive, bureaucratic, or political constraints or pathologies prevented them from capitalizing on these opportunities. Accurate signals of impending attack generally can be discovered in the intelligence pipeline after surprise occurs. Some people even manage to recognize these signals. Intelligence 'dissenters' – individuals who swim against the analytical or policy tide – often issue accurate warnings before disaster strikes only to be ignored by fellow intelligence analysts or policymakers. Prior to the Tet Offensive, for instance, civilian analysts in Saigon developed an accurate estimate of North Vietnamese and Viet Cong intentions, only to have their analysis dismissed as far-fetched by analysts at the headquarters of the Central Intelligence Agency.[34] Occasionally, intelligence analysts might even get things right: US intelligence analysts surprised the Japanese Navy at Midway. But the American miracle at Midway was made possible by the American disaster at Pearl Harbor. According to Handel:

Arrogance and a sense of invincibility blinded the Japanese, who did not consider their opponent worthy of much attention. On the other hand, the Americans, who had been humbled early in the war and who lacked both confidence and ships, knew that learning as much as possible about their enemy was imperative. There is no stronger incentive to encourage the appreciation of intelligence than fear and weakness (whether actual or perceived); conversely, victory and power reduce one's motivation to learn about the enemy, thus bringing about the conditions that may eventually cause defeat.[35]

What changed in the months following Pearl Harbor was that the Japanese had adopted the attritional mind-set characteristic of the strong, while US analysts and officers recognized that they needed force multipliers to overcome their disadvantage in numbers, equipment, morale, and experience.

The American experience at Midway thus offers some insights into possible ways of avoiding future surprise that US policymakers and analysts might use to great benefit. The outcome of the Battle of Midway raises an important question: why did the same analysts and intelligence organizations fail so badly in their task prior to Pearl Harbor yet succeed so well in its aftermath? Was it war alone that concentrated their minds? In the past, most observers have identified cognitive, bureaucratic, or political problems as a source of intelligence failure. But the pathologies and bureaucratic and cognitive limits to analysis often identified as the source of intelligence failure might simply be consequences of a more fundamental causal force. The theory of surprise suggests that it is the initial cognitive framework created by the relative power position of the parties in conflict that sets the stage for surprise to occur. In other words, if strong parties began to view conflict from the weaker party's perspective, while weak actors kept war's dialectic in mind, then surprise would become less likely. Christensen's analysis of the potential Chinese threat ends on a similar note: Chinese officers and officials should be encouraged to visit Pearl Harbor to take note of the fact that it is a mistake to count on a lack of American resolve in war.[36] One might also think about modifying the tour to include the surrender deck of the battleship *Missouri* to suggest that once the effect of surprise fades, the dialectic of war returns.

Clearly, reversing the cognitive predisposition that accompanies one's position in a conflict is no small or simple matter. Midway suggests that it might be possible to alter this fundamental bias quickly, although it is not apparent whether this change in mind-set can be accomplished quickly enough or completely before disaster strikes. The theory of surprise suggests, however, that at least a 'theoretical' path to reducing the likelihood that surprise will be attempted or succeed is available.

Conclusion

Handel began his 1977 article in *International Studies Quarterly* with the observation that the theory of surprise would be better at explaining, rather than preventing, disaster. He turned to Hegel's famous passage to capture this shortcoming: 'The owl of Minerva begins its flight when dusk is falling . . . man can perceive the conception of actuality . . . only when the actuality has already been fully unfolded and has indeed become cut and dried.'[37] One can only add the observation that things in fact did become pretty cut and dried on the morning of 11 September when the old bird returned home to roost. Millions of people in real time experienced surprise, which was accompanied by an inability on the part of nearly all concerned to interfere with the airplane hijackers. War, for a moment, became a matter of administration, a phenomenon in which it was possible for a few people to destroy the World Trade Center with the aid of a box cutter in just two hours. The very brilliance of such an audacious surprise attack showed that the assumption that people, groups, or states would not dare do such a thing was flawed, if not downright stupid. Usama bin Ladin, after all, had established a track record of attacking US interests and targets and made no effort to hide the fact that he intended to attack Americans in the future.[38] The fact that we could have seen the attack coming simply adds insult to injury. Handel would of course suggest that this sort of thing is inevitable, that this is what it means to be a victim of surprise.

It is too much to expect that surprise can be prevented in the future. But the theory of surprise can identify when it is likely to occur, who is likely to find the element of surprise attractive as a basis of policy or strategy, and who is likely to be its victim. It also explains why the beginning of the end for al-Qaida came when the first New Yorker noticed an aircraft heading toward the World Trade Center. The trick now lies in making operational use of the theory of surprise.

NOTES

1 A host of factors also bedevils those wishing to achieve surprise. For efforts to organize the body of theory related to intelligence and surprise see Michael Handel, 'The Politics of Intelligence', *Intelligence and National Security*, vol. 2, no. 4 (1987), pp. 5–46; James J. Wirtz, 'The Intelligence Paradigm', *Intelligence and National Security*, vol. 4, no. 4 (1989), pp. 829–37.

2 Robert Jervis, *Perception and Misperception in World Politics* (Princeton, NJ: Princeton University Press, 1976); and Richards J. Heuer, Jr, *Psychology of Intelligence Analysis* (Washington, DC: Center for the Study of Intelligence, Government Printing Office, 1999).

3 The 'Ultra syndrome' is the tendency to become over-reliant on a clandestine

source of information that has proven to be useful in the past, while the 'cry-wolf syndrome' is the tendency for repeated false warnings to desensitize an audience to subsequent alarms; see Ephraim Kam, *Surprise Attack: The Victim's Perspective* (Cambridge, MA: Harvard University Press, 1988).

4 Walter Laqueur, *A World of Secrets: The Uses and Limits of Intelligence* (New York: Basic Books, 1985).

5 For a similar argument about the prospects for a theory of deception see Barton Whaley and Jeffrey Busby, 'Detecting Deception: Practice, Practitioners, and Theory', in Roy Godson and James J. Wirtz, *Strategic Denial and Deception* (New Brunswick, NJ: Transaction, 2002), pp. 181–221.

6 Michael Handel, 'Intelligence and the Problem of Strategic Surprise', *Journal of Strategic Studies*, vol. 7, no. 3 (1984), pp. 229–30.

7 Surprise, however, cannot overcome gross incompetence (troops that cannot conduct basic maneuvers), or negligence (weapons that will not work or vehicles that will not run) on the part of the attacker.

8 Edward Luttwak, *Strategy: The Logic of War and Peace* (Cambridge, MA: Harvard University Press, 1987), p. 8.

9 Although in both instances US forces can be said to have benefitted from techno-logical surprise. On that phenomenon see Michael Handel, 'Technological Surprise in War', *Intelligence and National Security*, vol. 2, no. 1 (1987), pp. 1–53.

10 Handel often made the similar point that 'the weaker side has a very strong incen-tive to compensate for his weakness by resorting to the use of stratagem and sur-prise as a force multiplier'. Michael Handel, 'Crisis and Surprise in Three Arab–Israeli Wars', in Klaus Knorr and Patrick Morgan, eds, *Strategic Military Surprise* (New Brunswick, NJ: Transaction, 1983), p. 113.

11 Richard Betts, *Surprise Attack: Lessons for Defense Planning* (Washington, DC: Brookings Institution, 1982), especially pp. 88–92.

12 In his writings, Handel often stated that Clausewitz was no fan of intelligence, deception, and surprise, but he also often noted that since the early nineteenth century, changes in technology, logistics, and communications had increased the attractiveness of surprise in war. In 1996, for instance, he wrote: 'While for Clausewitz, surprise was rarely achievable on the strategic level but was more fea-sible on the operational or strategic levels, today the opposite is true . . . . the devel-opment of radars and other sensors have made operational and tactical surprise easier to prevent.' Michael Handel *Masters of War*, 2nd revised edn (London: Frank Cass, 1996), p. 131.

13 After all, one of the would-be hijackers apparently was already in police custody prior to 11 September 2001.

14 William McRaven, *Spec Ops Case Studies in Special Operations Warfare: Theory and Practice* (Novato, CA: Presidio Press, 1998).

15 Samuel Eliot Morison, *The Two-Ocean War: A Short History of the United States Navy in the Second World War* (Boston, MA: Little, Brown, 1963), p. 67.

16 In the revised edition of his seminal volume, Luttwak makes the same point: 'mil-itary leaders whose forces are altogether superior may be quite justified in spurn-ing surprise, for the sake of ample preparations to use their full strength with the simplest methods, to minimize organizational risk'. Edward Luttwak, *Strategy: The Logic of War and Peace*, revised edn (Cambridge, MA: Harvard University Press, 2001), p. 13.

17 According to Luttwak, 'In a manner itself paradoxical, it is those who are materi-ally weaker, and therefore have good reason to fear a straightforward clash of strength against strength, who can most benefit by self-weakening paradoxical conduct – if it obtains the advantage of surprise, which may yet offer victory.' Luttwak, *Strategy*, revised edn, p. 14.

18 Michael Handel, 'The Yom Kippur War and the Inevitability of Surprise', *International Studies Quarterly*, vol. 21, no. 3 (1977), p. 468.

19 Handel, 'Crisis and Surprise in Three Arab–Israeli Wars', p. 113.

20 Another important effort to link levels of analysis is Robert Putnam, 'The Logic of Two-Level Games', *International Organization*, vol. 42, no. 2 (1988), pp. 427–60.

21 Barton Whaley, 'Conditions Making for Success and Failure of D&D: Authoritarian and Transition Regimes', in Roy Godson and James J. Wirtz, eds, *Strategic Denial and Deception: The 21st Century Challenge* (New Brunswick, NJ: Transaction, 2001), p. 67.

22 James J. Wirtz, *The Tet Offensive: Intelligence Failure in War* (Ithaca, NY: Cornell University Press, 1991).

23 According to Jervis, 'A person is less apt to reorganize evidence into a new theory or image if he is deeply committed to the established view.' Jervis, *Perception and Misperception*, p. 196.

24 Special National Intelligence Estimate 85–3–62, 'The Military Buildup in Cuba' (September 1962), pp. 1–2, 8–9; and James J. Wirtz, 'Organizing for Crisis Intelligence: Lessons from the Cuban Missile Crisis', in James G. Blight and David Welch, eds, *Intelligence and the Cuban Missile Crisis* (London: Frank Cass, 1998).

25 Betts, *Surprise Attack*, pp. 87–149. This also is the point at which the theory of surprise can integrate the existing literature and competing theories of surprise into a unified explanation of the phenomenon.

26 Richard Betts, 'Surprise Despite Warning', *Political Science Quarterly*, vol. 95, no. 4 (1980/81), pp. 551–72; and Michael Handel, *The Diplomacy of Surprise: Hitler, Nixon, Sadat* (Cambridge, MA: Center for the Study of International Affairs, 1981), p. 144. Roberta Wohlstetter's use of a metaphorical 'signal to noise' ratio was an effort to show how accurate 'signals' could always be found in an intelligence system, along with extraneous information described as 'noise'. Signals would have to grow stronger than this background noise before they could be perceived accurately. Ariel Levite offered a dissenting opinion on the issue, that surprise often occurred because of a lack of accurate warning, if not raw data, in an intelligence bureaucracy. See Ariel Levite, *Intelligence and Strategic Surprises* (New York: Columbia University Press, 1987).

27 Surprise can make war go away, but it rarely can prevent it from returning.

28 Stalin offered a similar judgment about the effectiveness of surprise, which provided him with an excuse for the denigration of the disaster of June 1941. For Stalin, surprise was a transient influence in war, not a permanently operating factor that could determine the outcome of a conflict. I would like to thank Dick Betts for offering this observation.

29 'State Department Cable on Secretary of State Dean Rusk Meeting with Soviet Ambassador Dobrynin to Give Kennedy's Letter to Premier Khrushchev, Announcing Discovery of Missiles in Cuba', contained in Laurence Chang and Peter Kornbluh, eds, *The Cuban Missile Crisis, 1962* (New York: The New Press, 1982), pp. 146–7.

30 James Blight's interview with Dean Rusk, 18 May 1987, in James G. Blight and David Welch, *On the Brink: Americans and Soviets Reexamine the Cuban Missile Crisis* (New York: Hill & Wang, 1989), p. 185.

31 Geoffrey Blainey, *The Causes of War* (New York: The Free Press, 1988).

32 Thomas J. Christensen, 'Posing Problems without Catching Up: China's Rise and Challenges for US Security Policy', *International Security*, vol. 23, no. 4 (Spring 2001), pp. 5–40.

33 Handel, 'The Yom Kippur War', pp. 461–2; and Richard Betts, 'Analysis, War and Decision: Why Intelligence Failures are Inevitable', *World Politics*, vol. 31 (October 1977).

34 Wirtz, *The Tet Offensive*, pp. 172–7.
35 Michael Handel, 'Intelligence and Military Operations', in Michael I. Handel, ed., *Intelligence and Military Operations* (London: Frank Cass, 1990), p. 39.
36 Christensen, 'Posing Problems', p. 36.
37 Cited in Handel, 'The Yom Kippur War and the Inevitability of Surprise', p. 462.
38 Kenneth Katzman, 'Terrorism: Near Eastern Groups and State Sponsors' (CRS Report to Congress, 10 September 2001), pp. 9–13.

5

'FORTITUDE' in Context: The Evolution of British Military Deception in Two World Wars, 1914–1945

John Ferris

Strategic deception is conventionally treated as a success story for Britain, with reason. Cases like FORTITUDE, the campaign which kept German forces from the front during most of the battle of Normandy, in the belief the main invasion was yet to come and would be struck by a mythical 'First United States Army Group' (FUSAG); or MINCEMEAT, the planting of a story on Adolf Hitler, through a dead man dressed as an officer and floated on a beach in Spain, that Sicily was not the target of Allied invasion in 1943 – these have become the stuff of legends. Those events were real and dramatic and they mattered – ghosts kept Germans from battle. The British appear clever, because they were; doubly so, because these triumphs were linked to ULTRA, the solution of high-grade German cryptographic systems, and to the 'double cross' system, by which British security controlled German espionage in the United Kingdom. The intersection of these successes marks a triumph in military history. Still, legend makes for bad history, and problems remain in the study of deception, despite the work of scholars, especially the late Michael Handel.[1]

The causes are legion. Too few scholars have addressed the topic critically; until 1996, the record was largely out of the public domain, and much of the evidence there was overlooked. The study of deception sprang from a collision between a conceptually mature literature on strategic surprise and a fragmentary record of historical cases, filtered through the views of British practitioners. According to the latter, deception was practiced rarely in World War I, most notably in the Palestine campaign of 1917–18, but found its true home in World War II. Its creators were men of genius – Richard Meinertzhagen, Ewan Montagu, Dudley Clarke – who succeeded precisely because they were not organization men, marching to the sound of their own drum rather than to the deadbeat of bureaucracy. Technique was all; deception worked because of the artists' skill. The maestros were British and their success was unparalleled. This literature tends to be self-congratulatory, as if deception were innately British, but something that can be mastered by anyone who learns how to think like an Englishman –

or lie like one. Such views echo in the good literature on deception during World War II, including the official British history by Michael Howard.[2] Overgeneralization from these British instances has affected policy-oriented works and contemporary military doctrine on strategic surprise and deception. Much can be said for British deception, and for the principles its practitioners distilled from experience; but many states have practiced deception, and some have scored remarkable results against their enemies – including Britain. FORTITUDE was a triumph of technique, but how does it compare in effect with the German cover for Operation BARBAROSSA, or to Soviet operational deception on the eastern front in 1943–45? Again, deception has been a conventional practice for bureaucracies, with geniuses playing just one part, and the lessons learned in one world war were carried over to the next. Study of the record in context will illuminate the nature of deception, the conditions in which it works – how technique interacts with circumstance – and its value for policymakers today and tomorrow; it will illuminate what British deception really was and how it affected events. There were roots to FORTITUDE; they merit study.

Before 1914, British officers linked deception to security. A standard text by a celebrated soldier, Garnett Wolesley, noted patrols behind enemy lines might tap its telegraph system and send commands, 'ordering him to concentrate upon wrong points, or by giving him false information, you may induce him to move as you wish'.[3] The latter idea also was part of Victorian and Edwardian views on communications intelligence. During the decade before 1914, the founding memoranda for the counter-intelligence and intelligence services that became MI5 and SIS discussed deception in war and peace, as British and Indian Army Directors of Military Intelligence (DMIs) did in staff exercises and lectures.[4] These ideas were theory, not put into practice, and often naive. Nonetheless, the professional literature described advanced principles of intelligence and basic ones of deception, and advocated the idea of making an enemy act on deceptive messages: here lay the roots of MINCEMEAT. In 1914, intelligence officers and commanders knew the value of controlling another side's agents, and the close links between deception, security, and surprise. The conversion of these principles into practice took some time, and it occurred haltingly throughout World War I. Though the evidence on that process is fragmentary and uncertain, some matters can be proven and other possibilities raised.

Before the war, MI5 had aimed not to control agent networks but to smash them. In 1914, led by Colonel R.J. Drake, it did so. By 1915, it had adopted standard 'steps to hoodwink the Germans'. So, 'to keep the German Government in ignorance of the arrest of their spies for as long a time as possible', MI5 forwarded 'faked letters' to their masters. How far this practice extended is uncertain. According to its internal history, written from incomplete records, MI5 passed such material for the purposes of security, to deceive secret services rather than statesmen.[5]

However, according to a well-informed witness, Admiral Hall, the Director of Naval Intelligence (DNI), Drake used controlled agents in August 1914 to cover the movement of the British Army to France, and MI5 continued this process systematically throughout the war. 'Only 14 enemy agents shot. After they had been disposed of, their reports home were continued and even their pay drawn. Sometimes it became difficult to kill them off when desired. One had to lose his life in a bus bombed by a Zeppelin.'[6] Hall also claimed that he and Drake had made the German authorities anticipate amphibious assaults through controlled agents, deliberate passing of code systems so that the enemy could read misleading communications, and systematic leaks to the press and neutral diplomats. This evidence must be treated with caution, but material from Hall's colleagues and official records support much of this story.[7] In these instances, sophisticated technique had no effect, because it did not support real operations. The one exception to that rule is also the best documented: a combined effort by the army and navy 'to attract the enemy's attention to the possibility of a landing on the Belgian coast, with the object of inducing him to hold reserves in that area' during the Somme campaign.[8] It appears to have worked as planned – British General Headquarters (GHQ) in France noted that during the deception the Germans did move forces to the Belgian coast – but to no great effect.[9]

By 1916–17, generals and intelligence officers practiced strategic deception through multiple sources. In January 1917, for example, GHQ Egypt informed the Military Intelligence Department (MID) of the questions German intelligence had asked 'one of our agents who managed to get himself in their employment'. The MID replied with shrewd advice; someone had already considered such matters:

> As to the information you give, this must depend on your plans. You should minimize importance operations to agent if you are able to continue them on the lines recently suggested. On the other hand, you should exaggerate future plans if you consider that you cannot continue them for much longer. Generally speaking, the policy is to keep the Turks guessing everywhere, and questions should be answered accordingly. There is no objection, in order to give your answers appearance of truth, to your giving information about some units which should be partly true and partly false, and should fit in with suggestions contained in the first paragraphs of this telegram. You should let me know exactly what you send so that partial corroboration may be given from here should opportunity occur.

Instead of passing the whole story through one account, suspiciously bare, GHQ Cairo provided bits which, seen in the light of the whole by the enemy's staff, indicated Britain could not sustain another major operation across the Sinai, covering its intention to do precisely that. This campaign of misdirection may have continued. Two months later, before the first battle of Gaza, the MID informed GHQ that 'information upon which we can depend' showed 'what the Germans are endeavoring to learn from their spies in Egypt'.[10] This episode shows sophistication of technique, backed by useful means to monitor the enemy's response, through solutions of Turkish and German ciphers. More may be said of the army's use of strategic deception, had so many records not been slaughtered; more can be said about its practice of operational deception.

The most celebrated instances occurred in the Middle East. In August 1917, General Allenby defined a strategy to break the Turkish lines in southern Palestine. While the real cover for this endeavor was its risk and unexpectedness, he multiplied his chances through security and deception. He aimed to 'disclose such evidence of activity as would cause the enemy to be apprehensive of an attack against his right center and right' – the coastal area near Gaza where the enemy would expect attack – while hiding all deployments toward the real target, Beersheba.[11] Allenby's secret intelligence chief, Colonel Meinertzhagen, found a means to deliver false messages directly to the enemy. He rode alone toward enemy lines, provoked an enemy patrol into pursuit and fled, dropping a haversack containing misleading documents, which the enemy captured and believed – these indicated the attack would fall on Gaza. The 'haversack ruse' is the best remembered aspect of deception from Palestine, but it capped a greater process, as MINCEMEAT would do a generation later.[12] Deception at the third battle of Gaza worked in technical and operational terms; it made operations more complete and less costly – the enemy swallowed the bait, and the assault broke its defenses. Ten months later, a similar deception campaign covered British operations in northern Palestine. In terms of security and the relative power of British forces, deception was less significant here than at Gaza – matters might have gone much as they did without it – but, again, it was practiced with skill and worked in technical terms.

The greatest instances of operational deception occurred on the western front. During 1918, the effect of attrition and changes in operational styles made breakthrough easier to achieve than before; but developments in security and deception had made enemy intentions and capabilities more difficult to penetrate. Any defender could crush any attack and wreck the enemy's limited strength in storm troops – if it could determine where and when the assault would come and in what strength. Surprise characterized almost every successful attack of 1918. It was biased in favor of the side with the initiative, multiplying the operational advantages that gave it that position. The aims were generally to confuse the enemy, and, particularly, to conceal the movement of reinforcements just before an assault. Typically, a defender could not locate the enemy's reserves – between 10 and 20 per cent of its forces – in rear areas. The defender usually could detect preparations for major operations, but neither invariably nor with certainty; and the side with the initiative simultaneously prepared for several major attacks up and down the front. If an attacker could double without detection its strength (especially in élite formations) on a ten-mile sector for three days, a cheap and dramatic breakthrough was possible. A defender who could locate only 80 per cent of the enemy's divisions stood next to disaster; but one who could uncover the enemy's intentions was well on the road to triumph. The achievement of surprise hinged on many interdependent factors, such as spreading rumors among one's own troops, so as to blind the most dangerous of human intelligence sources, one's men as prisoners; and degrading technologically based intelligence services, through refinements in physical camouflage, the registration of artillery, and signals security.

Above all, surprise turned on a transformation of the idea and nature of security and deception. Before 1914, war was envisaged as short, decisive, uncertain, one's forces out of contact with the enemy until encounter battle suddenly settled the struggle, with intelligence hard to find and easy to block. Hence, security and deception were seen as distinct but related matters: one seeking to conceal everything about anything, the other adding a twist of misdirection to an environment of confusion. By 1918, these two matters came to share a common core, though each also had distinct elements, from years of experience with most of both sides fighting constantly hundreds of yards apart, and possessing excellent intelligence on each other. During 1917, both sides possessed near-perfect knowledge of each other's order of battle, and an extraordinary grasp of its operational intentions. Security and deception changed in response to these conditions, becoming artificial means to replace the confusion once natural to war, but stripped from the western front. Security became focused; deliberately aiming to let the enemy see many things, perhaps even the location of 90 per cent of one's forces, so long as it knew nothing about those matters one absolutely wished to hide, such as the deployment of assault forces. Even if no misleading signals were transmitted, focused security was inherently deceptive; in any case, it was linked to an unprecedented practice of deception, which in turn was directed largely to bolster security. When combined, these matters hid truth, showed truth, and created uncertainty about truth; but on the western front, unlike in Palestine, they did not create lies. Techniques of specific misdirection were minor parts of this arsenal, the real aims being to combine confusion in general with absolute secrecy about one's real intentions. Deception and focused security were not uniformly effective, but they were used by both sides before every major attack of 1918. Success in this sphere was usually a precondition for surprise. Focused security and deception, born in 1917, became standard in international military thought after 1918.

The British and German armies most emphasized these practices. They alternately led the world in this endeavor, with the scales of the balance wavering continually between them. Their techniques became surprisingly sophisticated: not until 1943 would these again be superseded. Thus, to mislead the Italians before the Battle of Caporetto and the Western Allies before the 'Michael' offensive of March 1918, Germany created phantom armies through signals deception. Britain intended to do the same for its projected operations of 1919. Ultimately, Germany pursued a more ambitious policy of deception but, because this proved extraordinarily difficult to execute, its approach was no more effective than Britain's simpler and more easily sustained one, which was strikingly similar to its style of operational deception during 1944. In any case, under the right circumstances, elementary techniques could provide extraordinary surprise. Merely to camouflage the movements of several corps for a few days, or prevent the enemy from detecting preparations for attack over a limited time and space, might matter if the date was 8 August 1918 and the place, Amiens.[13]

By September 1918, GHQ had defined deception as intrinsic to security, the two as essential to surprise, and the latter as fundamental to victory. It aimed constantly to mislead the enemy about strategy and operations, through rigorous control over every indicator of intentions and capabilities, to give the enemy a false picture through overlapping sources.[14] In order to achieve these ends, 'Security Sections' were established from divisions to GHQ, to coordinate all forms of security and deception, merged as 'negative, positive and confirmatory camouflage'. Meinertzhagen controlled this organization, and guided it with the most mature statement of the principles of deception and focused security to survive from the Great War:

> The ultimate goal of security is to produce an element of surprise. This can only be effected by preventing the enemy divining our real plan, whilst at the same time feeding him with sufficient material to induce him to believe he is in possession of our real plan.
>
> Whereas the primary duty of the Intelligence Section is to gauge the enemy's intentions and the means at his disposal to carry them out, in other words to pick the enemy's brains, Security feeds the enemy with material served up in as acceptable form as possible. A security officer must never lose sight of the fact that he is dealing with a trained Intelligence Officer at the enemy's headquarters and that badly prepared camouflage will have the same effect on a trained Intelligence Officer as badly served food – it will be refused or if accepted will not be digested. A study of enemy methods of security and a knowledge of the enemy's personal characteristics is a necessary basis for successful security. A security officer should constantly frame his mind to impersonate the enemy and judge of the quality and quantity of material that is likely of acceptance or rejection . . .
>
> Camouflage gives a wide field for an imaginative brain and can be

exercised to a second and third degree; if channels of leakage and methods of camouflage are carefully controlled, both the enemy and our own troops may become so confused and gorged with material that they are unable to assimilate it. This produces a clogged and inoperative brain, incapable of seeing clearly what our plans are.

As means to achieve these ends, Meinertzhagen emphasized signals deception, the provision of misleading information to one's own troops and physical camouflage, the best means to confuse the primary sources of field intelligence.[15] However, with the German collapse, this organization was not tested; the British would not again reach this standard of operational deception until 1944.

One can make some general, perhaps conservative, statements about British deception during the Great War. Generals and intelligence officers applied advanced principles and most of the techniques of World War II. They used knowledge of the enemy's expectations to mislead him and to guide their own attack. Intelligence was always used to monitor the effect of deception, though no such source could match ULTRA – the quality of supporting intelligence was the main difference between British deception in the two world wars. The classic game of controlled agent and deception was played on occasion. The Belgian coast gambit of 1916 compares favorably with many British deception plans of 1942–45. Strategic deception may have been practiced more than we know; but not as intensively and extensively and constantly as during 1939–45. Operational deception was practiced constantly, much as in World War II, albeit with more focus on security than misdirection. The most effective modes were simple, aiming to cover the movement of perhaps 100,000 men and 500 guns for two days. The object was confusion rather than misdirection. Confusion proved a powerful tool; misdirection harder to achieve, though still possible, and when so doubly powerful. Deception was a weapon for every attacker and a problem for every defender, and a factor on every battlefield during 1917–18.

World War I gave Britain much experience in deception, and its authorities thought about it, but not as modern military institutions would do. During 1919–39, deception had an odd place in British doctrine. Neither the Royal Navy nor the RAF (Royal Air Force) emphasized the matter: expecting wireless silence to be the norm, they misunderstood the basis of operational deception for war at sea and in air. Their officers knew of deception, but were not taught about it. Though the army better remembered lessons and distilled principles, it too lost much. No accounts by its leading practitioners were disseminated. In November 1918, the MID intended to synthesize the lessons of the war in a new manual: one of its four parts was to be 'Counter-Intelligence and Security', with a chapter on deception. *The Manual of Military Intelligence in the Field, Provisional,*

1921, however, followed another model. Like other such volumes during 1923–25, it mentioned deception with little detail or reference to principle. Fortunately, the leading relevant manual of the interwar years, *The Manual of Military Intelligence in the Field, 1930*, treated the matter better. It defined deception and security as essential to surprise, emphasized the need 'to ensure that any information which either leaks or is put through to the enemy is of such a nature that he forms wrong deductions', and discussed technique (rumors, the press, 'false information', 'deliberate deception', and 'agents in hostile and neutral countries'). It also defined a sound body of principles to govern 'a false scheme for secrecy and deception of the enemy'. The latter must:

i   Conform to the general plan of operations and allow for developments that may subsequently arise.
ii Be secure from disclosure by subsequent events.
iii Be a reasonable alternative to the actual operation to be carried out.
iv Be thought out to the minutest detail.
v   Supply the enemy with some correct information that, while it cannot disclose our true plan, will help to confirm his belief in the false one.
vi Suit the enemy's psychology.[16]

Arguably, given the role of doctrine with the British military during the interwar period, lessons were best passed on through brief definitions. These manuals devoted greater attention to other aspects of intelligence, providing little more of value. Nor was doctrine the only way to transmit lessons. Popular literature on British intelligence made ample reference to deception, especially the 'haversack ruse'; the latter had more influence as a model for future actions than as a factor in past events, because it reinforced the traditional idea that deception could deliver a false message direct to the enemy and so lead it to disaster. Around this event crystallized all the British ideas of what they had done with deception, and could do again.[17]

The stem of continuity lay elsewhere: the personal was policy. Commanders of 1939–45 had been middle-level officers during 1914–18, working in institutions that used intelligence and deception effectively. Memoirs by intelligence officers often suggest their conventional fellows disparaged these issues; those views are caricatures. Most officers thought intelligence and deception significant matters in which Britain had an edge. Many, especially the generals in the Middle East during 1940–42, over-rated their significance – rather than reactionaries muddling through, they were would-be revolutionaries, convinced intelligence and maneuver would transform war. Again, in 1940–45, relatively few people guided British deception, perhaps 100, many of whom had prior experience with deception or had worked in institutions concerned with it. Postwar intelligence services, far larger than before 1914, were marked by continuity of personnel and aimed to maintain their lessons from the conflict. Central among them for MI5 and SIS were controlled agents. In the 1930s, MI5 watched all foreign spies it knew in Britain without arresting them, to ensure it could disrupt or control their networks at need. As war broke out, it destroyed the *Abwehr*'s (German military intelligence) intelligence system in Britain, and made its main source, SNOW, a controlled agent. MI5 immediately used him and sought to palm other doubles onto the enemy, so as to control any network the *Abwehr* might establish. The same opportunity soon occurred with a man working for the *Abwehr* and the Italian *Servizio Informazione Militare* (SIM), Penato Levy, from whom stemmed Britain's most important controlled agent in the Middle East, CHEESE; in both cases SIS was key.[18]

The War Office maintained expertise in the theory of covert war, which in 1938–39 a sub-section, MI(R), began to handle, and well. Three MI(R) officers worked in deception during the war: Colonel Edward Combes, on the Inter-Services Security Board (ISSB), Joan Bright, in the London Controlling Section (LCS), which coordinated deception across the globe, and its director in the Mediterranean theater, Colonel Dudley Clarke. Colonel John Bevan, head of the LCS during 1942–45, had been an intelligence officer in 1918, attempting to penetrate German operational deception. Nor was there continuity merely with intelligence officers. Archibald Wavell was key to the link in deception because, as a staff officer in Palestine during 1917–18, he had witnessed deception in action, given intelligence and maneuver a place in the Army's Field Service Regulations of the 1930s, and, as GOC Middle East in 1939–41, had rebuilt an intelligence system on Allenby's model, rather than the one current in London.

The personal nature of this continuity had consequences. It ensured people in this field had expertise, and worked at cross-purposes. During 1914–18, authorities handled deception in different ways, from which stemmed distinct traditions; these resurfaced without harmonization during 1940. MI5 adopted a centralized approach toward the control of agents, primarily concerned with security but knowing its links to deception. From GHQ in 1918 stemmed a thorough, centralized approach, linking deception to security, focused on defense as much as attack, on the long term, the big picture, but without great experience in application. The Allenby tradition, transferred through Wavell, was a variant, with more emphasis on fluid tactics, the attack, and decision through one engagement. These last characteristics were even more true of the NID's tradition, influenced by Hall's buccaneering approach to bureaucracy, freewheeling gambits, concern for attack above security, and love for the unexpected and the big victory. These traditions had much in common; each had strengths and weaknesses; yet they had different attitudes about how deception should be organized and linked to security and strategy. Their debate and its ultimate resolution shaped the structure of British deception. During 1939–42, four traditions of deception worked their way through decision-makers in dozens of organizations and two locales. British authorities reinvented the wheel three times in four years before the car started to roll; time was wasted but when it came, the right men directed it.

The first spin was made by the Inter-Services Security Board, an institution run by the War Office for the Joint Intelligence Committee (JIC), which coordinated intelligence for the Chiefs of Staff (COS). The ISSB wished to be GHQ's 'Security Section' of 1918 writ large; it aimed to establish a centralized and high level of strategic security within the British Empire, and held that to be incomplete without misdirection. Possibly through Combe's influence, it acted on the 1930 intelligence manual. The ISSB first addressed deception in a report in February 1940, as damage control for the abortive expedition to Finland, which soon became a defeated operation in Norway. It sought to pursue a campaign of deception through a compendium of techniques from the first great war, and applied these ideas to a characteristic element of the second: to cover an amphibious assault, through procedures similar to those around OVER-LORD. The ISSB report held that the existence of an expeditionary force could not be concealed, given the 'considerable amount of speculation and "pointers" in the press'. 'What is urgently needed is to build up the alternative cover' – that these forces were bound for the Middle East. This 'will take time to achieve their effect', and aim to 'start the enemy looking for confirmatory details which action by the various Ministries, it is hoped, will supply . . . Otherwise there is a grave risk that the enemy will get a fairly complete picture of our real intentions and interpret the smaller efforts at bluff as being a belated attempt.' Among the means 'for a campaign of bluff on the higher levels' were an editorial in *The Times* demanding operations in the Middle East, to be immediately denied by the Foreign Office, backed by a highly publicized muddle over censorship and 'a high-grade whispering campaign', the passing of the cover to the diplomatic correspondents of London papers, an indiscreet speech 'in character' by a leading minister, inaccurate leaks to the (then-neutral) Italian government and to the Turkish Naval Attaché, 'which will certainly be cabled to Ankara in the Turkish cipher, which is not secure', and misinformation to British naval and mercantile personnel. The ISSB also intended to exploit the 'double cross' system, noting 'MI5 control certain delicate channels of communication whereby approved items of information may be passed to the enemy.' The report ended with a warning: this effort could be conducted effectively only if the ISSB was 'empowered to act on their own responsibility on the lines set out above', and if 'the highest authority' controlled leaks by ministers 'and other authorities on that level'.[19] With the JIC's approval, the ISSB acted on these proposals, flexing special channels while the News Department of the Foreign Office started 'a general press and rumor cam-

paign'. A month later, to cover operations in Norway, the ISSB attempted
to send misinformation 'to Germany via MI5, to Scandinavia via MI6' and
to Italy through the Foreign Office and 'Admiralty (possibly) by the broken
code to enquire from C.-in-C. Mediterranean for officers with good local
knowledge' – passing disinformation through a cryptographic system it
knew to be compromised.[20]

In early 1940, a body aware of the embryonic 'double cross' system and
of the secrets of British intelligence (with the salient exception of the work
on Enigma of the Government Code and Cypher School (GC&CS)) was
coordinating all activities for deception and security. The JIC and the COS
made the ISSB responsible 'for the co-ordination of all measures for preventing leakage of information to the enemy, and for the preparation of,
and executive action in connection with, measures designed to deceive the
enemy as to our plans and intentions'.[21] It was ready to act on these duties.
On 27 April, the ISSB considered a three-week-old request from the JIC
asking how to keep 'the enemy in constant doubt as to which of several
areas might, at a given moment, become the theatre of Allied operations',
and to define 'the main lines upon which a long-term policy for deceiving
the enemy might be framed'. It responded with a doctrine for deception,
following the GHQ tradition, and the 1930 intelligence manual. 'The
primary purpose of misleading the enemy is (1) to cause him to waste his
resources by making unnecessary or incorrect dispositions, both as a
general policy and in the particular event of an actual proposed operation,
or, (2) to restrain him from some action which he might otherwise take.
Attempts to mislead which are unlikely to compel a response from the
enemy serve little or no purpose.' One must 'persuade the enemy of a probable or possible intention to strike in a particular direction when, in fact,
that is not our intention'. At the same time, the intention must be one
which will appear to the enemy as intrinsically possible. Deception could
not be separated from power. 'Too much should not be inferred from the
demonstrated power of Germany to threaten and mystify. Though assisted
by technique and geographical position, this power is, in the main, a
product of her military strength.' The Allies, conversely, could not strike
anywhere on a large scale:

> If no major offensive action is contemplated this year, the develop-
> ment of a *long-term* policy of mystification is virtually impossible. It
> could not be otherwise than one of complete bluff, and it has
> throughout been considered that any long-term policy should be
> founded on a basis of truth. In the circumstances the Board consider
> that mystification must for the present at any rate be confined to a
> 'hand to mouth' basis . . . there appears to be little opportunity at
> present for active mystification, and until more suitable opportunities
> present themselves the Board consider that they should concentrate

upon the building up of channels of communication. Though this may have for the most part to be confined to the peddling out of comparatively minor information the Board consider that such action will materially assist in establishing these channels . . . a mystification policy cannot be produced ready-made, and likewise the machinery for mystification cannot be created fully-fledged but must be slowly built up from comparatively small beginnings.

Britain must prepare the means for deception, through the ISSB, which should know of major operations when they were in the early planning stage, while a 'nucleus' was needed to handle deception in the Middle East.[22] These ideas were reasonable, but ignored. The ISSB had introduced the principles and practice of deception to the JIC. For the next 18 months, it did as much deception as any other body; during 1942–45 it was one of the two main bodies to execute deception plans prepared by other agencies.[23] Nonetheless, the organization of British deception veered in another direction, away from the tradition of GHQ toward that of Admiral Hall. For 18 months, whenever Whitehall confronted the chance to coordinate deception, it declined to do so.

Means rather than aims drove deception – but not far. Offensives were impossible, but controlled agents grew rapidly. The *Abwehr* expanded its networks in an amateurish way, and MI5 collared the lot. Similar problems wrecked the *Abwehr*'s work in the USSR, and perhaps aided Soviet deception.[24] To reflect this growth in prospects, MI5 created a section to manage the 'double cross' system, 'W. Branch', later renamed 'B1A'. MI5 feared that the system might wither, and the *Abwehr* be driven to establish new, perhaps uncontrolled, networks – if not used for deception, the system might lose its value for security. Yet the services would not transmit minor pieces of true information to the *Abwehr*, fearing chicken feed would strengthen the sea eagle; they were reluctant to pass even disinformation. In October 1940, the JIC passed MI5's requests for policy about the use of controlled agents to a rump of its members, the heads of the SIS and military intelligence services. The 'W-Committee' established a new body under its control, the 'XX Committee', chaired by John Masterman of B1A, with representatives from the SIS, the Service Intelligence Directorates, GHQ Home Forces, and the Home Defence Executive (representing civil departments), to coordinate the information fed to controlled agents. Under the pressure of John Godfrey, DNI and custodian of Hall's tradition, the 'W-Committee' removed double agents and deception from the normal machinery of state. It took itself (renamed the 'W-Board') and the 'XX Committee' out of the JIC system, to preserve security and to ensure the 'double cross' system would be used. It thought the service intelligence directors, and they alone, would release enough true but trivial intelligence to maintain the credibility of the double agents.

Middle-level officers assumed the right to control policy, without reference to ministers or their superiors (although the chiefs of staff and the Prime Minister individually approved the decision).[25] This was contrary to constitutional theory and to practical sense. After the war, a British master of deception, Ewan Montagu, held that events had proven 'how wise the W-Board was to keep such matters informal and in the hands, on both the working and the supervisory level, of people who knew what they were doing'; at the time matters looked more chaotic. Masterman acknowledged the system odd, but wrote, 'Broadly speaking bad men make good institutions bad, and good men make bad institutions good': Michael Howard added, 'The men who ran the Twenty Committee were good.'[26] Eighteen months passed before these men made this system work, and only after it changed. During the interim, deception was successful only when a normal unit ordered that it be done by an official who could coordinate all its actions and knowledge – like Montagu, in charge of the Admiralty's internal circulation of ULTRA, member of the 'XX Committee', and secretary of the 'W-Board'. Alas, no one else had anywhere near this concatenation of knowledge, except the intelligence chief at GHQ Middle East during 1940–41, John Shearer – until 1943, not even Dudley Clarke knew of ULTRA (beyond 'ISOS' and 'ISK', solutions of *Abwehr* traffic).

No one in London had responsibility for deception until October 1941. That position received power only in July 1942. Then, the man made the office, through personality and liquid lunches. In order to conduct deception, many agencies and more departments had to be coordinated. This would have been difficult in ordinary times – doubly so in this one, in which Britain faced annihilation. The organization of and over intelligence was in chaos; agencies exploded in size, their command systems imploded under the weight, and, as they failed, they triumphed. 'Double cross', ULTRA, and deception became self-contained silos so secret that few people knew any of them and fewer all of them – hardly anyone knew what could and should be coordinated. These developments created grounds for new demarcation disputes, especially between the two central agencies involved with controlled agents. MI5 and SIS had cooperated well regarding that matter between 1914 and 1939, but during 1941 they almost wrecked the 'double cross' system. No one knew who controlled the system. SIS and MI5 squabbled over which should control 'double agents' abroad – each acting with justification. Less justifiably, SIS's slowness in distributing 'ISOS' and 'ISK' to B1A endangered the best 'double agent' of the day, TRICYCLE.[27]

In such circumstances, MI5's best efforts could not be good enough. At the first meeting of the 'XX Committee', on 4 January 1941, Masterman noted 'a real danger that the "double agent" system which has been built up may be allowed to collapse because no adequate use is made of it': 'the

losses involved in releasing information are outweighed by the gains accruing from the successful working of the system'. Most of his arguments
were defensive, aimed at controlling enemy intelligence. Still, deception
was the great aim: 'if, and only if, confidence on the enemy's side has been
established in a particular "double agent"', could s/he be used to deceive
'at an appropriate moment'. But 'only by constant planning in advance
and by the maintenance of an adequate flow of consistent and plausible
reports to the enemy can the "double agent" system be kept in being and
made available for effective use'. The 'double cross' system should be used
to pass disinformation on air matters, the issue that, *Abwehr* question-
naires indicated, most interested the Germans. Again, Masterman noted,
how could the 'XX Committee' achieve its aim of 'long-term operational
deception – e.g. with regards to large-scale raids or invasion of enemy territory. But this needs time, & careful planning.' 'We may construct ingenious plans, but how to put them into effect?' The XX Committee needed a
link with people who controlled real planning.[28] No one answered
Masterman's question; this silence stalled deception.

In 1941, Britain stood a poor third in global deception. Higher authorities did not define a policy. Contrary to their hopes, the service directors
of intelligence could not use the 'double cross' system. The Royal Navy
and the RAF authorized limited plans; the army felt unable to do anything. Working on its own initiative, but with the approval of army and air
intelligence, MI5 planted false documents on the *Abwehr*, including a
memorandum on 'divisional signs', one of the first steps in deception on
the army's order of battle.[29] Such efforts had no immediate impact. MI5
feared 'double agents' were passing material so innocuous as to compromise their plausibility. Meanwhile, elementary problems in signals security crippled operational deception. Only in March 1940 did the MID
branch responsible for signals intelligence and the GC&CS begin to consider wireless deception. The RAF did not begin to do so until July 1940.[30]
Signals deception was possible for the Royal Navy in 1941, for the Eighth
Army by 1942, but for no other branch of the army or the RAF until mid-
1943.[31] During 1941, Britain's main form of deception was the spreading
of rumors at home (aiming to confuse uncontrolled observers) and the
Dominions (hoping to shape Japanese perceptions of imperial policy, a
step closer to propaganda than deception).[32] When high authorities
thought of deception they referred to war by rumor, to procedures unlike
those famous in later years.[33] Meanwhile, other states applied deception to
the two greatest events it has ever affected.

In 1940–41, Hitler selected and his subordinates executed the most
sophisticated and centralized effort of deception ever attempted to that
date, to cover their attack on the USSR – a double deception, aiming to
convince Whitehall that a full-scale assault would strike Britain, and
Moscow that German forces were deployed in eastern Europe simply to

prevent Britain from realizing it would be attacked! This campaign was controlled by regular authorities, able to monitor and recalibrate their activities through two excellent sources, diplomatic reports on Soviet decisionmakers and imagery on Red Army deployments. The means were identical to those defined by the ISSB in 1940 – including a publicized muddle over censorship, as Berlin police clumsily seized copies of the 13 June 1941 edition of the Nazi Party newspaper, *Volkischer Beobachter*. The first step was to deceive one's own troops and to have them conduct operations that would indicate attack. Next came carefully phased troop movements, a sharp and sudden bombing campaign against Britain in May 1941, and a cascade of rumors through diplomats and the press, geared specifically for appeal to the Kremlin. On 5 June, the Nazi propaganda minister, Joseph Goebbels, provided this dictate to guide the German press: 'The Führer has decided that the war cannot be brought to an end without an invasion of Britain. Operations planned in the East have therefore been cancelled. He cannot give any detailed dates, but one thing is certain: The invasion of Britain will start in three, or perhaps five weeks.' One of his subordinates claimed to have floated so many credible rumors 'that in the end there wasn't a bugger left who had any idea of what was really up'.[34] They exaggerated their own success. This scheme failed everywhere except where it counted – thus it mattered. In the month before 22 June 1941, many Soviet commanders and foreign intelligence services and governments had seen through the effort, but not the men who mattered. To fool Joseph Stalin was to 'bugger' the USSR. The deception campaign achieved its aims of misdirection because the highest levels of Soviet leadership were incompetent, so much so that success may have been unnecessary – Stalin might have been fooled simply by security. Germany had all the advantages of launching a surprise attack in peacetime, against a regime fearful of provoking Hitler, certain of its own power, and hostile to the state Germany was already fighting.

The USSR was not the only victim of this deception – Britain too expected a renewed German offensive in the west until a month before BARBAROSSA. Then, it did penetrate the cover, no mean feat: in June 1941, for example, RAF Y and the GC&CS drew sound conclusions when they observed that massive amounts of bogus Luftwaffe wireless traffic were suddenly being transmitted in France.[35] Yet Whitehall's failure to realize German intentions until late in the day had consequences: Britain kept most of its forces in the United Kingdom, starving the key theaters of 1941–42, Egypt and Malaya. These problems were multiplied by a further and little-known campaign of deception in Asia. Standard works on the outbreak of the Pacific War mention Japanese deception, but in passing. When correlated, the evidence shows that Anglo-American intelligence failed largely because Japanese deception succeeded.[36]

Japanese officers applied deception to cover the outbreak of the Pacific

War with some skill and more success. This achievement is remarkable because Japanese espionage lacked a sophisticated ability to monitor and correct deception, though its tactical information was razor-edged and real time, while British and US intelligence had excellent sources of which Tokyo knew nothing. The effort developed in a loose fashion, though no more so than with Britain in 1941. In deception as with strategy, the Imperial Japanese Army (IJA) and the Imperial Japanese Navy (IJN) knew each other's plans but cooperated only in the broadest of senses. The score was written in Tokyo, but the commanders of the attacks on Pearl Harbor and Malaya remained free to improvise on the theme. Their efforts were linked simply because they supported different parts of one scheme, and used the same negotiations in Washington to gain strategic surprise. These consisted of several covers thrown together, but not interwoven – fortunately for them, given the unsuspected success of Anglo-American intelligence. The diplomatic cover was largely penetrated, and the naval one partly so, but cuts in one did not slash the other; had FORTITUDE been compromised to the same degree, the rents in its parts might have exposed the whole.

From its inception, the first priority in IJN planning against Pearl Harbor, as a key figure, Commander Genda noted, was 'maintaining utmost secrecy, so as to prevent any leakage of the plan'. Focused security and deception were central to the IJN; less so to the IJA. On 3 September 1941, Japanese leaders discussed their war plans against Britain and the United States. To attack Malaya, held General Sugiyama, Chief of the General Staff, Japan had to strengthen its forces and bases in Indochina. The War Minister, General Tojo, retorted, 'If you do that, our plans will become known.' A Naval Staff officer asked, 'Can't you pretend you are going to Kunming' – or cover Japan's intentions by indicating that the forces in Indochina aimed to cut the Burma Road. 'We can't hide everything', Sugiyama replied. Soon, Japanese leaders decided they must do just that – until 30 days before Japan attacked, it 'must carry out military preparations as secretly as possible, conceal our intentions, and refrain from sending additional forces to southern French Indochina'. By 8 October, noted Sugiyama, they were 'sending out propaganda to the effect that our troops will not be going into southern French Indochina, and that many troops will be going into northern Indochina for the purpose of attacking Kunming'. Later, Japanese officers emphasized the need to keep plans 'secret and deceptive' until surprise was achieved.[37]

Documentation on the execution of these intentions is thin. The holes in the record make it hard to distinguish British and US mistakes from cases where they fell prey to deception, or where such efforts worked but not as intended. They also create uncertainty about basic issues. In the 24 hours before the start of the Pacific War, Washington and London confronted two threats in the Pacific: one heralded, one silent, one hiding the other. One cannot even prove this coincidence was intended, or by whom. The evidence must be used cautiously; still, some matters are proven and others plausible. Security and deception were effective more because of the way they were integrated into Japanese planning than the sophisticated delivery of misleading messages. Until 12 days before the start of the Pacific War, most Japanese forces maintained normal procedures. Then followed widespread attempts at confusion, coupled with extraordinary security about the move toward Hawaii of Japanese aircraft carriers, and a feint to conceal the destination of combined forces (based on the Twenty-Fifth Army under General Yamashita) sailing southward from Hainan. These aims were pursued by normal authorities, not specialists, who ably applied standard techniques. They misled their own personnel as a means to spread rumors, gave false radio indicators, and spread disinformation by manipulating their relations with other states – negotiating with Washington after the final decision for war, ordering the French administration in Indochina to assist an invasion of Thailand from Cambodia. The Japanese were able to taint British and US sources, though they do not seem to have controlled them.

In order to cover the attack on Pearl Harbor, the IJN spread disinformation through military personnel, diplomats, and the foe, via elaborate procedures for security and misdirection, at the edge of its competence. Few knew the plan. Carriers followed a route from Japan to Hawaii rarely frequented by ship or plane; unless detected, they would not be suspected. They adopted *strictest radio silence*, even disabling sets by 'taking off fuses in the circuit, holding and sealing the keys'. Simple deceptive efforts (maintaining the usual numbers of sailors on leave and aircraft at bases and levels of radio traffic) indicated all was normal with the fleet at home; a Japanese liner ostentatiously sailed to Los Angeles to indicate relations were not broken.[38] Anglo-American intelligence and Japanese security crippled this effort at deception. Code breaking informed Washington and Whitehall that Japanese negotiations were merely hiding an attack against someone, somewhere, although this cover may have helped to lull the authorities in Hawaii. In the five weeks before the attack, the IJN twice changed its call signs, confusing the adversary's analysis, while much of it sailed to the Marshall Islands and Indochina, deliberately without camouflage. The IJN conducted extraordinary security, displayed major moves to the south, and simulated the normal presence of the main fleet around Japan. In this elaborate affair, techniques of deception achieved a mixed success and those of security a great one. In Washington, naval intelligence concluded the main Japanese fleet remained in home waters; in Hawaii, that the IJN was massing on the south. The IJN sold each of its narratives to different agencies but not the center of their plot, that its aircraft carriers were in home waters. From 16 November, US signals intelligence lost the Japanese carriers and so advised its superiors – not the best means for

Japan to gain surprise, when every sailor knew carriers could hammer ships in port. This failure shows inexperience in signals deception. The IJN failed to realize the need to simulate calls between carriers, so they would not be lost after a sweeping change in security; and to control everything associated with them. US signals intelligence in Hawaii thought the IJN's carriers near the Marshall Islands because destroyers, previously linked to them but no longer, were detected in that region.[39] So ambiguous was the evidence that years later intelligence officers still differed over Japanese deception. The director of radio intelligence at Pearl Harbor denied Japan had made any 'attempt . . . to practice radio deception in any of its forms', whereas his superior said, 'they thought of everything'.[40] Despite these technical failures, the IJN achieved its main aim: the Pacific Fleet took no actions to detect surprise or to avoid it.

This success was mostly to the credit of IJN security, but that is not the end of the story. Deception conducted by the Japanese Army was important to the assaults on Malaya, and Pearl Harbor. During the last three months of peace, British authorities received a host of reports on Japanese intentions, few indicating the truth, more reflecting the ideas Japan wished its foes to believe. In October, from the time of Sugiyama's 'propaganda', many reports indicated Japanese forces in Indochina would occupy Kunming – which, to spread disinformation, were their orders until 3 December.[41] Until mid-November, British authorities accepted Kunming as the target, as did some US ones to 7 December, a success for Japanese deception, though of secondary significance.[42] The great failures of assessment in London and Singapore and, to a lesser extent, Washington, were the beliefs Japan could not yet attack Malaya, nor do so until after it had seized Thailand. Deception did reinforce these attitudes – one British report noted that Japanese soldiers in Hainan expected to attack Bangkok, again reflecting disinformation, while Japanese authorities had a fair understanding of British attitudes about Thailand, which Yamashita's staff exploited on 7 December – the question is, to what degree?[43]

From October, Japanese ground forces in Indochina built up steadily, preparing to coerce Thailand and move overland to Bangkok when Malaya was attacked; meanwhile, air bases in Indochina developed rapidly but air strength remained low until reinforcements deployed from late November; on 4 December, the Twenty-Fifth Army set sail. The Japanese revealed many indicators about Thailand but few against Malaya until 25 November, when the latter mounted quickly. In the classic manner of deception, evidence on a real but secondary action was advertised while that for the major attack was hidden. This approach sidestepped the danger that the French administration in Indochina would inform Britain of Japanese actions, because it could see little more than the cover – thus, it became an unwitting conduit for disinformation. The only risk lay in observations about the construction of air bases. Even if the French accu-

rately reported Japanese air strength just before the attack, strategic surprise would not be compromised. Though the main concern was security,
deception was built into Japanese planning; perhaps the effect was more
substantial than the intent was sophisticated, perhaps not.

How far the dissemination of disinformation aided this effort is unclear.
British intelligence picked up rumors from many sources that reinforcements to Indochina were intended to coerce Thailand. Some may have
come from deception. Most were echoes of the truth, about Japanese
deployments against and negotiations with Thailand; and they coincided
with the reports of reliable sources, unknown to Tokyo. The Japanese used
Thai affairs to cover the attack on Malaya, but apparently in an episodic
fashion. If they did so systematically, which is unlikely, if intriguing, they
scored the greatest known triumph of deception. Throughout the period,
Britain understood Japanese capabilities in Indochina, with one key exception; it was influenced by an erroneous, perhaps deceptive, report that
Japanese air-base capacity would not become dangerous until February
1942. The mask slipped before the attack, but still in time. By 28 November,
British intelligence, wrongly, had located the Fifth Japanese Division,
known to be trained for seaborne assault, in southern Indochina (in fact, it
was with the Twenty-Fifth Army in Hainan); forces in Malaya quickly went
on alert. At Pearl Harbor and Singapore, mistaken assessment thus compromised operational deception more than accurate analysis. The cover
was all that could be seen until late in the day; only a good intelligence
service looking precisely at the real danger could see it, and false reports
abounded. So well did Japan hide the real danger that its problem was how
the adversary might react to imaginary ones. By 2 December, British intelligence in Singapore had reported Japanese air strength in Indochina had
risen sharply. By 7 December, it had predicted an imminent attack on
Malaya by 513 Japanese aircraft, against a true strength of 650; a fair
assessment.[44]

The combination of security, deception, and self-delusion wrecked
Britain in Asia. In the six months before the Pacific War, Whitehall saw no
threat. Accurate intelligence on Japanese actions in Indochina from 28
November did not prevent strategic surprise, because these moves were
timed to avoid that danger. Britain understood capabilities but not the key,
intentions. So convinced were the authorities in Singapore that Thailand
was the target that they did not request air reinforcements until two days
after the Pacific War broke out; nor Whitehall offer them. Britain thought
air power would defend Malaya against Japan. When war broke out, it had
just 252 aircraft in the first line and immediate reserve in Malaya, 38 per
cent of the 672 machines deemed necessary for defense, creating immediate disaster. That could have been avoided had Britain accurately understood the situation, though it lacked the forces needed to prevent Japan
from taking Singapore, sooner or later. On 7–8 December, a Japanese feint

multiplied the scale of the disaster and destroyed Britain's thin chance of staving off slaughter. The authorities in Singapore appreciated that if Japan wished to attack Malaya, it first must seize the southeastern Thai port of Singora. They wished to occupy Singora before Japan took it; but they dared not do so if this might prevent the United States from joining Britain, and feared this would occur if they invaded Thailand without cause. Yamashita's command loosely understood these concerns, and exploited them. In April 1942, it announced it had covered its attack by exercising 'the greatest care in leading the enemy to believe that the transports were heading for Bangkok in Thailand. Thus 20 odd transports left the base heading North, but on the way the course underwent a 180 degree change, and then sped southward directly toward Singora.'[45] This effort was successful, aided by luck and the fact Britain had just five reconnaissance aircraft in Malaya. They detected Japanese vessels moving on Bangkok, but lost contact in bad weather. Convinced these forces were moving on that city, British commanders threw those aircraft into the area between Bangkok and the last sighting of the convoy. Thus, they lost any ability to detect the Twenty-Fifth Army until it landed, or to hammer it at sea with air strikes and warships, or to pre-empt it at Singora; misread Japanese intentions crippled British capabilities. Though this feint appears to have originated within the Twenty-Fifth Army for local purposes, its effect was strategic. This sighting, flashed to London and Washington, drew decisionmakers before the Pacific War to focus on Thailand, and to ignore danger elsewhere, particularly because solutions of Japanese diplomatic traffic had just indicated that Japan might simulate an attack on Thailand in order to lure Britain into invading first, leading Bangkok to declare war and justify a Japanese incursion. Most likely, this double hook was baited by coincidence; nonetheless, it had the consequences of FORTITUDE. Britain was deceived as much here as anyone ever was during World War II. Deception shaped the campaign's start and its end. In February 1942, Yamashita used a feint against the northeastern shores of Singapore Island to cover the assault on the northwestern side, luring British forces to the wrong place, lulling them at the decisive one, though so blooded was the lion that this action merely hastened the kill.[46]

Japanese deception shaped some, perhaps many, British intelligence reports before the Pacific War – not most. Anglo-American intelligence penetrated parts of these efforts; those which worked did achieve their end. They reinforced the misconception that Japan could not attack Malaya before March 1942, and tainted analysis in Washington, where Thailand was thought to be Japan's next target and British intelligence was trusted. Deception, backed by successful campaigns of focused security, prevented Britain from taking effective action as Japan attacked, and it loomed behind the intelligence failure over Pearl Harbor. Given the limits to Japan's knowledge of the perceptions or intelligence of its adversaries, its efforts rarely worked as expected, but usually for unanticipated reasons, forming an alloy with reports beyond its control or understanding. This wrecked many of its efforts and let one work with unforeseen effect. Yet proportion is necessary. German and Japanese campaigns of security and deception reinforced British decisions to deny Malaya the military strength deemed necessary for defense against Japan. Feints broke Britain's faint chance to defeat the Twenty-Fifth Army. On the greatest of issues, however, Whitehall and Washington were deceived, but that was not why they were blind. Strategic surprise was suicide, not assassination, and it was overdetermined – the effect stemmed from more causes than it needed. The key issues were Anglo-American preconceptions and Japanese success in concealing the precise nature of its intentions; much the same might have happened without deception, though, as things were, it was useful and influential. Ironically, the excellence of Anglo-American intelligence made itself inadequate. So great was Anglo-American faith in their power and intelligence that they doubted the adversary could do anything they did not know. Only absolutely true and trusted material about intentions at the heights of Japan, or on the real movements of the carriers or the Twenty-Fifth Army, could have freed US and British strategy from preconception; this was lacking. Reports about intentions were not conclusive, nor was truth drowned by deception; reports about capabilities were good and accurate – except the killing thrusts.

Britain's record in deception during 1941 was mediocre on attack and poor on defense. The tide turned in 1942 for two reasons: power – combined with the United States, the Commonwealth finally could take the initiative against Germany; and inspiration – from a subordinate command, based in Cairo, Egypt was an odd place to base deception, because of the extraordinary problems with security. A small British garrison controlled a quasi-independent government and a people of dubious loyalties. When British forces overran General Pescatori's headquarters in February 1941, they discovered that some member of the Egyptian cabinet had leaked him Britain's defense plan for the forward position of Siwa, from which much might have been inferred.[47] Against this, Britain had ample experience of managing Egypt, and the means to do so, including a small internal security service, which, by 1939, had become 'Security Intelligence Middle East' (SIME). SIME manipulated its Egyptian counterpart through 'subsidies', monitored the activities of the *Abwehr*, and achieved a triumph: it controlled or neutralized Axis human intelligence in Egypt. It also began to coordinate deception and controlled agents at the same time as MI5 did.[48]

GHQ Middle East approached intelligence in a manner unlike that of Whitehall. Wavell's memories of the procedures of 1917–18, his initiatives and those of Shearer, produced a personalized rather than a bureaucratized system, in which intelligence officers worked closely with each other and with commanders and with latitude; few people were involved, so coordination was easy. Shearer was of mixed quality as an intelligence chief, perhaps too forceful and self-confident, but able, imaginative and trusted by his chiefs; his role in deception was positive. Wavell, again, was a mixed blessing; too focused on grand strategy, intelligence, deception, surprise, and maneuver and too little on training. He planned the blows that broke the Italian empire in Africa; and he brought deception into their heart. 'One of our most powerful aids to victory will be surprise. Every means by which we can preserve secrecy and deceive the enemy must be studied. The plan and intentions must be confined till the last moment to as few persons as possible; and everyone must understand that the lives of his comrades and the success of the war may be imperiled by careless-ness.'[49] He aimed to launch a series of offensives: first, COMPASS, a raid to hammer Italian forces in northwestern Egypt, though the scale of that victory was unexpected; then, attacks from Sudan and Kenya to annihi-late Italy in Ethiopia; and, finally, the deployment of forces to other objec-tives in Greece and Palestine.

Wavell covered these intentions with Britain's first exercise of deception since 1918 – two of them. These campaigns were practical, more than any-thing undertaken in London during 1940–41, because they were intended to cover immediate actions, demanded by a regular authority and devised by an expert (the same man, Wavell), and handled by men who could coor-dinate all actions and knowledge. British intelligence also could monitor the effect of these deception campaigns in progress, though far less so than nine months later, and not much more so than in 1918. The first program covered COMPASS, by indicating an attack in the desert was impossible. Wavell 'attempted, through certain channels known to my Intelligence, to convey to the enemy the impression that my forces in the Western Desert had been seriously weakened by the sending of reinforcements to GREECE and that further withdrawals were intended'.[50] SIME ran this campaign, through bribed journalists, press leaks, and misinformation leaked to pro-Axis elements in Cairo and the Japanese consul; SIME exploited insecurity as a tool for deception. This campaign was augmented by secrecy – few knew of the operation – to which its commander, General O'Connor, largely unaware of Wavell's cover but equally convinced of the need for surprise, glued a thick layer of security.[51]

Wavell's second deception plan, CAMILLA, begun after the unantici-pated success of COMPASS, supported the assault on Ethiopia. Deceiving his own men was a central means to fool the enemy. His staff was ordered to plan an attack on British Somaliland, but also on Ethiopia – just in case. 'The following is a picture of my plans and intentions that I should like to put across to the other side', Wavell told Shearer. He was determined to reconquer a colony to save a career: 'I got a rocket from the Government and nearly lost my job at the time of the loss of SOMALILAND. I have orders to recapture it as soon as resources are available, and am most anxious to remove this blot on my reputation. (I think this state of mind might appeal to the Italian.)' He would attack British Somaliland with the Fourth Indian Division, currently in Egypt, and the South African Division, in East Africa – both formations central to Wavell's real offensive against Eritrea and Ethiopia. This cover could be spread through journalists, troops, and civilians, 'the usual matters' of military movements and misleading wireless traffic, and the passing of misleading messages. 'We have probably bust the channel we used before, but it should not be impossible to find others and there are many ingenious methods of carelessness with important documents.' Again, false information was planted on the Japanese consul.[52] Thus, the Italians would be led to believe Wavell thought operations in Ethiopia logistically impossible; that no attack would occur until the Fourth Indian and the South African Division were ready to strike British Somaliland, by sea – conveniently, two Indian brigades really would be shipped from Egypt by sea to Port Sudan. (The third, notionally held back in Cairo until just before the amphibious assault, its movement the indicator of imminent onslaught on British Somaliland, would move secretly by river transport up the Nile.) – while any preparations for the true attack would support, then cover. As Wavell noted, 'The advantage of it seems to me to be that the greater part of it is true, the enemy will see for himself that the greater part of it is actually being done. What we want is for him to place the wrong interpretation on what he sees.'[53] This campaign was executed by SIME under the direction of a new officer. In November 1940, the War Office had sent Dudley Clarke to visit commands in West Africa and the Middle East, to discuss paramilitary forces and 'various MIDDLE EAST GENERAL STAFF (R) matters previously dealt with in WAR OFFICE by MI(R)'.[54] While Clarke had experience with paramilitary forces, Wavell already had many experts developing them. He needed help in other areas, and asked that Clarke, whom he had commanded years earlier, oversee deception, escape, and evasion at his headquarters. From service in MI(R), Clarke understood deception in theory but had no practical experience. In CAMILLA he learned more than he taught; throughout 1941, he worked under the direction of Wavell and Shearer, and left operational deception to force commanders. Not until 1942 was he his own master, and that of deception.

The attacks in Egypt and Ethiopia caught the Italians by surprise, which British authorities credited to deception. Though they did not realize it, soon they had evidence to demonstrate that these efforts had failed, or not worked as intended, but that also showed the road to success. O'Connor's forces captured a host of Italian military documents, which showed the enemy had grossly overestimated British strength. In April 1940, the Italians assessed imperial British forces in Egypt at 68,000 men – not far off, if one added British regulars, raw Australians, and Egyptian troops into one sum.[55] In the second half of 1940, the Italian calculations went awry, however. Britain maintained four infantry divisions and one armored division in Egypt, Palestine, Sudan, and Kenya, augmented by paramilitary and garrison forces; it planned at most to raise that strength to ten infantry and two armored divisions by June 1941.[56] The Italians overestimated British strength on the front by up to 50 per cent; but the real problem was estimating formations behind it. By 4 October 1940, SIM and the Italian Tenth Army calculated that 800 aircraft and 15 Common-wealth divisions (including two Egyptian ones) stood in Egypt – 300 to 400 per cent above the real strength! – while several more divisions would arrive imminently (just one was on the way). In the autumn of 1940, Italian intelligence thought Britain had transferred from Egypt four divi-sions each to Palestine, Sudan, and Kenya, and another force to Greece, but that reinforcements had entirely replaced this outflow. Though material from the COMPASS cover may have entered into this equation, the product was contrary to Wavell's intentions: the Italians thought Britain stronger in the desert than it actually was, not weaker.[57]

The cover for COMPASS may have worked in technical terms – the enemy might have picked up indications of capabilities and believed them – but it was swamped by reports from sources outside British control, and it did not affect Italian actions as Wavell had hoped: the Italians would probably have done the same had there been no deception at all. Nor does the subtle dissemination of material on British intentions appear to have reached the Italians; they were surprised by the British actions, but for their own reasons. Tactical security covered COMPASS, not strategic deception – O'Conner's actions thus mattered more than Wavell's.[58] The story was different with CAMILLA, a more sophisticated plan, which joined strategic and operational deception to tactical secrecy. Clarke expected Wavell's original cover 'to have worn very thin by 16th Jan. and have evaporated altogether by the 24th', when GHQ ceased to support it. Old actions, however, still may have echoed on, augmented by a new cover, created and executed without reference to Clarke. Between 9 and 15 February 1941, on the front between Kenya and Somaliland, the force commander in Ethiopia, Alan Cunningham, deployed a few platoons, armored cars, dummy tanks and wireless operators, to simulate the pres-ence of the notional 4 (African) Division, a deceptive force equal to his entire strength, while security swathed the forces poised to invade Ethiopia and Eritrea. The effect was mixed – the Italians were confused and their forces scattered, too weak to block the main axes of British advance, but this stemmed from bad strategy, poor intelligence, and focused security more than from deception.

Meanwhile, the efforts of Wavell, Clarke and Cunningham at specific misdirection failed by succeeding: so convinced were the Italians of an attack on British Somaliland that they did not hold or reinforce it –

instead, they abandoned it without a fight; not quite what the British wanted, though the effect still proved useful. During the second stage of the assault, in early March, again on his own initiative, Cunningham conducted a 'whispering campaign' to indicate a British advance on Addis Ababa, but it 'must have been somewhat negatived by the BBC which persisted in forecasting an advance on the capital via HARRAR' – his intention.[59] In Ethiopia, deception contributed to the enemy's confusion in a piecemeal rather than precise sense; it showed the limits to deception as much as its value. By then, Wavell and Clarke were focused on different issues and ignored these, while Cunningham concluded that techniques of deception successful against the Italians would automatically work against the Germans.

This lack of attention was unfortunate, because lessons could have been drawn from these experiences, and from evidence on the expectations of one of Britain's main adversaries in intelligence. Captured records showed that the Italians could determine, with fair accuracy, the strength of forces on their front, but not those in the rear or reinforcements; they had no good sources on these matters and accepted any account they received, so long as it was large. In assessing these issues, the SIM claimed to work on conservative estimates, but actually accepted the worst case every step of the way. It distorted the number of convoys reaching Egypt and the strength of soldiers in each convoy by up to 300 per cent; it assumed any stray battalion must belong to some division, in a theater where British units were scattered on garrison duty; hence, it was accurate about the number of Indian, Australian, and New Zealand divisions but exaggerated the British ones by 600 per cent! Wavell thought on too small a scale and the fine points of his deception were lost in the grossness of their intelligence failure. He hoped to make the Italians jump to the timings of one brigade's movement when they were wrong about the location of 20 whole divisions.

Underlying all of these technical errors were more fundamental ones: Egypt was a major theater for Britain, so it had to have substantial forces there; if not at the front, they should be in the rear.[60] Preconception determined assessment: the account of a powerful Britain justified the worst-case analysis and the passivity of Italian generals. Even more, Italians over-rated the British Army in size. The Commonwealth and the United States used their resources differently from European states: they placed more manpower in industry, infrastructure, air and naval forces, less in the army; Britain deployed fewer divisions to the European theater in 1939–45 than it had in 1914–18. By continental standards, the United States and the Commonwealth should have had 100 per cent more divisions than they did have; hence, the Axis were predisposed to exaggerate evidence on this issue – and open to deception. The order of battle deception could expand to fill a vacuum of expectations. These flaws in Italian assessment also characterized German intelligence; the British would not realize the scale of these opportunities for 18 months.

How far this Italian evidence shaped British deception is uncertain, but no one seems to have realized its value. Clarke did not refer to this material, though, he stated; a captured Italian diary had inspired his first step in Britain's most breathtaking technique of deception, the deceptive order of battle, which ultimately led the OKH (*Oberkommando des Heeres*, German Army High Command) and the OKW (*Oberkommando der Wehrmacht*, Wehrmacht High Command) to believe that the Commonwealth and the United States possessed twice as many divisions as they actually did. That diary inspired him to fool the enemy about the presence of an airborne brigade and an armored division; captured German documents soon led him to fabricate an infantry division on Cyprus. The full evidence at hand might have led him to realize he could pursue this effort faster and further. Certainly, he did so when intelligence records captured during the CRUSADER offensive showed the enemy had swallowed these lies. In 1941, Clarke simulated the presence of a corps in the Middle East, when the enemy was ready to swallow an army.[61] This failure shows the confusion in GHQ Middle East, where responsibilities and possibilities swamped a few able officers.

Between March and July 1941, deception advanced in a haphazard fashion. Wavell had Clarke improvise several covers at the last minute, which failed, showing the desperation of the commander's position, his tendency to over-rate the ease of the tool, and the limits to Clarke's capabilities. Against this, Clarke's branch received another four officers and was named 'Advanced Headquarters A Force' – Britain's first specialist office for deception since 1918 (though initially devoting much time to escape and evasion); meanwhile, technique moved past Meinertzhagen. Clarke simulated the presence around Egypt of a force equal in size to that really in the desert – a notional Tenth Armoured Division and 1st SAS Brigade – and their intervention in the battle ('Plan A-R') when the expeditionary force under Erwin Rommel entered the fray. To augment SIME's defensive manipulation of pro-Axis elements in Cairo, Wavell attacked the *Abwehr* in its regional bastion. Clarke visited Istanbul to pass 'A-R' to the *Abwehr* and to build networks for future disinformation. He developed nine sources 'in direct contact with the Axis [which] could be used to plant the particular type of information which would come most naturally from the special circles they frequented'; varying in nationality and profession, including Greek, Hungarian, Turk, Iraqi, Russian, Swede and journalist, banker, carpet-seller, diplomat, and stenographer.[62] These sources in Cairo and Istanbul were used regularly to pass disinformation to the *Abwehr* and SIM. SIME added controlled agents and playback to its repertoire, as it discovered captured agents became 'living decanters'.[63] By the autumn of 1941, SIME had reinforced this wine with CHEESE, a network centered on a British controlled agent working for the SIM and the *Abwehr*, with notional links to GHQ Middle East.

Meanwhile, ISOS and operational ULTRA became available in Cairo, illuminating the enemy's intelligence, plans, and expectations, while new procedures emerged to control these powers. Wavell left the theater, to command the Indian Army. His replacement, General Auchinleck, loved intelligence and deception, but was less interested in running it. He delegated these matters to Shearer, the only officer in the Middle East with full access to all intelligence secrets and to Auchinleck's plans. Shearer could coordinate all the actions of and knowledge in a personalized system of decisionmaking, and link deception to operations. Soon, he and Clarke devised the first British deception campaign of 1939–45 to meet the standards of 1918 – indeed, to exceed them. They developed the first instance of classic British deception in World War II, with the material in each secret silo multiplying the effect of the other: ULTRA providing information on the enemy, double agents and other channels spreading deception, and ULTRA and ISOS monitoring enemy intelligence, combined with all the traditional components for camouflage and security in the field.

In July 1941, Auchinleck decided to relieve the besieged outpost of Tobruk in the autumn and, if possible, to annihilate enemy forces in Libya. Meanwhile, his forces were badly trained, and he wished to deter Rommel from attacking Tobruk; his intelligence indicated immediate German intentions were cautious.[64] Hence, he ordered Clarke to pursue COLLECT, a plan to simulate an imminent offensive from Egypt into Libya; its notional date was postponed three times in three months. Later, the deception sought to indicate a build-up of strength in Jarabub, on the center of the Libyan–Egyptian frontier. The aim, in Clarke's words, was to make the enemy think twice before attacking, to 'force him into urgent and premature defensive preparations . . . to keep him on the defensive all through the Autumn. What was more, we hoped also that by crying wolf several times in succession, we might lull him into a sense of apathy and false security by the time the real CRUSADER was ready to go in.'[65] 'A' Force began to spread this cover through its tentacles, initially physical preparations and rumors in Cairo, but later via more sophisticated means. Shearer monitored the effect of this campaign, mostly through ULTRA. Intelligence showed deception was working as hoped. Shearer wrote, 'the activities of the Germans on each (of the three dates in the cover) indicated that they expected to be attacked by us on that day. From an analysis of all available data there can be no doubt that the selected dates put out by us for a British offensive were accepted by the Germans as authentic.'[66] These events fed the faith at GHQ Middle East, where deception shaped Auchinleck's planning for CRUSADER. 'We are trying by every means in our power to mislead the enemy as to our intention to attack and as to the date on which we may attack.' His first orders stated that, 'In order to deceive the enemy as to the direction of our main blow, the original deployment will be made on a wide front from the coast to JARABUB.' At the top of the list of requirements for victory was surprise, and of its means, deception.[67] His field commander, Cunningham, 'did not think it possible to conceal the fact that an offensive was toward . . . I therefore concentrated on trying to conceal the time and direction of the attack.' He did so by seeking to convince the enemy that Britain's main force, an armored corps, would thrust from Jarabub rather than laterally along the coast, through a carbon copy of Allenby's cover at Beersheba, using all forms of physical disclosure and camouflage except radio means, impossible because signals personnel were inadequately trained.[68]

To this cover Shearer glued another. Enthusiastic exponents of deception worried this story might have undesired echoes: Churchill feared that 'false alarms' might make the Germans reinforce the theater, Auchinleck that they might spur Rommel to attack Tobruk before Britain was ready. Shearer held that the enemy might doubt a deception carried through sources to which it had reacted unnecessarily three times before. He possessed a new channel of disinformation, CHEESE, and believed some Axis authorities but not Rommel thought an attack imminent. Hence, Shearer made Britain's first application of the 'double cross' system to operational deception, and, through an untested and complex technique, the 'double bluff'. In Clarke's words, this 'was an ingenious plan, but not an easy one to implement'; 'it was the first time we had tried one and subsequent experience taught us to avoid the double-bluff until all other possibilities had been exhausted'. Shearer 'hoped to induce the enemy to interpret such signs of our *real* preparations which he might detect as being merely bogus ones for the purpose of keeping up the Deception'. Old channels spread the story of an imminent offensive (though the Jarabub deception distorted time and place). Meanwhile, the CHEESE network told its masters these preparations were part of a campaign of lies, and no offensive could occur until the end of 1941. Shearer knew these actions would wreck the value of the CHEESE network, with unfortunate consequences for Levy, then negotiating with SIM in Italy. Ironically, Levy had just been jailed in Rome for currency speculations; yet his network survived and he lived, in Clarke's words, 'to bask in his Italian sunshine on the remuneration awarded to him by the British Government'.[69]

Cunningham and Auchinleck believed that their 'cover story' had blinded the enemy up to the onslaught.[70] They were half right. It kept the Germans confused and sometimes alarmed about British intentions, but this did not affect their plans to attack Tobruk. Throughout October–November, *Panzer Group Afrika* noted the movement to the front of many forces, but missed two key formations, the New Zealand Division and the Seventh Armoured Division, and failed to realize an attack was looming. Despite this gross failure of intelligence, its forces were well placed to defend against that threat. The Italians missed details of British efforts but appreciated an attack was imminent, and deployed their mechanized forces effectively against it. Rommel was surprised, the Italians not; the enemy misunderstood the exact time and place of the British attack but was still well prepared for it. Deception hampered enemy assessments but not their actions, and its effect was less significant than that of mere security. This mixed success came at a price, however. CRUSADER was damaged because it relied so heavily on intelligence and deception, and Cunningham was ordered to 'deploy his forces on as wide a front as possible in order to deceive the enemy'.[71] The forces were widely distributed, yet too weak to win without concentration. When CRUSADER began, the Eighth Army's plan collapsed, its fragile system of command broke, and its forces divided themselves. The Jarabub deception fizzled out – a mechanized infantry brigade advanced 80 ostentatious miles and ran out of gas; though observed by the Luftwaffe, which overstated its strength, it did not affect Axis operations.[72] The planning for deception in CRUSADER was techni- cally brilliant, operationally irrelevant and sometimes counter-productive, as may be said of most deception conducted in the Middle East during 1940–41; yet these campaigns laid the foundation for FORTITUDE.

British forces in the Middle East had honed all the traditional techniques for operational security and deception, and tested new ones – the double bluff, the false order of battle, and the delivery of precise messages through controlled agents; the use of ULTRA to smoke out German preconceptions and monitor their reactions, and deception to stimulate the enemy to bad action. Whitehall thought these techniques innovative and exciting, and that they had worked as planned and with significance. It had faith in the British capacity to deceive, and mistakenly thought deception already had caused several Axis forces to be caught by surprise. Reports to this effect from the Middle East reached London during 1941, especially from July, when, for the first time in 15 months, Whitehall thought itself able to take the initiative. Wavell and Cunningham praised the matter. Shearer built up COLLECT to the MID and Churchill. Clarke's visit to London electrified the ISSB and the 'XX Committee' – an experienced practitioner was asking their help, offering his, and expressing confidence on technical issues. Tellingly, elementary forms of liaison had to be discussed for the first time; Clarke asked the ISSB for help to cover CRUSADER and whether the 'XX Committee' could 'arrange to plant a document on the Germans' and give him information 'about what the Germans knew or think about Middle Eastern matters'; the Committee replied that it could do so, though it did not fully inform him of the background to these matters, of ULTRA and 'double cross'.[73] The COS placed more emphasis on centralized and world- wide rumor campaigns. In October 1941, it established the LCS, within the Joint Planning Staff (JPS) and under a 'Controlling Officer', the politician Oliver Stanley, to coordinate deception and make it a sword.

In itself, this act had little value. The LCS's responsibilities were broad, its powers shallow. It did not control the activities of Montagu or Clarke, and did less deception than they or the ISSB; before July 1942, its only practical contribution was to coordinate cover plans between Cairo and London and help A Force's order of battle deception. Montagu, Whitehall's most seasoned deceiver, grumbled that no member of the LCS had experience in the matter, the COS did not know what it wanted to achieve or how, while the 'inflexible' system gummed up his gambits. There was truth to this complaint. The two-man LCS and the position of Controlling Officer were ineffective. Stanley failed to further the work or the LCS. Dennis Wheatley, one of these two men, noted that Clarke had sold deception, 'but nobody apparently asked him before his return to Cairo for any information about how he carried out his task and, of course, no guidance could be obtained upon this new type of planning from any military manual'. Hence, Wheatley created principles for something he had never practiced, ignorant of the material available in military manuals, but still defining similar views – proof that something was in the air. The LCS was treated as 'the most secret section in the whole building; kept absolutely incommunicado and not even allowed to tell the other members of the JPS what we were up to, although actually for several weeks we were not up to anything at all', except cooperating with the ISSB. The results were ludicrous. In March 1942, no member of a planning meeting for the invasion of Madagascar knew the COS had already approved a cover for the operation – hence, the commander created one of his own, which contradicted the official line. Wheatley, the lowest form of officer life – Pilot Officer RAFVR – had to tell a bevy of brass, 'Sir . . . With due respect, I fear I cannot agree to this.' Though the LCS received the minutes of the Defence Committee and the COS, and memoranda on high-level planning, for its first nine months it was denied the knowledge it really needed, about the existence of the 'double cross' system and ISOS (though, unofficially, Godfrey let Montagu give some ISOS to Bevan).[74] The LCS had no power, merely the possibility of influence; it could succeed only through persuasion and social skills. Wheatley thought the first man in charge of the section, Lieutenant-Colonel Lumley, an able officer who failed because he lacked social contacts. Aware of his impotence, Lumley left as soon as he could, as did Stanley, the latter replaced by Bevan. Combes, conversely, achieved influence for the ISSB by throwing lavish, leading to liverish, lunches at the restaurant 'Rules'. Wheatley followed this lead, using his cachet as a thriller-writer and his salubrious flat, with its well-stocked cellar, to host soirées where people central to strategy met Bevan – a convivial stockbroker, brother-in-law to General Alexander, who was well connected, well-off, and able to entertain those who could further his work at the 'old-boy level'.[75]

Bevan had other advantages; gamekeeper turned poacher, he understood how things had been done on the western front, how deception and intelligence and Whitehall worked. After a month in office he told Wheatley: 'Dennis, we are never going to get anywhere like this. We might just as well both be on leave for all the good we are doing. No one tells us anything or gives us orders. We have got to have a directive. And as no one else seems prepared to give us one, we must write one for ourselves.'[76] The COS gave Bevan authority to ask anyone he wanted to help him mislead the enemy in any way he wished, probably without realizing the significance of their action.[77] It was catalyst for a revolution in the role of deception. The time was ripe to act, thus, to deceive. The Western Alliance was ready and able to take the initiative, through the invasion of North Africa. An immediate operation was at hand; its success hinged on surprise, which Whitehall believed deception could provide. Enthusiasts like Wavell and Montagu wanted more action and centralization.[78] Spurred by Montagu's experiences with the LCS and its new head, the NID turned the balance. It backed Bevan and his approach, even suggesting he take over the 'XX Committee'. With wisdom his guide, Bevan declined this offer, which would have raised problems with MI5, hampering his work and to no avail, since B1A was eager for direction; instead, he worked with Masterman. Bevan had the sense to appreciate what must be done and what the LCS could do, to focus on bigger things and delegate the details.

Faced with the need for a practical solution to a real problem, Britain muddled through to a miracle, made on the 'old-boy level', official relations emerging from personal ones. The system remained personalized, but became effective; its personnel doubled in size, to 20 officers. Finally, Britain applied the powerful and unique edge in organization that it had forged since 1940. Deception was coordinated permanently, everywhere, by an institution of specialists, the most experienced on earth, rather than by regular authorities acting in an episodic and amateur fashion. A high-level synthesis emerged of all three forms of top-secret knowledge – ULTRA, 'double cross', and deception – and of all four traditions of deception, incorporating their strengths in an optimal fashion. Bevan brought the GHQ tradition of central control and the big picture to the right place, aided by his executive branch for security and cover, the ISSB; Masterman and B1A ran 'double cross', with the guidance they had always wanted. Montagu handled naval matters, while remaining free to develop original ideas, including the masterpiece of British deception, MINCEMEAT. For the next 18 months, Clarke dominated the main work of deception, buying time for Noel Wild and Roger Hesketh at Ops B, the deception planners for the Normandy offensive, to prepare FORTITUDE. Only after their integration within a greater system, when Britain had the initiative, did Masterman, Montagu, Clarke, and Hesketh achieve the successes that made their reputation – and that of deception. Genius flourished on the shoulders of bureaucrats.

Meanwhile, the most one-sided intelligence struggle in history occurred. The problem and prospect for both sides was amphibious assault on Fortress Europe. The Allies chose their beaches from a 1500-mile front by strategic criteria, assisted by sound intelligence on enemy expectations and power, and an extraordinary range of techniques and power for deception. What Shearer pioneered before CRUSADER became the norm for every Allied assault after the summer of 1942. The triumph of these attacks was not fore-doomed. Germany had sizable military power and some hope to stall defeat, if it could break the crust of Allied cover. This did not occur, because criti-cal problems were emerging in German intelligence. During 1939–41, it had met the needs of its country as well as British intelligence had done. By 1942, however, intelligence services suited to a sprint were gasping in a marathon, precisely as Germany, thrown on the defensive, needed good intelligence on Allied strategic capabilities and intentions. Its intelligence services did not meet these needs. German imagery and signals intelligence failed at strate-gic intelligence; this threw the OKW, OKH, and Hitler on to the unchecked word of the *Abwehr*, a corrupt and inefficient service, and agents under Allied control. A postwar SIS assessment held that the *Abwehr* 'gradually became a conspiracy to conceal the success of Allied deception', because of a broader context: it failed, but so did every branch of German intelligence, while Britain succeeded at deception and code breaking.[79]

With Britain able to build credibility for controlled agents and the enemy unable to see the truth, Germany could not get Allied intentions right. British lies mailed through the *Abwehr* blinded Hitler and the OKW before the attacks on Sicily and Normandy. Germany suffered from another and deeper failure: the willingness to swallow the order of battle deception. Every German decision of 1943–44 about where the Western Allies would attack, and how to manage the strategic defensive in Europe, assumed those enemies had more divisions than they actually did. These errors, built up from day to day, shaped the miscalculations about inten-tions; FORTITUDE would have failed had the enemy not believed an army group could remain entirely uncommitted in Britain after 6 June 1944. Germany accepted the false order of battle for reasons distinct from the mistakes about MINCEMEAT. It was not just the *Abwehr*'s corruption which wrecked Germany's position in the war of knowledge, or Hitler's faith in his own judgment; unchecked by good intelligence, the profession-alism of the German General Staff became a deformation. After the war, Hut 3, the GC&CS's intelligence office, held that 'the success of "special Means" seems to have been largely a fluke, the result of unexpected gullibil-ity at OKH/Foreign Armies West'. Field intelligence officers 'laughed uproariously when interrogator spoke of agents' reports available to the Germans – you controlled them all.'[80] Yet intelligence and operations pro-fessionals at the OKW, OKH, and Foreign Armies West were able men, far from gullible about *Abwehr* reports – with one exception. They expected the

United States and the Commonwealth to have far more divisions than actually existed; in order to do any serious work they had to reconstruct the Allied order of battle – what kind of professional could fail so elementary a duty? They found it easier to believe lies about large armies than truths about small ones; they had no reliable sources able to make them accept the truth (the main thing that prevented their Allied counterparts from making such errors); the only sources that addressed the issue told the professionals the lies they wanted to hear – because British intelligence knew what words German officers dreamed of having whispered in their ears. One of the few things that made the professionals trust the *Abwehr* was precisely its distorted reports of Commonwealth and US strength in divisions – they would have trusted the *Abwehr* less had it been more accurate on this point!

Triumph was not immediate. From July 1942, disorganization no longer blocked deception, but problems of organization remained. Initially, Bevan thought in traditional terms, developing covers for one operation after another, as the ISSB had done, and searching for means to spread rumors through neutral diplomats in London.[81] When he took office, B1A's controlled agents were at a low ebb, the older ones in eclipse, and the greatest, GARBO, just establishing himself. GARBO did little to cover TORCH, though this work boosted his credibility with the *Abwehr*. TORCH achieved surprise, but entirely because of security – which the ISSB handled – rather than deception or the LCS.

A simultaneous act of deception in Egypt had more sophistication and success. Experience with CRUSADER and afterward taught Clarke several key principles:

> the only purpose of any Deception is to make one's opponent ACT in a manner calculated to assist one's own plans and to prejudice the success of his. Too often in the past we had set out to make him THINK something, without realizing that this was no more than a means to an end. Fundamentally it does not matter in the least what the enemy thinks; it is only what line of action he adopts as a consequence of his line of thought that will affect the battle. As a result we resolved the principle that a Commander should tell his Deception Staff just what it is he wishes the enemy to DO – often a more difficult decision than would appear at first sight – while it is the duty of the latter to decide, in consultation with the Intelligence Staff, what he should be made to THINK in order to induce him to adopt the required line of action. After that it is necessary to decide what evidence must be created to make him think in the right way; and thus the complete Deception Plan is evolved.[82]

'A' Force knew how to play its instruments and to conduct the orchestra; finally, controlled agents and signals intelligence let British deception shape German operations. With other sources on his intelligence menu running thin, Rommel turned to a new diet. After months of rebuilding his credibility, on 2 July 1942 CHEESE received a radio message from his Axis controllers: 'Be very active these days. Good information will be well rewarded. From now onwards we are going to listen in every day for your signals.' Both sets of masters appreciated the taste of his response: SIME noted that Rommel 'insisted that the full text' of messages from CHEESE 'be relayed to him as soon as they were received by Abwehr station Athens. (This information was obtained by "Ice" intercepts of *Abwehr* signal traffic.)'[83] GHQ Middle East had one source it knew the enemy trusted, another to monitor what it expected to happen and thought was happening, real battles to fight, and useful lies to spread. CHEESE was controlled by SIME, his daily messages written by a committee under Clarke, their purport harmonized with physical camouflage behind the lines. He passed reports that blinded Rommel between July and October 1942, shaping the bizarre overconfidence that doomed the *Panzer Armée Afrika*.

Meanwhile, the Eighth Army developed a high level of security in the field and conducted operational deception successfully for the first time in the war, joining the techniques of Amiens and Gaza to those of A Force. Alexander and Montgomery, the new British commanders in Egypt, loved revolution less than their predecessors; they were less starry-eyed about intelligence and deception, but still regarded it as central to their style of war. The Meinertzhagen ruse, revived in the 'false going map', together with A Force and CHEESE, shaped victory at Alam el Halfa; as did a coordinated campaign of strategic and operational deception, including the first systematic use of wireless means since 1918, at El Alamein.[84] The main causes for this victory were bad German decisions and good British ones, the RAF and Commonwealth armies; deception and security were secondary, but significant. Rommel was the first victim of the power of British deception; more would follow.

Then, from the way things fell together, rather than intention, the British learned how to combine all their tools in every theater, to develop a new kind of deception with power never seen before – perhaps never to be seen again. Gambits were linked to the big picture. To an unprecedented degree, deception aimed for precise misdirection rather than confusion. Britain aimed to fool all branches of German intelligence. Because of the inefficiency of enemy aircraft reconnaissance everywhere and its signals intelligence in France, most of the effort in wireless deception and physical camouflage proved unnecessary. In 1943, the power of B1A and ULTRA rose dramatically, because of the success of GARBO and other agents, and against the traffic of the German Army. Britain learned fully how to exploit controlled agents and the order of battle deception and to monitor their success. Between March and July 1942, A Force established 'a permanent comprehensive Plan' to exaggerate the strength of Commonwealth forces in the Mediterranean theater by 30 per cent (eight notional divisions and other pieces); by December 1943, it had simulated the presence of 17 divisions. Captured Axis documents, especially the German assessment, *Die Britische Kriegsheer*, from April 1942 indicated the enemy was well informed on real divisions, but gullible about notional ones – it overestimated the number of Commonwealth divisions in the Mediterranean theater by 40–45 per cent.[85]

Meanwhile, faith in deception rose, finally with justification; before MINCEMEAT, Churchill grumbled, 'Anybody but a bloody fool would *know* that it's Shishily'; afterward, all saw idiocy to be exploited.[86] The United States left Britain to manage this effort for the alliance. Experts from the Mediterranean shaped deception in London, their influence magnified when seasoned commanders, de Guingand and Montgomery, took the helm at OVERLORD; de Guingand gave FORTITUDE its jagged edge, by insisting Ops B extend the FUSAG deception to tie down German forces in the Pas-de-Calais for weeks after the initial landing.[87] LCS informed high staff levels how deception and cover had worked with TORCH, and elucidated lessons drawn mostly from 'A' Force experiences; its proposals were enacted. By spring 1943, LCS coordinated all the strategic deception activities of the Western Allies in Europe and the Middle East, setting the stage for the most broad and integrated plan ever conceived in the field, BODYGUARD. Its aim was simple, 'To induce the enemy to make faulty strategic dispositions in relation to operations by the United Nations against Germany', and profound – to make enemy dispositions as little useful as possible against all real attacks.[88] GHQ's deception policy of 1918 was realized, but on a far larger scale.

One development was of paramount importance and accidental nature. In 1945, intelligence officers concurred that the success of deception rested on ULTRA.[89] That relationship developed haphazardly throughout 1943. From the spring, SIS, the NID, and the MID cooperated to give LCS monthly reports drawn from ULTRA, entitled 'German Appreciation of Allied Intentions', complete with analysis and selections of raw traffic.[90] The material was valuable to deception planning; one from spring 1943, noting German concern with an Allied threat to the Aegean and the Balkans, shaped the cover for MINCEMEAT. The British understood the threats that concerned the Germans and reinforced them, to cover their intentions to strike elsewhere.[91] Yet for months after this process started, no one fully informed deceivers and codebreakers of each other's existence. Hut 3 sent reports on German appreciations of the Allied order of battle 'to Commands abroad in the rather vague hope that someone on the operations or security side would find them of value'. Only in November 1943 did it discover 'A' Force, and the 'general verdict in the Mediterranean . . . that "A" force is one of the great successes of the war'.[92] Years later, Hut 3 concluded that 'A' Force had been almost entirely

dependent on ULTRA material for discovering German reactions, but had
been totally unaware that Hut 3 could have substantially supplemented its
services and greatly assisted their problems. It changed that situation. 'As
a result of the visit, many scraps of MSS (Most Secret Sources) Intelligence, hitherto looked upon as valueless, gained new meaning.'[93] Such
material was fundamental to the order of battle deception and FORTI-
TUDE. Solutions of Japanese traffic on 28 May 1944, showing Hitler had
swallowed FORTITUDE, inspired GARBO's message of 8/9 June, which
led the OKW to believe the main attack was yet to come, and so keep its
troops in Pas-de-Calais and out of the battle – until it was lost.[94]

Thus emerged the greatest campaign of deception ever mounted. As
they stood on the strategic defensive for 18 months, Germans were confused and misdirected; each day they accepted false proof the enemy was
stronger than it was; each week they expected attacks that could not occur.
Britain exploited its knowledge of German fears to simulate imminent
assaults on Norway and the Balkans, pinning armies like butterflies.
Throughout 1943–44, essentially to handle these dangers, Germany maintained 200,000–400,000 combat soldiers above the level necessary for gar-
risons in those theaters. Given the level of German wastage, this force was
not large, nor insignificant; it matched the number of infantrymen in Italy;
in June 1944, as many Germans stood in Norway as in Normandy. How far
deception shaped these actions is hard to say, because of its nature and that
of the events. The Germans expected certain things; the Allies knew these
preconceptions and reinforced them, so the enemy would do what it was
doing, and overlook their intentions to strike elsewhere. This effort might
have been unnecessary; in its absence, Germany might have done exactly
what it did; what would have happened in such a world is unknowable,
because Britain strangled it in the cradle. This effort was a triumph of intelligence, which contributed to confusion. It was not necessarily a victory of
deception that sent Germans to the wrong places – just probably so.

Deception did keep Germans from the right places, and this did matter
– it was central to the war. The Allies could return to the continent only
through great seaborne assaults, a hard operation of war, against a strong
foe with time to prepare stronger defenses. The strategic success of these
assaults depended on the tactical situation at the sharp edge; even against
weak positions, attackers faced agonizing slogs or were pinned in their
beachhead for months, as at Salerno, Omaha Beach, or Anzio. Allied
navies and air forces were an insurance against annihilation, but in every
amphibious assault, the attackers easily might have suffered heavier casualties before they were able to break out, or have been denied the force
levels needed to do so, instead being sealed off and made strategically irrelevant (as occurred at Anzio and almost at Salerno, despite surprise). Such
failures might have triggered others in the key weakness of Allied forces,
the politicization of field command, which produced crises at Anzio and

Normandy. Every amphibious assault of 1943–44 would have faced greater problems had the Germans focused more of their defensive resources on the right beaches, or had 20,000 good soldiers more on the spot, or another 50,000 within two days' march; and Hitler had this power. With better knowledge of Allied intentions, Germany could easily have quadrupled its strength at Sicily in July 1943 or Normandy in June 1944. The war would have taken a different course had the Normandy beach-head been sealed off, five miles deep and 15 wide, had the Allies abandoned their attack on Sicily, or had every seaborne assault cost twice the lives it did. Intelligence and deception prevented such possibilities; instead, the Allies struck places known to be the least well defended of useful sites, where deception kept the enemy weak. Intelligence and deception sheltered Allied weak spots from enemy pressure, and eliminated much of the risk normal to seaborne assault. Intelligence and deception let attackers evade the enemy's defenses and engage its main strength only when they wanted to do so, and forced the enemy to improvise a response from a poor position. Intelligence and deception made these operations look easy when, in fact, they rank among the greatest and most risky in the history of war; so successful were they that some critics use them to prove the failure of Allied command and commanders. Here, intelligence and deception struck *Festung Europa* like lightning, transforming the balance of forces and of probability. These and the *maskirovka* (deception), which shielded Soviet offensives on the eastern front in June–July 1944, are the most successful and significant cases of deception in history. Germany would probably have lost the war in any case, but the price would have been higher, especially for the Western powers.

FORTITUDE continued to cover Allied operations until the end of the war, but Hesketh noted, 'when the German line stabilized at the end of September 1944 the day of strategic deception was over'.[95] One last piece remained, to cover the transfer of 1 Canadian Corps from Italy to the Netherlands; it failed. Hut 3 blamed this failure on Ops B, which 'might have blown both the cover-plan *and* 'Special Means', but for itself, 'A' Force and LCS.[96] Part of this claim may be true but not the whole – German forces in Italy detected the Canadian Corps' departure as it was occurring, before Ops B was involved – and it illuminates otherwise obscure points about Allied deception.[97] To mask the movement of a corps between two theaters combined operational security and strategic deception; the Allies hid real things less well than they created false ones, and had less success with operational than strategic deception – they did the hard thing better than the easy one.

At the strategic level, Allied security mastered all German sources of intelligence, the key means for misdirection were controlled agents, and the aim was to hide the strength and movement of forces across the seas, where notional formations were easy to simulate. At the operational level, Allied security was weaker, German intelligence stronger, and their main concern was forces on the front, or just behind it (where the long-term presence of notional formations was hard to simulate). German intelligence controlled two sources able to slash the shroud of misdirection, prisoners, and signals intelligence. In Italy, prisoners compromised most Allied attempts to hide the redeployment of formations. Wireless means were the central mode of operational deception; in this sphere British practitioners were able, but so too were their adversaries. Between October 1942 and May 1943, just one Allied force, the Eighth Army, had effective signals security. Although other formations improved in quality, still US, Polish, and Brazilian security remained poor to mediocre. Throughout 1944–45, signals intelligence gave the enemy key material. German intelligence was weak and easily deceived regarding amphibious assaults; otherwise, it usually knew when and where attacks would be launched (though not necessarily their strength), and when real formations had entered or left the peninsula.

In these campaigns operational deception was practiced as during 1918; again, its effect is hard to distinguish from those of security and normal failures of intelligence. In Tunisia, focused security (with deception tertiary) helped the Eighth Army achieve surprise for the defense at Medennine and the assault on the Mareth Line, which demolished German offensive capacity, and hastened the inevitable. Otherwise, in Tunisia and Sicily operational deception had little impact. 'A' Force and others practiced operational deception constantly during the Italian campaign, with mixed success. After interrogating German generals and intelligence officers, Allied experts concluded 'the enemy's overall "I" picture was at most periods fairly accurate. Serious gaps in the enemy's knowledge certainly existed, and it seems clear that he consistently overestimated Allied strength in ITALY; this led, however, to less operational inefficiency than might have been expected'.[98] German intelligence performed well in Italy; when its failures and the effect of Allied security are removed, however, little remains to the credit of deception. The main accomplishment, and a great one, was NUNTON, the cover for the battle of May 1944, which broke German defenses in southern Italy and forced the Germans to run for the north. Allied security and deception worked almost exactly as intended, with remarkable effect – on their own they neutralized the power of the enemy's defenses. After capturing the intelligence records of the German 14th Army, Allied headquarters in Italy held that the enemy was 'almost entirely blinded by the fog of war, misled as to where the main weight of our attack was to fall, he had placed his reserves where we wanted them'.[99] The Allies did not have overwhelming superiority, while German defenses were powerful, as had been proven by the bloody failure to crack them in previous months. Deception and security turned this balance – they were essential to this victory, which mattered to the war. It achieved the strategic purpose of maintaining pressure on the

Germans just before D-Day and inflicted serious losses on them, though a politicized Allied command fumbled its chance at annihilation.

In the rest of the Italian campaign, operational deception had little success, nor in the west after Avranches, for different reasons. For most of the time, Allied forces outran plans to conceal their activities, though the FUSAG deception continued to affect German strategy, particularly its maintenance of forces in Scandinavia. The enemy was usually confused about Allied capabilities and intentions, which sometimes damaged its defenses, more from intelligence failure than Allied actions. The Germans were often surprised, but less because of deception or even security than circumstances. After interrogating German signals intelligence personnel, Hut 3 concluded, 'the vast efforts' at operational deception 'were largely wasted', partly because US forces had poor signals security, easing enemy work against the largest army in the theater, mostly because German signals intelligence was so bad that it picked up neither real nor deceptive traffic (which had also rendered futile the wireless deception elements of FORTITUDE). The 21st Army Group had excellent signals security and wireless deception, but '[had] no evidence that the Germans were misled. There is evidence they were not even following.'[100]

During 1942–44, Britain conducted the greatest campaign of strategic deception ever known. Japanese and German strategic deception in 1941 were less sophisticated and more easy, covering surprise attacks that opened hostilities against states rather than assaults against an enemy already at war; nor did deception shape these successes as much as in the British case. No other state has ever come close to matching Britain's successes of technique or breadth of attack; but the issue is different when deception as a whole is judged by the criterion of effect. In operational deception it had no better a record than Britain or Germany in 1917–18, and was less good than that of the Soviets in 1943–45. During 1941, deception multiplied Axis power against the Allies more than it ever did Allied power against the Axis, though it was much easier do so in those circumstances than in the case of FORTITUDE. When one considers the effect of operational and strategic deception, the German performance was breathtaking, but still below the British standard of 1942–44; the cover for BARBAROSSA failed against Britain and perhaps was unnecessary against the USSR; Germany may even have gained more from operational deception than the Western Allies, but not much. Between September 1941 and February 1942, Japan used deception well and to significant effect, but the pursuit of feints shaped the Japanese disaster at Midway; afterward its effect was small. The Soviet performance during 1943–45 was close to that of Britain, perhaps too close to call. Deception mattered more to the greatest operations of the Western Allies, amphibious assaults, than to those of the USSR on land, and Soviet techniques were simpler and less precise, aiming more at confusion than misdirection. British intelligence, however, did believe the Soviets were passing disinformation to the *Abwehr* through a controlled agent in Bulgaria, Richard Klatt, as it may also have done through others in Russia.[101] Against this, the *maskirovka* that covered the Belorussian offensive, Operation BAGRATION, matched FORTITUDE in effect; deception probably killed more Germans in the east than the west, and during the last nine months of the war the Soviets gained more from it than did the Western Allies.[102] Above all, two of the greatest cases of deception in history struck the same enemy at the same time; in May–June 1944 the Germans were deceived on every front, and perhaps this hastened their end.

FORTITUDE had peculiar – almost bizarre – roots; rare British successes and German failures in intelligence, a personalized system for decisionmaking, which made the development of deception chaotic during 1940–41, and its power remarkable during 1942–44. FORTITUDE was grounded in ironies. Deception was not consistently valuable to Britain during 1940–45. It was almost useless when Britain stood alone and most needed help – during that period, deception aided the enemy. It had nothing to do with the turning of the tide; deception became significant only when the Allies had the initiative, but then it multiplied that surge in power. The British became so good at deception largely because they thought they already were. Their faith moved mountains; it sprang from their experiences of the Great War and ideas about the power of deceit. This faith led decisionmakers to credit deception for successes of security and failures of enemy intelligence and command; and to mistake the sophistication of their technique for its effect. Had British decisionmakers before June 1942 known how ineffective deception really was, they might not have taken the steps that did make it so deadly.

Deception is not hidden. Practitioners have analyzed their experiences; scholars, above all Michael Handel, have extended these insights. Both groups have shaped US doctrine on deception, which has been integrated into that about Command and Control Warfare (C2W), Operations Security, Information Operations, and Intelligence Preparation of the Battlespace. Collectively, these statements reflect the best practices of good practitioners, of Anglo-American intelligence during 1942–45. This US doctrine defines all aspects of intelligence as force multipliers, to be integrated into every aspect of planning and operations. Intelligence, psychological warfare, and operations security have a dynamic relationship with deception, the attempt to '*deliberately mislead adversary military decisionmakers as to friendly military capabilities, intentions, and operations, thereby causing the adversary to take specific actions that will contribute to the accomplishment of the friendly mission*'.[103] This doctrine for deception defines sound principles, distilled from Hesketh and Handel – 'centralized control'; 'security'; 'timeliness' in planning and execution; 'integration' of deceit with an operation; and, above all, 'focus' and 'objective', aiming to influence the right decisionmakers and to affect their actions – to treat the manipulation of intelligence and ideas merely as means to an end. It advocates a process that comes as close to that of 'A' Force as any bureaucracy can achieve. Practitioners must understand their foe's psychology, 'possess fertile imaginations and the ability to be creative while using and understanding each component of deception and C2W capabilities'; they must pass a story through many sources that an adversary will find believable, ideally by reinforcing its expectations.

This doctrine is powerful, but it has weaknesses that stem from the roots of its strength, the influence of the British tradition of deception, as reflected through FORTITUDE. The latter stems from so many unique circumstances that it is a poor guide to average practice. To treat it as normal is to assume deception is precise and predictable, that one will have edges equivalent to ULTRA, 'double cross', and the *Abwehr*, while the enemy's intelligence is castrated. These are tall assumptions. Again, 'focus' and 'objective' are fine principles: but in order to make key decisionmakers act as one wishes, one must know who they are, what they expect, how to reach them and how to know whether one has succeeded. This is not easy. Deceivers wrestle with uncertainties and pull strings they hope are attached to levers in a complex system they do not understand. Deception rarely has just the effect one wants and nothing else; the unintended cannot be avoided. US doctrine urges that this difficulty and others be resolved through risk assessment, but that is to mistake a condition for a problem. Reason is good, war games are fun; when assessment concludes, risks remain. Never when one deceives will one know all the unintended consequences in advance. Rarely will one know if deception has worked at the time one must act. Always, one should consider whether one is being deceived; but that is hard to prove and the effort confuses your intelligence. US doctrine leads students to aim at specifically misdirecting an adversary, to make it take exact actions. The best is a good target, but it is hard to hit; generally that occurs by aiming at the normal and easily struck outcome of deception, confusion. The rule of thumb is: act to confuse, aim to misdirect.

No aspect of intelligence theory is so well studied as deception, nor so much in need of it, for paradox rules the field. Deception exploits the psychology both of an adversary and of competition – the response of generals and institutions to war, with its environment of uncertainty. It overthrows its adversaries by exploiting inertia, their preconceptions, and their habits. One can throw only while remaining balanced; deception requires security, the ability to influence the rival's intelligence channels and, ideally, to control them all, and a good knowledge of its views, the best possible. Deception is natural to competition, with a record of success, varying dramatically from case to case. Strategic deception, an effort to mislead about one's core intentions and capabilities, or those matters which determine one's power or policies as a whole, has great effect in peacetime; less in war. Leaving aside cases such as amphibious assault, deception in war has affected operations more than strategy; though British deception had profound strategic effects in 1942–44, its only purely strategic deception covered its order of battle. British deception during 1942–44 does not represent the norm, but its apex. FORTITUDE was a fluke, though indicative. You cannot get there from here – but you can get somewhere. It is not easy to control the enemy's intelligence services, or to know its preconceptions and assessments of one's own intentions and capabilities. Otherwise, the security – as against the control – of information becomes the central element of deception. If the enemy cannot be fed only the information one wishes it to receive, one must deny it the material it cannot be allowed – certain knowledge of one's intentions and capabilities. Operational deception rarely centers on controlled agents, but on signals deception, the provision of misleading information to one's troops and camouflage. Modes of deception range from the manipulation of posture – playing a shell game with one's capabilities mostly but not entirely visible and one's intentions uncertain – to the delivery of precise messages. Of the two forms of deception – misleading the enemy as against confusing it – the former is the higher and harder art, but the lower form can be effective.

Deception is most easily conducted when one controls all the information about oneself, though even then bad assessment by the enemy may accidentally compromise one's lies. It can also be applied when such information is easily found, by using that fact; passing lies through leaks, hiding fundamentals in plain sight behind a flood of trivia, so exploiting what Michael Handel termed 'Type "B" uncertainty', the condition of suffering from too much data.[104] It can be sold to intelligence services and sent to key decisionmakers with astonishing ease and speed. Deception can be conducted without detection even when one's intelligence is average, while the enemy possesses good sources of which one knows nothing, as occurred with Germany and Japan in 1941; only intelligence or security services of rare ability can detect a competent campaign of deception. For a defender confronting deception, absolute accuracy about 90 per cent of matters is failure, while 99 per cent may not be a passing grade. Deception is easiest to conduct when one has good intelligence; but even when poorly served, one can still confuse. The ideal target is a mediocre intelligence service; a good one is hard to find and harder to fool; a bad one may not pick up the material one transmits, as with Allied efforts at wireless deception for FORTITUDE, or in the Pacific War.

In deception, attack is stronger than defense. It is easy to mount, hard to avoid. It aids the active party, which generally means the stronger side. Deception aims to affect a rival's behavior; it is useless unless one has actions to cover. Far more than intelligence, much like surprise, deception aids the side with the initiative, not the one reacting to it. Deception is a tool for the strong. Of course, every party in a complex competition has the initiative somewhere, and so can deceive there – terrorists might use deception to cover an attack on a superpower. Unlike intelligence, however, deception is useless to a reactive policy, unless one aims to simulate an active policy – not easy, but not impossible. An attacker can more easily mislead on key aspects of an operation than a defender, because it has the initiative; it determines which actions matter and why; deception can aid a defender only by affecting the attacker's actions. In order to deceive, an active party needs merely know how it will act, while a reactive party must know what its rival will do. This requires superior intelligence, and its application to deception.

One can never know how deception will work until it is tried; one may never know when it is being applied against one, or is succeeding – until it has; perhaps not even then. Deception does not pay a guaranteed return. It succeeds from a combination of factors, some in the enemy's control. One cannot deceive without the victim's cooperation, nor be deceived without one's own, nor avoid such cooperation. One can merely create the most favorable terms of trade, both ways. One cannot know in advance the nature of this combination of factors nor the effect of one's efforts; to deceive is to whistle in the dark. Rarely can the effort be shown to succeed through works, mostly through faith; yet faith is cheap. Deception costs a few creative minds, a scarce resource but a small one. Some 100 officers and 4,000 soldiers ran British deception and camouflage in 1942–45, a small investment given the return. Deception is easy for one to use, and for one's foe. It costs little more than security, for which it is essential in any case. Deception is one of the most effective means available to exploit successes in security or intelligence, including those one does not know one has achieved; often it succeeds for unexpected reasons, as minor aspects of a cover have major effect – the simplest of feints can kill. Deception may fail, but that will cause damage only when the enemy is far superior in intelligence, when it can use one's practice to deceive, so as to read one's mind. Such circumstances occur; rarely. Failures of deception cost less than those of security or intelligence. Just three things can withstand deception: superior power and initiative; intelligence of outstanding quality or else so poor that it cannot pick up misleading signals; an inability or unwillingness to act on any knowledge, true or false. Even when one succeeds in deception, probably one will not know it at the time, perhaps never, because deception reinforces actions already under way rather than causing anything new, because of its links with security and intelligence failures. Often one's actions at deception will have no effect; generally it will be a force multiplier – but by 1.0001 per cent or 150 per cent? – rarely it will strike like lightning.

NOTES

The AIR, CAB, FO, HW, KV, and WO series are held by the Public Record Office (PRO), Kew; and the L/MIL and L/WS series by the British Library. Citations from them appear by permission of the Controller of Her Majesty's Stationery Office. The AWM and 3/DRL series are held at the Australian War Memorial, Canberra, and the SP series at the National Archives of Australia, Canberra; all citations appear with permission of the copyright holders. The papers of James Edmonds and Richard O'Conner are held at the Basil Liddell Hart Center for Military Archives (BLHCMA), those of Admiral Hall and Winston Churchill at Churchill College, Cambridge, those of R.J. Maunsell at the Imperial War Museum, those of Alan Cunningham at the National Army Museum, and those of Claude Auchinleck at the John Ryland Library, Manchester; all citations appear with permission of the copyright holders.

1 Michael Handel, ed., *Strategic and Operational Deception during the Second World War* (London: Frank Cass, 1988). Another useful compilation is Donald C. Daniel and Katherine L. Herbig, *Strategic Military Deception* (Oxford: Pergamon, 1981).

2 Michael Howard, *British Intelligence in the Second World War, vol. V, Strategic Deception* (London: HMSO, 1990). For a good example of the memoir literature, see Ewan Montagu *Beyond Top Secret U* (London: P. Davies, 1978).

3 Garnett Wolesley, *The Soldier's Pocket-Book for Field Service* (5th edn, London: Macmillan, 1886), pp. 140, 169–70.

4 'Organization of Secret Service (Note prepared for the DMO on the 4th Oct. 1908)', KV 1/1; 1909, 'Intelligence Methods in Peace Time', KV 1/ 4; 'Intelligence in European Warfare', lecture by J.E. Edmonds, January 1908, 1V/1/1/ and 'Information in European Warfare', No. 389, undated, 1908–9, by Edmonds, 1V/2, J.E. Edmonds papers, BLHCMA; Report on Intelligence Exercise, Army Headquarters, India, 1913, L/MIL 7/11/47.

5 'MI5 Historical Reports, G Branch Reports, The Investigation of Espionage, Volume IV', KV 1/42, pp. 52, 165; 'MI5 Historical Reports, G Branch Reports, The Investigation of Espionage, Volume V', p. 197, KV 1/43; 'MI5 Historical Reports, G Branch Reports, The Investigation of Espionage, Volume 1', KV 1/39; Memorandum by Drake, MI5. G, 4.1.17, 'Rough Notes on the History of German Espionage in The Country', KV 1/46.

6 Memorandum, no author cited, but presumably Hall by internal evidence, 'RMS Otranto Rough Notes', 20/1/36, HALL 2/1.

7 'Second Rough Draft, Chapter Six, A Little "Information" for the Enemy', undated, *c.* 1932, HALL 3/ 4; Locock to Hall, 19.10 (year uncertain, but probably 1932), Hall 1/3; 29.11.32, unsigned letter, but Straus to Hall by internal evidence, Hall 1 /4; undated and unsigned memorandum, presumably by Hall, *c.* 1932, HALL 2/1.

8 Haig to Robertson, 4.9.16, 1(b) 4208, AWM 252/141, Australian War Memorial, Canberra.

9 'Second Rough Draft, Chapter Six, A Little "Information" for the Enemy', HALL 3/ 4; 'Chapter VIII, HALL 1/3; 'RMS Otranto Rough Notes', 20/1/36, presumably by Hall, HALL 2/1; Charteris to MacDonogh, 10.9.16, 18.9.16, WO 158/897.

10 GHQ Egypt to DMI, 11.1.17, 16.1.17, DMI to GHQ Egypt, 13.1.17, 24.3.17, WO 33/905.

11 Memorandum Z/77, 15.8.17, for GOCs XX and XXI Corps and Desert Mounted Corps; Egyptian Expeditionary Force (EEF) to Admiral Commanding Egypt and Red Sea Division, 14.9.17, WO 95/4368.

12 XX1 Corps General Staff War Diary, 5 and 6.11.17, XXI Corps to EEF 5.11.17,

WO 95/4490. The standard study of intelligence and deception during the Palestine Campaign is Yigal Sheffy, *British Military Intelligence in the Palestine Campaign, 1916–1918* (London: Frank Cass, 1998).

13 John Ferris, ed., *The British Army and Signals Intelligence during the First World War* (London: Army Record Society, 1992), pp. 17–21, 171–95, offers the clearest account of deception and intelligence on the western front, and reprints many relevant British and German documents, including those cited above.

14 Ibid., pp. 173–75, reprints the entire document.

15 Ibid., pp. 185–94, reprints the entire document.

16 Secret Supplement to Signal Training, 1925, WO 33/1073; *Manual of Military Intelligence in the Field, Provisional, 1921*, Secret Supplement 1 of *The Manual of Military Intelligence in the Field, 1923*, *Manual of Military Intelligence in the Field, 1930*, Ministry of Defence Library, Whitehall.

17 Ferdinand Touhy, *The Secret Corps: A Tale of Intelligence on All Fronts* (London: Murray, 1920), p. 213.

18 J.C. Masterman, *The Double Cross System in the War of 1939 to 1945* (London: Yale University Press, 1972), pp 36–46; F.H. Hinsley and C.A.G. Simkins, *British Intelligence in the Second World War,* vol. IV, *Security and Counter-Intelligence* (London: HMSO, 1990), pp. 41–2.

19 ISSB, Report No 1, 19.2.40, WO 283/1.

20 ISSB Special Meeting, 20.2.40, 8th Meeting 21.2.40, Extraordinary Meeting, 14.3.40, Appendix A, 19.4.40, WO 283/1.

21 Memorandum to War Cabinet, S.50/29, 16.3.40, L/WS/1/1542.

22 25th ISSB Meeting, 27.4.40, WO 283/1.

23 For one example of its daily work, 331st ISSB Meeting, 16.6.41, WO 283/4; A Force Narrative War Diary, entry 18.9.41, CAB 154/1.

24 Robert Stephan, 'The Role and Effectiveness of Soviet Combat Counter-intelligence During World War II', PhD dissertation, George Washington University, 1997, UMI Microfilms, Ann Arbor.

25 Hinsley and Simkins, *Security*, pp. 98–101; Masterman, *Double Cross*, pp. 61–5.

26 Memorandum by J.H. Godley *et al.*, 3.3.52, 'Double Crossing and Deception', CAB 154/104; Montagu, *Top Secret*, pp. 134–9; Masterman, *Double Cross*, p. 65, Howard, *Strategic Deception*, p. 9.

27 Hinsley and Simkins, *Security*, pp. 107–9, 119, 126–7.

28 Memo by MI5 (B.2a), 'Memorandum on the "Double Agent" System': unsigned memo, probably by Masterman (Chairman). 'General Statement' for First Twenty (XX) Committee Meeting, 2.1.41, Agenda, MI5 (B2a) for First 'Twenty (XX) Committee Meeting', 2.1.41, First Twenty (XX) Committee Meeting, 2.1.41, MI5 (B2a) to Findlater Stewart, Home Defense Executive, 7.1.41, KV 4/63.

29 Masterman, *Double Cross*, pp. 92–3, Hinsley and Simkins, *Security*, p. 107.

30 Butler to Denniston, 3.40, Denniston to Travis, 29.3.40, HW 14/4; 'Minutes of Conference on W/T Security', Air Ministry, 12.7.40, HW 14/6.

31 Bomber Command to Groups, 4.8.42, *passim*, AIR 14/467; 12th Army Mediterranean Expeditionary Force to Commands, 28.5.43, *passim*, AIR 23/5440; AFHQ Signals Instruction No. 33, 12.12.42, No. 71, 1.7.43, WO 204/1556; 18th Army Group to CGS AFHQ, 1.3.43, WO 204/1557.

32 331st ISSB meeting, 16.6.41, WO 283/4; Dominion Office to High Commissioners Canberra (No. 100) and Wellington (No. 91) 21.2.41 and Nos 101 and 92, 22.2.41, Australian Archives, Canberra, SP/12/1/429/8/4.

33 Admiralty to Commanders in Chief, WX. 3921, 16.9.41, AIR 20/291.

34 Donald S. Detwiler, Charles B. Burdick, and Jürgen Rohwer, eds, *World War II German Military Studies,* vol. VII (New York: Garland, 1979), MS3-C-059, pp.

3–4; MS #-C-059; Willi A. Boelcke, ed., *The Secret Conferences of Dr Goebbels: The Nazi Propaganda War, 1939–43* (New York: E.P. Dutton, 1970), pp. 174–5; Gabriel Gorodetsky, *Grand Delusion: Stalin and the German Invasion of Russia* (Princeton, NJ: Princeton University Press, 1999), pp. 295; cf. 53,135, 126–99. Gorodestsky's is the best account of the relationship among perception, intelligence, and deception in this case, though he underrates the role of ideology in the Soviet error; James Barros and Richard Gregor, *Double Deception: Stalin, Hitler and the Invasion of Russia* (deKalb: Northern Illinois University Press, 1995), and Barton Whaley, *Codeword Barbarossa* (London: MIT Press, 1973), are essential readings on this matter.

35 Air Historical Branch, *The Second World War, 1939–1945, The Royal Air Force, Air Ministry Intelligence*, Part II: Ch. 6, para. 58, undated; Hut 3 History, Section III, Development as a Research Organization (Spring 1940–Autumn 1942), HW 3/104.

36 Roberta Wohlstetter, *Pearl Harbor: Warning and Decision* (Stanford, CA: Stanford University Press, 1962), pp. 379–80; Louis Allen, *Singapore, 1941–1942* (London: Davis-Poynter, 1977), pp. 103, 107; Gordon W. Prange with Donald Goldstein and Katherine V. Dillon, *At Dawn We Slept: The Untold Story of Pearl Harbor* (New York: McGraw-Hill, 1981), p 444.

37 Nobutaka Ite, *Japan's Decision for War: Records of the 1941 Policy Conferences* (Stanford, CA: Stanford University Press, 1967), pp. 132, 154–5, 185, 224, 241–3; Prange, Goldstein, and Dillon, *At Dawn We Slept*, pp. 338–41; Donald M. Goldstein and Katherine V. Dillon, eds, *The Pearl Harbor Papers: Inside the Japanese Plans* (New York: Brassey's, 1993), pp. 14–15, 18, 140–2.

38 Goldstein and Dillon, *Pearl Harbor Papers*, pp. 142–3, 282; *Hearings before the Joint Committee on the Investigation of the Pearl Harbor Attack* (Washington, DC: US GPO, 1946), Part 14, p. 715.

39 *Hearings*, Part 10, p. 4836.

40 *Hearings*, Parts 27, pp. 37, and 28, p. 1588.

41 *United States Strategic Bombing Survey, Japanese Air Power* (Military Analysis Division, Washington, DC: US GPO, July 1946), p. 8.

42 The relationship among British intelligence, strategy, and the outbreak of the Pacific War is still murky. Serious accounts include Richard Aldrich, *Britain and the Intelligence War against Japan, 1941–45: The Politics of Secret Service* (Cambridge: Cambridge University Press, 2000); Antony Best, *Empire Under Siege: British Intelligence and the Japanese Challenge in Asia, 1914–1941* (London: Palgrave, 2002); Ong Chit Chung, *Operation Matador: Britain's War Plans against the Japanese, 1918–1941* (Singapore: Times Academic Press, 1997); John Ferris, 'The Singapore Grip: Preparing Defeat in Malaya, 1939–1941', in Ian Gow and Yoshi Hirama, eds, *The History of Anglo-Japanese Relations, 1600–2000*, vol. III, *Military Relations* (London: Palgrave, 2003); and John Ferris, 'Student and Master: Britain, Japan, Airpower and the Fall of Singapore, 1920–1941', in Brian Farrell, ed., *Singapore, Sixty Years On* (Singapore: 2002).

43 For Japanese policy and its understanding of British perceptions, see E. Bruce Reynolds, *Thailand and Japan's Southern Advance, 1940–1945* (New York: St Martin's Press, 1994), pp. 53–81, esp. n. 77.

44 AC 34799, TEL 383, 7.12.41, *passim*, AIR 40/2618; COIS, 5.12.41, 0500, FEW Serial No. 215, *passim*, FO 371/27767; memorandum by MI2c, 'Order of Battle – Japanese Forces in the South, 3 Dec. 1941', *passim*, WO 208/1080. Chung, *Matador*, pp. 218–33, provides a good account of these British assessments.

45 *The Japanese Times and Advertiser* for 8.4.42, 'Brilliant 70–Day Drive of Imperial Forces down Malay Peninsula to Singapore Told', allegedly quoting Yamashita. According to an unsigned and undated covering note, from an investigation con-

ducted during the occupation of Japan, presumably by Australian officers, that report actually was written by one of Yamashita's senior staff officers, Colonel Tsuji, and vetted by his chief of staff (AWM 27/118/15, Australian War Memorial, Canberra). Tsuji pursued another feint, using Japanese soldiers in Thai uniforms to overwhelm British soldiers on the Malayan border near Singora, but this effort was abandoned (Masonubu Tsuji, *Singapore: The Japanese Version* (New York: St Martin's Press, 1960), pp. 64–6, *passim*).

46 Stanley Falk, *Seventy Days to Singapore* (New York: Putnam's, 1975), pp. 224–9; Tsuji, *Singapore*, pp. 223–39.
47 Memorandum by MI2a, 12.2.41, 'The Siwa Leakage Case', *passim*, WO 208/501.
48 Brigadier R.J. Maunsell, 'Security Intelligence in Middle East, 1914–1934 and 1934–1944', IWM, 80/30/1; Hinsley and Simkins, *Security*, pp. 149–51.
49 Memorandum by Wavell, 15.12.40, 'Operations in Western Desert October to December 1940. (Notes on Genesis and Working Out of 'COMPASS' Plan', CRME/1553/G (O), WO 169/16). Howard, *Strategic Deception*, relies for its evidence on deception in Egypt during this period essentially on the 'A' Force Narrative War Diary (CAB 154/1), and overlooks other useful sources on the matter. That 'Diary' is not in fact, a contemporary document, but a postwar account based on contemporary records. Hence, Howard's account of deception in the Middle East from June 1940 to December 1941 is not entirely authoritative. Special care also must be taken with two works by one of Clarke's subordinates, David Mure, *Practise to Deceive* (London: William Kimber, 1977) and *Master of Deception* (London: William Kimber, 1980); while valuable and often accurate, these books are wrong on many issues, some significant, and cannot be taken for granted.
50 Brigadier R.J. Maunsell, 'Security Intelligence in Middle East, 1914–1934 and 1934–1944', pp. 17–20, IWM, 80/30/1.
51 Memorandum by Wavell, 15.12.40, 'Operations in Western Desert October to December 1940. (Notes on Genesis and Working Out of 'COMPASS' Plan', CRME/1553/G (O), WO 169/16); Memorandum by O'Connor, 'Ist. Des. Campaign', *c.* 1972, *passim*, General O'Connor Papers, 4/2/70, BLHCMA.
52 Wavell to Smuts, 28.12.40, Memorandum by Wavell, 15. 12.40, 'MOST SECRET AND PERSONAL', for DDMI, 'CAMILLA', Alan Cunningham Papers, National Army Museum, 8303/104/7' CAB 154/1, 'A' Force Narrative War Diary, entry 18.12.40.
53 Ibid.
54 War Office to Middle East GOC, W. Africa 19 and 20 Military Missions, 3.11.40, WO 169/20.
55 Appendix 'B' to GHQ ME Intelligence Summary No 245, 20.1.41, WO 169/924.
56 War Office to GHQ Middle East, 20.10.40, No 85856, WO 169/21.
57 Appendix 'B' to GHQ ME Intelligence Summary to No 247, 22.1.41, WO 169/924; 'Through Italian Eyes, A Series of Extracts from Daily Intelligence Summaries of the Tenth Italian Army from July to December, 1940, Captured in the Western Desert', ND, Australian War Memorial, AWM 54/423/4/95.
58 Memorandum by Cunningham, 'Notes on Operations in EAST AFRICA from 11th February, 1941, to 3rd July, 1941', 8303–104/14.
59 Ibid. 'A' Force Narrative War Diary, entry 18.12.40, CAB 154/1.
60 'Through Italian Eyes'.
61 'A' Force Narrative War Diary, entry 11.1.41, 7.6.41, CAB 154/1.
62 'A' Force Narrative War Diary, entries 11.1.41, 1.2.41, 6.4.41, 26.4.41, CAB 154/1.
63 Maunsell, 'Security Intelligence'.
64 Mideast to Trooper, 7.7.41, I/79781, Blamey Papers, 3 DRL 6643/1/2B 6; Weekly Review of the Military Situation, Nos 57, 58, 30.6.41, 7.7.41, WO 208/1559.

65 'A' Force Narrative War Diary, entry 17.7.41, *passim*, CAB 154/1.

66 'A' Force Narrative War Diary, entry 17.7.41, CAB 154/1.

67 Auchinleck to Churchill, 18.10.41, Auchinleck papers, No. 391; Auchinleck to Cunningham, 2.9.41, 'Western Desert Offensive, Autumn 1941', CRME/1775/G (O) Memorandum by Auchinleck, 30.10.41, 'CRUSADER', Cunningham Papers.

68 'Minutes of a Conference Held at GHQ Eighth Army on 6 Oct 41 at 1100 Hrs'; memorandum by Cunningham, 28.9.41, 'Appreciation of the Situation by Commander Eighth Army in the Field – 28 Sep 41', 8303–104/19, Cunningham Papers.

69 Auchinleck to Cunningham, 10.10.41, 8303–104/19, Churchill telegram to Shearer, T572, 11.9.41, 'Private and Secret', CHAR 20/42B, Winston Churchill papers; 'A' Force Narrative War Diary, entries 25.9.41, 20.10.41; Winston Churchill papers.

70 John Ferris, 'The "Usual Source": Signals Intelligence and Planning for the Crusader Offensive, 1941', *Intelligence and National Security*, vol. 14, no. 1 (1999), pp. 84–118.

71 'Eighth Army, Report on Operations', WO 201/358; GHQ, Middle East, to Eighth Army, 2.9.41, 'Crusader, Note by C-in-C, MEF', 30.10.41, 8303/104–18.

72 Memorandum by Brigadier Reid, 29th Indian Brigade, 27.11.41, WO 201/378.

73 409th and 416th meetings of the ISSB, 24.9.41, 1.10.41, WO 283/5; 40th XX Committee Meeting, 2.10.41, KV 4/64.

74 Montagu, *Top Secret*, pp. 133–5, 139; Dennis Wheatley, *The Deception Planners: My Secret War* (London: Hutchinson, 1980), pp. 27–49. This memoir is accurate on the main points, though Wheatley's memory of the words in conversations 30 years past no doubt is colorful.

75 Wheatley, *Deception Planners*, pp. 28–32, 60–2.

76 Cited in ibid., pp. 64–5.

77 Howard, *Strategic Deception*, Appendix 3, p. 243.

78 Wavell to Churchill, telegram 12461/C, 21.5.42, CHAR 20/75; Hinsley and Simkins, *Security*, pp. 127–37.

79 Memorandum by Trevor Roper, 'The German Intelligence Service and the War', 1945, CAB 154/105.

80 Hut 3, 'History', p. 418, HW 3/120.

81 Memorandum by London Controlling Section, 4.12.42 'Suggestions for Dinner Table Talk, Winter 1942–43', CAB 154/32; (COS)42(216) (0) 26.11.42, 'Torch: Deception and Cover Plans', CAB 81/76.

82 'A' Force Narrative War Diary, entry 18.2.42, CAB 154/1.

83 'A' Force Narrative War Diary, entry 2.7.42, CAB 154/1; Maunsell, 'Security Intelligence'; Hinsley and Simkins, *Security*, pp. 166–7.

84 C.A. Borman, *Divisional Signals: Official History of New Zealand in the Second World War* (Wellington: War History Branch, 1954), pp. 310–11.

85 Hesketh, 'FORTITUDE', Ch. 1, p. 2; 'A' Force Narrative War Diary, entries 10.3.42, 6.2.44.

86 Montagu, *Beyond Top Secret U*, p. 142.

87 Roger Hesketh, 'Introduction', in Roger Hesketh, 'FORTITUDE, A History of Strategic Deception in North Western Europe, April, 1943 to May, 1945', 208.

88 COS (43) 779 (O) (Revise) 25.12.43, Hesketh, 'FORTITUDE', Appendix 1, 4373.

89 Memorandum by NID 12, 28.9.45, 'German Deception', ADM 223/298.

90 Memorandum by NID 12, 20.7.45, 'German Appreciation of Allied Intentions', ADM 223/298; for copies of these reports, see CAB 154/76, 95–6.

91 'The Abwehr and Allied Intentions May 1943', CAB 154/95.

92 Hut 3, Memorandum No 569, 27/12.43, HW 3/125.

93 Hut 3, 'History', pp. 89, 135–6, HW 3/119.

94 Hesketh, 'FORTITUDE', Ch. XXII, p. 2, n.4.

95 Ibid., Ch. XXXIII, p. 153.

96 Hut 3, 'History', p. 418, HW 3/120.

97 WO 204/11457.

98 WO 204/11457. My assessment of German intelligence and Allied deception in Italy rests on the records of interrogation contained in this document.

99 Memorandum by Nalder, 'Wireless Cover and Deception in the Italian Campaign', c. 1945, CAB 154/103; Howard, *Strategic Deception*, pp. 161–2.

100 Hut 3, 'History', HW 3/120.

101 Memorandum by Trevor Roper, 'German Intelligence Service', CAB 154/105; Stephan, 'Combat Counterintelligence'.

102 David Glantz, *Soviet Strategic and Operational Deception in the Second World War*, (London: Frank Cass, 1989).

103 Joint Chiefs of Staff, Joint Pub 3–58, *Joint Doctrine for Military Deception*, 31.5.96 (under revision as of time of writing, July 2002); Joint Pub 3–13.1, *Joint Doctrine for Command and Control Warfare (C2W)*, 7.2.96; Joint Pub 3–54, *Joint Doctrine for Operations Security*, 24.2.97; Joint Pub 3–13, *Joint Doctrine for Information Operations*, JCS, 9.10.98; Joint Publication 2–01.3, 24.5.00, *Joint Tactics, Techniques, and Procedures for Joint Intelligence Preparation of the Battlespace*, taken from the Joint Chiefs of Staff website.

104 J.R. Ferris and Michael Handel, 'Clausewitz, Intelligence, Uncertainty and the Art of Command in Modern War', *Intelligence and National Security*, vol. 10, no. 1 (January 1995), pp. 1–58.

6

Intelligence Failure and the Need for Cognitive Closure: The Case of Yom Kippur

Uri Bar-Joseph

'For me, the week between 1 October and 6 October, in the Southern Command, was the most normal week. I did not see anything irregular.' (from the testimony of Lieutenant General David Elazar, the IDF Chief of Staff, in the Agranat investigation committee)[1]

On 5 October 1973, about 24 hours before the Yom Kippur War broke out, Israel's Directorate of Military Intelligence (AMAN) distributed an immediate Military Intelligence Review. Titled 'Alert Status and Activity in Syria and Egypt as of 051000 Oct. 73', the document summarized a long list of warning indicators that should have led any experienced person to the conclusion that the two states had completed all the preparations for attack and were on the verge of launching it. Indeed, at this stage, five of out of the six senior analysts of Syrian and Egyptian affairs in AMAN's Research Division estimated that war was either certain or highly likely.[2] But none of AMAN's political and military consumers was aware of it. For them, the consensus of Israel's sole intelligence estimate[3] was expressed in paragraph 40 of the document, which said:

> Although the mere taking of an emergency deployment at the Canal front implies, allegedly, warning indicators for an offensive initiative, to the best of our estimate no change took place in Egypt's estimate of the balance of forces with the IDF. Therefore, the probability that they intend to resume fighting is low.[4]

The officer who wrote this paragraph, Lieutenant Colonel Yona Bandman, was the head of Branch 6 (Egyptian and North African affairs) of AMAN's Research Division and the agency's prime estimator for Egyptian affairs. Since entering office in mid-1972, he had been a major pivot of the dominant estimation in AMAN, according to which Egypt would not initiate a war unless certain conditions were met – primarily the acquisition of attack airplanes and surface-to-surface missiles that were capable of attacking Israel's air force bases and other strategic targets. Twenty-four hours before war started, when all available information indicated that this conception was no longer valid, Bandman saw no reason to change his mind. He continued to believe so until its outbreak.[5]

Had Bandman been the sole devotee of this conception this could have been merely an anecdote. But he was not. A more central and no less ardent believer in the conception was the Director of Military Intelligence (DMI), Major General Eli Zeira, who served, *ex officio*, as the government's intelligence advisor. Less than three weeks before the war, he was certain that 'the Egyptians understand that they cannot present any serious military threat to Israel', and that they would not gain such an ability at least until 1978.[6] On the morning of 6 October, despite clear evidence of preparations for war, he continued doubting its outbreak and estimated that even if the Egyptians opened fire, they would not attempt to launch a ground offensive into the Sinai. The head of AMAN's Research Division, Brigadier General Arie Shalev, another true believer in the conception, agreed by now that a war with Egypt was probable but, nevertheless, assessed that Syria would join it only at a later stage, and only if the fighting in the south went against Israel.[7]

In contrast to the rather cohesive assessment in AMAN's higher echelon, many lower-ranking analysts estimated in the week or so before the war that the military activity on Israel's northern and southern borders was for war.[8] For various reasons their voices were not heard. This was one of the main causes of Israel's strategic blunder.

This chapter addresses only partially the question of why AMAN spoke with just one voice to its consumers. Moreover, it does not attempt to describe and analyze the quality of the intelligence information that Israel's intelligence community collected before the war and the way in which it was processed by AMAN. I discuss these more comprehensive aspects of the subject in other works.[9] Instead, this chapter asks a different question: Why did some of the agency's analysts estimate the situation correctly and regard war's probability as high or even certain, while others (mostly in higher ranks) erred completely? By focusing on this question, this chapter deviates from the common wisdom of students of surprise attacks, who look for general pathologies in the warning–response process in order to explain the intelligence failure. Instead, it suggests that idiosyncratic behavior – of two intelligence officers in the case of 1973 – constitutes the best explanation for the Israeli fiasco. Consequently, the aim of this chapter is to: (1) analyze the present body of literature on the 1973 intelligence debacle and its deficiencies; (2) describe and explain the main cause of the failure – the behavior of DMI Zeira and head of Branch 6, Bandman, the two officers who determined, more than anyone else, the poor quality of the intelligence product that the policymakers received – and show the impact that their action had on the decisions that were taken

by the Chief of Staff and the Defense Minister; (3) attempt to explain
Zeira and Bandman's conduct by using recent theoretical findings from the
field of cognitive psychology.

The Literature and its Deficiencies

Along with the German attack on the USSR in June 1941 ('Barbarossa')
and the Japanese attack on Pearl Harbor six months later, the coordinated
Egyptian–Syrian attack of Yom Kippur is considered a classic example of
a successful surprise attack and a costly intelligence failure. The similarity
among the three cases is obvious: despite ample evidence concerning the
ability and the intention of the initiator to launch an attack, the intelligence agencies that were involved failed to provide a timely and accurate
warning. Much of the puzzle concerning the Soviet case is explained,
however, by the German deception plan, which convinced Stalin that the
attack would be delayed until war with Britain was over and that prior to
its initiation Hitler would submit an ultimatum. Stalin's dictatorial style
and the purges of Moscow's intelligence community, prior to the war, constitute another important explanation. Neither deception, nor dictatorial
rule, nor purges played a role in the case of Pearl Harbor.[10] Here, surprise
is largely explained by the Japanese success to conceal the main element of
their attack: its target.

Neither deception nor concealment can provide a good explanation for
Israel's 1973 intelligence failure. Syria had no deception plan at all.
Though a number of works emphasize an Egyptian deception plan – at
the center of which stood the attempt to conceal operational preparations
for war under the disguise of a routine exercise ('Tahrir 41')[11] – its overall
quality was poor. By 3 October, AMAN's SIGINT unit ('Unit 848' – later
known as '8200') collected enough evidence to show that in actuality no
exercise took place. By 5 October, this was even more obvious.[12] The same
is true with regard to concealment. Despite extensive Egyptian and Syrian
attempts to prevent Israel from gaining information about their plan to go
to war, on 2 October AMAN disseminated an updated version of the
Syrian war plan.[13] The detailed Egyptian plan to cross the Canal was in
its possession more than a year before.[14] Prior to the war, moreover,
AMAN collected hundreds of warning indicators by visual (VISINT) and
signal (SIGINT) means of collection. Mossad human sources (HUMINT)
provided a number of high-quality warnings about the intention to launch
an attack.[15] As Israel's official investigation of the war concluded: 'In the
days that preceded the Yom Kippur War, the Research Division of
Military Intelligence had plenty of warning indicators that had been supplied to them by AMAN's Collection Division and by other Israeli collect-
ing agencies.'[16]

This, indeed, has also been the conclusion of most students of Israel's 1973 failure. Hence, and with the lack of a 'conspiracy theory' to explain it, the focus has been on two types of explanation. The first suggests that the failures at the war's beginning were not the product of a lack of warning, but rather the outcome of poor operational preparations for war. The second holds that the source of Israel's military setbacks was the poor quality of the intelligence warning and attempted to explain it in various ways.

The approach that minimizes the impact of the intelligence failure on the war's outcome suggests three main deficiencies to explain the military defeats:

1. Over-optimistic assumptions by IDF (Israel Defence Force) planners, who believed that 300 tanks, without effective air support from the Israeli Air Force (IAF) (which would first have to destroy the Egyptian and Syrian SAM layouts), would suffice to stop the Egyptian ground offensive.[17]
2. The decision to forgo the pre-emptive air strike at the beginning of the war, for which the IAF paid dearly afterwards.[18]
3. Technical and doctrinal surprises, primarily the effectiveness of Soviet personal antitank weapons, which became the deadliest enemy of Israeli tanks in the southern front, and the Egyptian and Syrian air-defense systems, which prevented the IAF from gaining control in the air.[19]

A close look at these arguments shows their poor explanatory quality. Prior to the war, AMAN assumed that it would be able to provide a strategic warning four to six days before it broke out,[20] and this was the foundation for the war plans. According to plan *Sela* ('rock'), the IDF was to deploy three divisions in the Canal theater of operations during this time-span: one division (252), made up of three regular-service tank brigades (about 300 tanks), was to deploy in the front line, and two reserve divisions (143, 162) were to deploy in the rear, primarily for a counter-offensive. Deployment in the Golan Heights, according to this plan, was to take about 48 hours. Division 36 (combined of regular and reserve forces) was planned to defend the front line, and a reserve division was to deploy in the rear for a counter-offensive.[21] Plan *shovakh yonim* ('dovecote') was the codename for deployment in the south under a worse-case scenario, in which warning for war was given only 24–48 hours prior to its inauguration. It called for an immediate deployment of Division 252, and the mobilization and deployment of the two reserve divisions, which, so it was assumed, would enter into combat only after war had started. In the north, plan *gir* ('chalk') called for the deployment of more than a division in the Golan Heights within 48 hours.[22] The worst-case scenario, known simply as 'catastrophe', involved the breakout of war without any warning. No planning was done for such a situation. The Chief of Staff and his deputy assumed that in such circumstances a combination of defense by the regular army, improvisation of rapid deployment of reserve forces, and maximal use of the IAF against the Arab ground offensive would be the only solution during the war's first day or two.[23]

As this evidence shows, the IDF had no plans for defense by regular forces alone if early warning was provided. However, when war did actually start, the main problem was not lack of reserve forces in the front, but the inappropriate deployment of the regular army. Because of the poor quality of the intelligence warning, the forces in the Golan (almost two tank brigades) were deployed for a local clash rather than for war. As some analysts assess, had these been deployed according to plan 'chalk', they could have blocked the Syrian advance.[24] The situation in the south resembled the 'catastrophe' scenario even more. The force that manned the Bar Lev line was a second-rate reserve force rather than the élite paratroop soldiers that were to replace it according to plan 'dovecote'. Although the Chief of Staff ordered the commander of the Southern Command, Major General Shmuel Gonen, to deploy for war about seven hours earlier, only three out of the 300 tanks of Division 252 were in their positions when war began; the rest began to deploy only thereafter.[25] Behind Gonen's decision to delay deployment was his belief (influenced by estimates that he had heard from Zeira that morning) that war was still not certain.

Division 252 lost about 200 tanks during the war's first 16 hours, mostly to personal anti-tank weapons. The Egyptian *Sagger* anti-tank missile systems and RPG-7 rocket launchers were so effective because the first crossing waves of their operators met no resistance and had ample time to secure the same positions originally prepared for the Israeli tanks. They then destroyed these tanks when approaching the same positions or when trying to rescue the soldiers who were not supposed to man the Bar-Lev line. In this sense, a combination of a poor-quality intelligence warning and Gonen's series of mistakes, rather than an over-optimistic planning for war or a technological surprise, 'gave the Egyptians the best conditions to start the war – better than they ever dreamed about'.[26]

Lack of strategic warning rather than doctrinal surprise was also the cause of failures to destroy Egyptian and Syrian air defenses. The IAF had planned and exercised a large-scale operation to destroy the anti-aircraft layout along the Canal since the end of the War of Attrition in the summer of 1970. Titled *tagar* ('quarrel'), it was planned to last six hours, through which four flights were to be taken: preparation (destruction of anti-aircraft guns and of air bases' runways to isolate the main battlefield); destruction of the surface-to-air missile (SAM) layout; location and destruction of remaining SAM batteries; and destruction of incoming reserve batteries. The operation called for a massive ground and airborne electronic-warfare (EW) support, a reconnaissance flight shortly before the operation in order to locate the mobile SA-6 batteries, and good weather. Following the build-up of a similar SAM layout in the Golan front, IAF planners prepared a similar operation titled *dugman* ('male model') for its destruction.[27]

Four months before the war, Defense Minister Moshe Dayan assured the IAF Commander that in case of war he would be allowed to strike pre-emptively.[28] But, on the morning of 6 October, probably because he still doubted the inevitability of war, Dayan objected to such a move and the Prime Minister accepted his decision. Despite this setback, on the morning of 7 October, the IAF started carrying out '*tagar*.' However, while the first flight (which proved to be successful) was still underway, Dayan, who was by now anxious about the dire situation in the Golan, gave the order to cease the operation and to focus all aerial efforts on blocking the Syrian ground offensive. A few hours later, without EW support and a reconnaissance flight, the IAF carried out '*dugman-5*'. The result was a catastrophe. Only one out of the 31 Syrian SAM batteries was destroyed, at the cost of six F-4 *Phantoms* and three A-4 *Skyhawks*. As a result, the IAF avoided similar attempts until the war's end.

The available evidence shows, then, that neither a doctrinal surprise nor the decision to veto a pre-emptive air strike were the causes for the IAF's difficulties throughout the war. Its inability to carry out its missions was, first and foremost, the outcome of the poor quality of the intelligence warning. It caused Dayan to doubt the need for a pre-emptive air strike, and then it led, though indirectly, to his order to cease '*tagar*' in order to save northern Israel from a Syrian invasion.

Two conclusions arise from this discussion: (1) Israel's defeats in the war's first stage were due to the poor quality of intelligence warning rather than other causes; and (2) this failure was the result neither of insufficient information, nor of high-quality deception. Indeed, as most academic students of this fiasco concluded, at the root of the 1973 blunder stood certain pathologies, which were found in similar cases as well. Michael Handel, probably the most prominent student of the surprise of Yom Kippur, identified nine 'paradoxes' in his works on intelligence, which preclude the possibility of avoiding strategic surprise.[29] Some of these – such as the difficulties involved in differentiating 'signals' from 'noise', the 'sounds of silence', self-negating prophecy, over-reliance on an intelligence agency with a good reputation, and 'alert fatigue' (a.k.a. 'cry-wolf syndrome') – were highly visible in 1973. In addition, Handel regarded the politicization of the intelligence process as another major source for failure.[30] While he was certainly right about it, another type of political interference with intelligence, that is, 'intelligence action taken consciously by intelligence makers in contradiction to their professional role',[31] is even more relevant here. Indeed, the information that has become available only in recent years shows that the unprofessional interference of DMI Zeira with the intelligence cycle on the eve of the war was, probably, the most devastating factor that prevented Israel from being ready when it came.

In his specific studies of Yom Kippur, Handel identified three 'noise barriers', which distorted the signals that had to pass through them. The first of these barriers involved various other threat sources in the international and regional systems as well as too quiet an international environment (for example, *détente*), which averted the victim's attention from the real threat and destroyed its ability correctly to assimilate the signals of the coming attack. The second barrier was created by the initiator's attempt to conceal its plans and to mislead the victim with regard to its real intentions. The last barrier was the noise generated unintentionally by the victim, which further hampered the proper assimilation of the signals of the impending threat.[32] Not surprisingly, the interaction among the three barriers led Handel to conclude that 'surprise can rarely be prevented'.[33] More than ten years later, he repeated this conclusion, adding that this was so 'because at the root of the problem – the weakest link in the intelligence process – is human nature'.[34]

Most academic students of the case of Yom Kippur could not escape a similar conclusion.[35] Yet, while the consensus among them is that the failure was the outcome of human nature and strategic errors, none of them attempted to penetrate the 'black box' in which the intelligence process took place, in order to link specific destructive behavior by specific officers to a specific result.

The Human Factor: Penetrating AMAN's 'Black Box'[36]

In the summer 1973, three officers largely determined Israel's national intelligence estimate regarding the likelihood of war. Two of them were relatively new in their positions. DMI Eli Zeira entered office on 1 October 1972, after a few years' service as the military attaché in Washington DC. Previously, he had headed AMAN's Collection Division, commanded the IDF's sole active-duty paratrooper brigade, and had served in various senior positions in the G (general staff) branch of General Headquarters (GHQ). In the mid-1950s, he served as military assistant to Chief of Staff Moshe Dayan and, as a result, Dayan knew him well, respected him more than any other IDF officer, and saw him as the next chief of staff.[37] The head of Branch 6 (Egyptian and North African affairs), Lieutenant Colonel Yona Bandman, entered office in the summer of 1972. Earlier, he had served in various positions in the Research Division. The third key officer was the head of this division, Brigadier General Arie Shalev, who had served in this position since 1967.

The importance of the three men was derived not only from their formal roles, but also from what was believed in summer 1973 to be their earlier success. In April–May 1973, following a number of warnings from reliable HUMINT sources, Israel's political-military élite (mainly Golda Meir, Dayan, and Elazar), as well as officers in AMAN and the Mossad, reached the conclusion that Egypt was likely to launch war in the coming months. By contrast, AMAN's official estimate, as determined by Zeira, Shalev, and Bandman, was that the likelihood of war remained low.[38] As time passed, the validity of this assessment became evident, and policy-makers such as Dayan, who in May ordered the IDF to prepare for a war in the summer,[39] assessed in July that no war would take place within the next decade.[40] The professional prestige of Zeira and Bandman – the two most ardent believers in the idea that in the coming years Egypt would not perceive itself as capable of launching a war – reached its height in the summer 1973, not only within AMAN and the IDF, but also among policy-makers. Had Zeira and Bandman been more prudent professionally, this would have constituted a minor problem. But they were not. The combi-nation of their high informal status with certain personal characteristics and peculiar beliefs regarding their professional duties created unique circumstances that allowed them (together with some other officers in AMAN) to lead the whole country astray.

Both Zeira and Bandman were highly intelligent with excellent verbal skills. The men also enjoyed 'a good chemistry' with one another and both held in high esteem the professional skills of the other. Zeira regarded Bandman as an estimator of international caliber, and Bandman respected Zeira as a decisive director who knew how the intelligence product should be made and provided to consumers.[41] But they were also arrogant, over-confident, and authoritarian types, as reflected in their professional think-ing and action. What follows is a discussion of some of the main patterns of their thinking and behavior, and its impact on the making of Israel's national intelligence estimate on the eve of the Yom Kippur War.

Mode of Estimation

Zeira and Bandman tended to view the complex Arab–Israeli environment in terms of Popperian 'clocks' – that is, as a regular, orderly, and highly predictable physical system – rather than 'clouds', which represent 'highly irregular, disorderly, and more or less unpredictable' systems.[42] This ten-dency was most critical and best expressed when it came to Egypt's mili-tary weaknesses. Since October 1972, when Zeira entered office (and, ironically, Sadat decided to go to war), neither Zeira nor Bandman ever questioned the conception that without having a fighter-bomber force capable of attacking IAF bases, and surface-to-surface missiles with enough range to reach Israel (for the purpose of deterrence), Sadat would avoid a major military initiative. Since such conditions were not to be met for some time, they assessed, even in mid-September 1973, during the next five years, the Egyptians were unlikely to estimate 'that they have the capability to occupy the Sinai desert or a part of it, since this means an overall confrontation with Israel'.[43] Hence, it was their conclusion that no war was possible.

Other experts, who took into account not only this factor, but also other military and political considerations, painted their estimate in shades of gray. Dayan, who understood well that Sadat was under growing political pressures as long as the 'no war, no peace' situation continued, believed (until summer 1973) that the Egyptian leader might take military measures to alter the *status quo*.[44] Major General Aharon Yariv, Zeira's predecessor, who had a reputation for being a prudent estimator, assessed in mid-1972 that the present situation was likely to last until mid-1973. Then, it was possible that Sadat would perceive a limited military option as a feasible move.[45] The head of the Mossad, Zvi Zamir, estimated in April 1973 that the Egyptian Army bridged many of the gaps that prevented it from launching a war and was now more capable than ever before to take such action.[46] The Chief of Staff had estimated in August 1972 that, despite the expulsion of the Soviet personnel from Egypt, the continuation of the *status quo* would increase Sadat's frustration and that during 1973 he might initiate war.[47]

Managerial and Organizational Style

Zeira and Bandman's tendency towards authoritarianism and decisiveness was well felt here. Both lacked the patience for long and open discussions and regarded them as 'bullshit'. Zeira used to humiliate officers who, according to his opinion, came unprepared for meetings. At least once, he was heard to say that those officers who estimated in spring 1973 that war was likely should not expect promotion.[48] Needless to say, such a behavior discouraged open and frank debate – a necessary condition for the making of good intelligence.

Bandman, though comparatively less influential in AMAN, used to express, either verbally or in body language, his disrespect for the opinions of others. He was also known for his total rejection of any attempt to change a single word, not even a comma, in a document that he had written. For an organ whose task is to produce balanced estimates that reflect the views of the organization as a whole, this was a rather unproductive pattern of behavior. But this was not unique to Bandman alone. Neither he nor Zeira was ready to provide consumers with estimates other than their own. Consequently, policymakers were not aware of the fact that there were in AMAN contradictory assessments regarding Egyptian and Syrian war intentions. Here, however, other senior officers, primarily the head of the Research Division and his two assistants, were to share the blame. Their impact was less relevant in assessing Egyptian intentions, where Bandman's estimates ruled out those of others; it was more important when it came to Syria, since the officers of Branch 5 (Syrian affairs) tended to estimate that Assad was gearing for war. But, since the consensus in AMAN was that Syria would not go to war without Egypt, and since the agency's dominant assessment was that Sadat did not perceive himself as being capable of going to war, the command of the Research Division avoided providing consumers with the divergent assessment of the officers of Branch 5. This managerial style was established in AMAN, mainly under Zeira. His predecessor, Yariv, was known for his openness to divergent opinions and, as a rule, always provided consumers not only with his own assessments but with contradictory ones as well.

Beliefs About Professional Duties

The common wisdom holds that the duty of the intelligence officer is to provide consumers with the most precise intelligence picture that he or she can. If available information portrays an intricate and ambiguous picture, then it should be described to policymakers precisely as such. Zeira and Bandman thought differently. As Zeira explained it to some *Knesset* (Parliament) members a few months before the war:

> The Chief of Staff has to make decisions and his decisions should be clear. The best support that the DMI can provide him with – if this is objectively possible – is to provide an estimate that is as clear and as sharp as possible. It is true that the clearer and sharper the estimate is, then, if it is a mistake, it is a clear and sharp mistake – but this is the risk of the DMI.[49]

Bandman viewed his duty similarly. Believing that providing consumers with all courses of action that were available to the enemy was unprofessional behavior, he thought that the intelligence advisor's duty was to provide the consumer with the clearest estimate.[50] In line with this belief, he insisted 24 hours before fire started on adding his personal assessment (paragraph 40) to AMAN's review of Arab military readiness. To the members of the Agranat investigation commission, he explained:

> I wrote the first version of this document without paragraph 40, and I felt that I had to add it. I felt that if I did not include paragraph 40 I would betray my duty. In other words, it is not enough that I should come and point out the information. I assessed that from a pure military perspective I had all the indications needed for offensive intentions; but as far as intentions were concerned, my estimate remained

the same, that they do not perceive themselves as capable of attacking. They attacked 24 hours later, but this is something else.[51]

The belief that consumers should be provided with a clear intelligence
picture corresponded closely to Zeira's and Bandman's tendency to view
the world in terms of 'clocks' rather than 'clouds'. AMAN's documents
and oral presentations before the war vividly reflected this combination. It
seems, however, that when receiving information that contradicted the
dominant conception, clarity was sacrificed for the sake of preserving
belief. We shall return to this pattern of behavior later.

Zeira's tendency to prefer clarity to precision reflected his belief that he
knew far better than his consumers which intelligence product should be
provided to them. But, it also went far beyond this – as expressed in two
of his modes of conduct on the eve of the war.

The first was Zeira's tendency to avoid providing the Chief of Staff and
the Defense Minister with critical information that indicated that war was
a real possibility. On one such occasion, in the early hours of 1 October,
he decided to hold a warning that had been received from a reliable
Mossad source that said that Egypt and Syria would initiate war the next
day.[52] The head of the Research Division, who reported this to him, suggested that he call the Chief of Staff so that the Northern and Southern
Commands could be put on alert. Zeira thought differently and informed
Elazar and Dayan about the warning only when he met them later that day.
When asked by Dayan why he had acted so, Zeira responded that the
warning had been checked out and that, since AMAN's experts concluded
that neither Egypt nor Syria was capable of launching a war the next day,
he had decided to delay its delivery. Then he added: 'In principle I do not
think that we should distribute information at night which we deem to be
groundless. It would suffice to do it in the morning, together with an evaluation of its meaning.'[53]

In another instance, about 20 hours before the war, Zeira decided to
delay the dissemination of information from SIGINT sources, which
clearly indicated that the Soviets had begun their emergency evacuation
from Egypt and Syria because of their clients' intention to launch war.
Explaining the decision to delay this information, he told the members of
the Agranat investigation commission:

> I saw no reason to alert the Chief of Staff at 11:00pm to tell him that
> there is such a message, and to add what we wrote later, that the
> source was not our most reliable one and that there were mistakes . . .
> And it should be remembered that when making this decision I knew,
> and the Chief of Staff knew that the whole IDF is at the highest state
> of alert . . . This was how I felt that night and, I assume, that the Chief
> of Staff felt similarly . . . . So the Chief of Staff would have seen it

and, I assume, would have said: fine . . . . But the whole army stands ready? Fine.[54]

When taking this decision, Zeira was aware of the fact that in a series of discussions earlier that day the Chief of Staff had said, repeatedly, that after putting the regular army on the highest state of alert, all he needed now was one more war indicator to request the mobilization of the reserve army. By deciding to hold this warning from Elazar, Zeira must have realized that he took a Chief of Staff's decision. This, of course, was far beyond the realm of his professional discretion by any standard but his own.

While denying his immediate superiors critical information at the most critical moments was, by itself, peculiar, another series of decisions derived from Zeira's unusual perception of his professional duties led them even further astray. On 1 October, and perhaps also the following day, the Chief of Staff asked him if all AMAN's means of collection were operating. Dayan asked him a similar question on 5 October. What both had in mind were certain means – sometimes referred to as 'Israel's national insurance policy' – which were to be operated only at times of tension and were likely to generate high-quality warning indicators had Egypt or Syria intended to launch an attack. Zeira let both understand that the 'special means' were activated, while, in reality, he gave an order to avoid their operation.[55]

By acting in this way, Zeira prevented critical information from reaching his superiors. But, the real implication of his action was far worse. Since Dayan and Elazar knew the potential of these means, and since they believed that they were operational but produced no warnings, their belief that the military preparations were not for war was strengthened. The Chief of Staff said so when learning, after the end of the war, that the 'special means' remained inactive until a few hours before it began. The Agaranat Commission found Zeira's behavior in this case a reason to ease Dayan's responsibility for the fiasco. The Commission avoided, however, investigating this issue and accepted Zeira's allegation that he misunderstood his superiors' questions.[56] Given that the Chief of Staff asked him specifically about these means,[57] and that since 1 October the heads of AMAN's Collection and Research Divisions as well as Unit 848 had demanded that he activate these means, his claim seems to be quite groundless. Here, again, a combination of over-confidence, a unique *Weltanschauung* of professional duties and dogmatic beliefs concerning Arab war intentions, led Zeira to a professionally unacceptable and damaging form of conduct.

Denial of Inconvenient Information

Under some of the circumstances that came to light at that time, neither Zeira, nor Bandman, nor other officers who believed that war was unlikely could ignore the information indicating that their conception might be invalid. In such situations, they used various techniques to bridge the gap between information and belief. As the theory of cognitive dissonance predicts, this was done by adapting reality to belief rather than the other way around. In some cases, it was simply done by phrasing assessments in the form of hard evidence. Thus, after reporting at noon on Friday that the Egyptian Army was at its highest state of alert, the head of Branch 6 added, without any hard information to support it, that:

> The Egyptians continue to fear an Israeli intention to exploit the ['Tahrir'] exercise and the 'Ramadan' fast for an offensive air action. These fears increased towards the morning of 5 October 73, probably following the air photograph sortie conducted by our planes yesterday, October 4th, and similar sorties on October 3rd.[58]

Here, at least, Bandman had no new evidence to refute his notion. But four paragraphs later, when summarizing activity at the front, he wrote: 'Routine activity was observed this morning along the Canal sector.'[59] All the reports from observation posts along the front, however, told an opposite story: massive movements of heavy weaponry, including tanks, to positions on the front line; senior Egyptian officers' reconnaissance of Israeli strongholds; large numbers of soldiers getting organized for some kind of action; blackout in the town of Port Said in the northern sector, and so on. 'Towards the evening of Yom Kippur', a battalion commander testified after the war, 'the line became full to capacity.'[60] By any standard, this could not be considered as a 'routine activity.' The 'Tahrir 41' exercise could not account for it either: activity in former 'Tahrir' exercises was very different from the action taken by the Egyptian Army in early October 1973.[61]

When asked why he disregarded these reports, Bandman gave a typical answer: 'The nature of the Command's collection capability implies its low value. We [in the Research Division] analyzed the situation from Cairo's perspective and not from the perspective of the Firdan [bridge on the Canal].'[62] Post factum, Bandman would maintain that he had ranked collection sources by his own order of reliability: SIGINT and air photographs came first, then open sources, and, lastly, HUMINT sources.[63] In the case of Yom Kippur, the best warnings came from Mossad HUMINT sources. This helps explain why they were never incorporated into Bandman's reports. But one may also wonder whether Bandman (and others) ranked HUMINT sources so low for purely professional considerations. It is also possible that they were ranked in this order because they usually contradicted the view that war was impossible.

Much like Bandman, who produced documents in which no conflict between estimate and information existed by disregarding the latter, Zeira showed a similar pattern in oral discussions. A good example is the way he explained to the Prime Minister, on Friday at noon, why the Soviets were conducting an emergency evacuation from Syria and Egypt. Zeira suggested three answers: '(1) the Soviets assess that Israel intends to attack ... (2) the Soviets reached the conclusion that Egypt and Syria intend to attack ... (3) a crisis in Soviet relations with Egypt and Syria.'[64] Then, probably after realizing that neither the first explanation nor the third made much sense, he added: 'The Soviets may nevertheless think that they [Egypt and Syria] intend to attack since they don't know the Arabs well enough.'[65] One has to take into account the Soviet stand in Syria and Egypt in order to grasp the true meaning of these words. Since the mid-1950s, the USSR had provided these two clients with all their military needs; Soviet military and intelligence personnel served in advisory capacities to senior officers mainly (in 1973) in Syria, but also in Egypt; and, if the war turned against them, Sadat and Assad were certain to demand that the Kremlin intervene militarily on their behalf. Hence, the notion that they would launch a war without informing the Soviets first was absurd. Yet, Zeira ignored this inference when it did not suit his beliefs.

In the early hours of Yom Kippur, after receiving an excellent warning from the Chief of the Mossad, the Chief of Staff ordered the IDF to prepare for a war that would start at around sunset. By now, Zeira's belief in the validity of the conception was badly shaken. And yet, even at this point, when every piece of information indicated war, he was reluctant to forgo it. At around 5:15a.m. he told Elazar that he assumed that ultimately there would be no war.[66] Shortly afterwards, after describing the Arab war plans, he added that, 'politically, Sadat does not need war'.[67] And in a discussion with Dayan and Elazar, at around 7:00a.m., he repeated this estimate, adding that 'the impression is that the Egyptians and the Syrians are training, or that this is a coordinated exercise, or a coordinated war'.[68] Shortly afterwards, Golda Meir heard from him that the Egyptian and Syrian layouts suited defensive and offensive deployment, with more indicators for the latter. Here, Zeira added: 'They are ready, they know that they cannot win the war. Sadat is not in a situation where he must start war. No political pressure and no domestic one.'[69] Implicitly, what Zeira kept on saying was that he saw no reason to change his estimate. If war broke out, it would be Sadat's mistake, not his.

Zeira's claim that Sadat did not need to go into a war that he was going to lose received a professional boost from the head of Branch 6, who repeated a similar argument at the same time. At a certain stage, the head of Branch 6 refused to add to a newly produced document the estimate that war was now very likely. In a rather unusual procedure, another officer added this estimate.[70] The clearest indication that Bandman and Zeira were of the same opinion, even at this stage, is an intelligence review submitted to Zeira by Bandman about three hours before the war began, which estimated its likelihood as low. Before approving its distribution, however, Zeira consulted his predecessor, Yariv, who arrived at his office. Yariv advised him to avoid its dissemination and Zeira accepted the advice.[71] But, the mere fact that he was willing to consider the distribution of this review – when almost everyone else accepted that war was certain and when the whole country was gearing up for war – is a good indication of his dogmatism, as well as his utmost trust in Bandman's professional qualifications and discretion.

Not much has changed since then. In 1992, Zeira published his war memoirs, which aimed at cleaning his name. The book totally ignores his mistakes, and the role they played in leading Israel astray, and turns Golda Meir, Dayan, and Elazar into the prime culprits in the Yom Kippur fiasco.[72] Similarly, Bandman, who found no major mistakes in his professional conduct before the war, was hardly ready, 25 years later, to admit that he and others were dogmatically 'locked' into the belief that war was unlikely.[73]

Summary

The most important point that comes out of the testimony given by Chief of Staff Elazar before the Agranat investigation commission was his lack of awareness, until a day before war started, that threatening developments were taking place on the Egyptian front: 'For me', he said 'the week between October 1st and October 6th, in the Southern Command, was the most normal week. I did not see anything irregular.'[74] Elazar had believed, since becoming Chief of Staff in early 1972, that war with Egypt was probable during his tenure. On Friday morning, immediately after receiving a detailed report about the massive deployment in the south – the first report of its kind for at least two weeks[75] – he realized that the situation on the Egyptian front was anything but normal. As a result, he ordered the IDF for the first time since 1967 to enter its highest state of alert.

After having received accurate reports about the Syrian build-up since early September, Elazar and Dayan were aware of a potential clash in the north and, until Friday morning, they focused their attention there. But since Syria could not launch a war without Egypt, and since the situation in the south was 'most normal', all that could be feared in the north was a limited act, perhaps a Syrian attempt to occupy a civilian settlement or an IDF stronghold. Elazar and Dayan were aware of the real situation in the north but not in the south, since the analysts of Branch 5 reported accurately every new development in their sector. By contrast, as already described here, war information concerning Egypt was either not reported at all, or reported partially and wrapped in calming assessments that were phrased as hard facts rather than mere beliefs. This unprofessional conduct was the main cause for Elazar and Dayan's misunderstanding of the true nature of the threat that they faced in early October, and, ultimately, for Israel's heavy losses during the war's first days. Zeira and

Bandman shared prime responsibility for it. Needless to say, they did not want to mislead their superiors and yet they did. Their conduct was motivated not only by an unusual perception of their professional duties, but also by total closure to any information that contradicted their beliefs. Explaining this closure is the subject of the last section of this chapter.

The Human Factor: Explaining the Behavior of Zeira and Bandman

A number of cognitive psychology theories – primarily the theories of confirmation bias, cognitive dissonance, and heuristic judgment – offer good explanations for the human tendency to make judgmental errors in complex situations. According to the theory of confirmation bias, individuals tend to look for, and attach more importance to, information that validates their existing beliefs and tend to ignore information that invalidates them.[76] Similarly, the theory of cognitive dissonance maintains that in situations in which an individual is confronted with information that contradicts a dominant belief that he or she holds, this individual will tend to adopt the information in a way that suits his or her belief rather than alter belief to suit the new information.[77] According to heuristic judgment theorists, the individual's need to make mental shortcuts in processing information in complex situations – which is done through mechanisms such as availability representativeness, or anchoring – is another cause of judgmental errors.[78]

These explanations are not mutually exclusive, although their explanatory quality varies from one case to another. For example, the fact that AMAN documents did not properly reflect the magnitude and the volume of information that indicated war, while amplifying calming information, can be partially explained by the theory of confirmation bias. The impact of the mechanism of cognitive dissonance was better felt in situations in which information that contradicted the dominant theory could not be ignored. A typical example is the way AMAN's analysts, and Zeira himself, acted when having to explain the Soviet emergency evacuation from Syria and Egypt two days before the war started. Though Soviet knowledge about an Arab decision to go to war was the most reasonable explanation, they diminished its value, since it challenged their dominant belief. The use of the heuristic judgment mechanism – in this case it was the mechanism of availability – came into effect in the attempt to explain this Soviet act as a sudden crisis in Moscow's relations with its two clients – a repetition of the July 1972 expulsion of Soviet personnel from Egypt.

Useful as these explanations are, they do not provide us with a satisfactory answer to the question why some analysts in AMAN regarded the probability of war as high or even certain, while others, who were exposed to precisely the same information, believed its likelihood was low – even nil.

Or, more specifically, why the agency's chief analyst for Egyptian affairs submitted, two hours before the beginning of the war, a review that repeated the clearly invalid conception, while his deputy for political affairs estimated that war was certain by the beginning of that week, and his deputy for military affairs reached this conclusion when learning about the Soviet evacuation.

Cognitive psychology theorists offer a number of possible explanations to this question. The most useful approach seems to be laid out in Kruglanski's theory of the epistemic process. Specifically, his concept of the 'need for nonspecific closure', that is, a concept that 'represents the desire for a definite answer on some topic, *any* answer as opposed to confusion and ambiguity',[79] seems to be highly relevant to our subject matter.

According to Kruglanski, the epistemic process starts with a question that the individual has on a certain topic of interest. In order to find an appropriate answer, he or she generates a number of hypotheses and tests their validity through collection and analysis of relevant information. When concluding that a logical consistency between the available information and a specific hypothesis has been reached, the human tendency is to stop looking for additional answers. This ends the epistemic process – a situation termed by Kruglanski as 'epistemic freezing'. Certain circumstances, primarily the arrival of new information that is inconsistent with the current hypothesis, may increase the tendency to generate an alternative hypothesis, to 'unfreeze' the process.

The level of the need for closure or its avoidance is the function of situational, as well as personality-based, variables. Situational variables that increase the need for closure include: time pressure, concrete deadline, and need for action; exogenous aspects such as environmental noise, and endogenous aspects such as a perception of information processing as effortful, dull, and unattractive; the perceiver's organismic state, primarily the state of fatigue; attribution of high value to closure by significant others; and a requirement for judgment on the topic under discussion. When opposite conditions are present the need for cognitive closure is lowered. In addition, the need to avoid closure is heightened if the cost that is involved in a premature closure is clear.[80]

Five characteristics were found to heighten the need for closure on the personal level: preference for definite order and structure in the individual's environment; discomfort with ambiguous situations; a need to make an urgent and decisive judgment; the desire for secure and stable knowledge (that is, knowledge 'that can be relied on across circumstances and is unchallenged by exceptions or disagreements'); and closed-mindedness, that is, 'an unwillingness to have one's knowledge confronted (hence rendered insecure) by alternative opinions or inconsistent evidence'.[81]

Some of the situational variables that heighten the need for closure were clearly present in AMAN's epistemic process before the war. Time pressures, concrete deadlines, and the need for action typify any intelligence process, particularly in emergency situations. AMAN's analysts were under constant pressure to provide consumers with an updated intelligence picture and, as the possibility of war started to loom large, time pressure and the need for action became even more influential. Physical fatigue was also a dominant factor, since, under time pressure, analysts continued to work through the night. For example, in a discussion in the office of the head of the Research Division on Friday at noon, one of the principal believers in the conception expressed some doubts about its validity. But Shalev decided to postpone the debate until Sunday, since everybody around was 'dead tired'. They had not had any sleep the night before, when ongoing discussions had been held to explain the Soviet emergency evacuation.[82] Esteem and appreciation for closure were highly present. DMI Zeira and some of his assistants expressed this not only before the war and in its aftermath, but, as noted, also many years later. This created an atmosphere in which avoidance of closure became a highly undesirable situation. As a result, junior officers who doubted the validity of the conception refrained from expressing their authentic beliefs in formal discussions, but talked about it informally among themselves.[83] Of course, to judge the situation was precisely the task of intelligence officers involved, though not necessarily in the decisive manner in which some of them performed.

On the other hand, a number of situational variables that favor a high need for closure were not there. Although the intelligence process on the eve of the war was effortful, it was far from being deemed as dull or unattractive. All participants perceived it as highly important for the fate of the nation, interesting, and lively. They regarded themselves as the chosen few, a serving élite that had to make critical decisions in a highly secretive environment. Accordingly, everyone was aware of the potential cost that was involved in their estimates. Some, however, tended to lower the cost of a possible mistaken judgment, as exemplified in Zeira's explanation for his decision to delay the delivery of critical information to the Chief of Staff on Friday afternoon, arguing that its timely delivery would have had no real effect on the situation.[84]

While situational variables conform only partially to favorable conditions for a high need for closure, the personality variables – as far as Zeira and Bandman are concerned – fully match the creation of such an environment. The two had had, as was so well reflected in their own words, a high preference for definite order and structure in their environment and a strong need to avoid ambiguous situations, particularly ambiguous estimations. Similarly, the behavior of both men reflected a need to make judgments in an urgent and decisive manner. As Zeira noted in his memoirs, his inability to give a clear explanation for the Soviet evacuation on Friday morning, 'was the first and the only time [throughout his tenure] that I told the Defense Minister that I [had] no explanation for a certain problem'.[85] Both, moreover, had a desire for secure and stable knowledge, as reflected by their persistent rejection of any information that challenged this knowledge. Furthermore, both were impatient for ongoing discussions and tended to react aggressively to alternative opinions.

All in all, then, the information that we have on the character traits of Zeira and Bandman indicates that both had a high need for cognitive closure and that, as a result, they reached the phase of 'epistemic freezing' at an early stage of the epistemic process – in fact, more than a year before war broke out. Their high need for closure also explains why they were the last in AMAN to unfreeze the process. Combined with their critical role in shaping Israel's national intelligence estimate on the eve of the war, and their *Weltanschauung* regarding their professional duties, this set of circumstances seems to provide the most plausible explanation for Israel's intelligence fiasco on the eve of the Yom Kippur War.

Conclusion

This chapter has used information that only became available recently in order to shed new light on Israel's 1973 intelligence failure. Its specific conclusions lead us to three others of a more general nature. First, the evidence presented here reconfirms the main assumption of the dominant school in the study of surprise attack, that the incorrect comprehension of the meaning of available information prior to attack, rather than the lack of such information, is the principal cause for this type of intelligence failure. Second, that theories that explain this incorrect understanding by a plethora of explanations of a general nature tend to ignore idiosyncrasies in the conduct of key individuals that may provide a better solution to the intelligence-failure puzzle. Although this study is focused on the Israeli case, there is ample evidence to show that such conduct contributed significantly to similar results in other intelligence failures as well.[86] Finally, the third conclusion derives from the first two: the tendency to try to prevent intelligence failures by increasing investments in collection or by reorganization of specific agencies and the community as a whole is like looking for a coin under a street light, rather than where it was actually lost. The problem lies, as Michael Handel noted, in human nature. A prudent manning of key intelligence positions by the most suitable personnel seems to be a less costly and more efficient solution to the problem. In other words, the use of certain methods of psychological screening – methods that are now used by many civilian organizations – in order to select to senior positions in the intelligence community officers with low or medium need for cognitive closure is certainly a necessary means to prevent the recurrence of fiascos such as Israel's intelligence debacle of 1973.

NOTES

The author thanks Richard K. Betts, Thomas G. Mahnken, Arie Kruglanski, Nir Evron, and Joshua Teicher for their comments on earlier drafts of this chapter.

1 Investigation Committee – The Yom Kippur War, *An Additional Partial Report: Reasoning and Completion to the Partial Report of April 1974* (hereafter, *Agranat*), 7 vols (Hebrew; Jerusalem, 1974), Vol. II, p. 268.
2 This information is based on interviews I conducted with: Lieutenant Colonel (in October 1973) Avi Ya'ari (head of the Syrian Branch, Branch 5); Lieutenant Colonel Yona Bandman (head of the Egyptian Branch, Branch 6); Lieutenant Colonel Zusia Kaniazer (head of the Jordan and the Arab Peninsula Branch, Branch 2); Mr Albert Sudai (head of Egyptian political section in Branch 6), and Major Yaacov Rosenfeld (head of the military section in Branch 6). In addition to Ya'ari, Sudai, and Rosenfeld, the heads of the Syrian political and military sections also estimated that war was either certain or highly likely.
3 In 1973, AMAN held a monopoly over Israel's national intelligence estimate. Assigning estimation functions to the Mossad, the Foreign Office, and the IDF's local commands began in 1974, as one of the main lessons from the Yom Kippur intelligence blunder.
4 Branch 3 + 5 + 6 + Israeli Air Force (IAF) Intelligence Division + Israeli Navy (IN) Intelligence Division, Immediate Military Intelligence Review, 'Alert Status and Activity in Syria and Egypt as of 051000 Oct. 7', para. 40 (private collection).
5 Kaniazer's interview; Alex Fishman, 'Even Today He Does Not Believe that War Broke Out', *Hadashot*, 24 September 1993 (Hebrew).
6 Directorate of Intelligence/Research Division, 'The Implication of Arab Arming with New Weapons – a Platform for GHQIDF (in Response to DMI Request)', 17 September, 1973 (private collection).
7 Interview with Brigadier-General Aria Shalev (the head of AMAN's Research Division in 1973); interview with Colonel Aharon Levran (assistant for operations to the head of the Research Division), Sudai's interview; Ya'ari's interview.
8 In addition to the names of the analysts mentioned in note 2, some others who estimated that war was imminent were Brigadier General Rami Luntz (head of the intelligence division of the Israeli Navy), Major Amos Gilboa (Basic Branch), and Major Ilan Tehila (head of the Soviet political section in Branch 3).
9 Uri Bar-Joseph, *The Watchman Fell Asleep: The Surprise of the Yom Kippur War and Its Sources* (Hebrew; Tel-Aviv: Zmora-Bitan, 2001) (under translation into English); 'Israel's 1973 Intelligence Failure', *Israeli Affairs*, vol. 6, no. 1 (Autumn 1999), pp. 11–35; 'Israel's Intelligence Failure of 1973: New Evidence, A New Interpretation, and Theoretical Implications', *Security Studies*, vol. 4, no. 3 (Spring 1995), pp. 584–609; 'The Wealth of Information and the Poverty of Comprehension: Israel's Intelligence Failure of 1973 Revisited', *Intelligence and National Security*, vol. 10, no. 4 (October 1995), pp. 229–40.
10 See, for example, Edwin T. Layton with Roger Pineau and John Costello, *'And I Was There': Pearl Harbor and Midway – Breaking the Secrets* (New York: William Morrow, 1985), pp. 228–9.
11 For example, Amos John, 'Deception and the 1973 Middle East War', in Donald C. Daniel and Katherine L. Herbig, eds, *Strategic Military Deception* (New York: Pergamon, 1981), pp. 317–34; Aharon Zeevi, 'Deception in Egyptian Yom Kippur War Plan', an MA thesis (Tel-Aviv University, Faculty of Humanities, the Zalman Aran School of History, History of the Middle East Section, September 1980). Zeevi, who served as an intelligence officer in 1973, was nominated in 2001 to be the Director of Military Intelligence.

12 Yoel Ben-Porat, *Neila (Locked-On)* (Hebrew; Tel-Aviv: Edanim, 1991), pp. 64, 117–18; interview with Lieutenant Colonel Shabtai Brill. In 1973, Colonel Ben-Porat was the head of Unit 848 and Brill was its operations officer.

13 Branch 5, Special Intelligence Review No. 104/73, 'A Syrian Plan to Occupy the Golan Heights – an Estimate', (October 2, 1973) (private collection); interview with Yaari.

14 Eli Zeira, *The October 73 War: Myth against Reality* (Hebrew; Tel-Aviv: Yediot Ahronot, 1993), pp. 68–9, 210.

15 For a detailed and updated discussion of this information, see Bar-Joseph, *The Watchman Fell Asleep* (Hebrew). For a partial discussion of this information, see Bar-Joseph, 'Israel's Intelligence Failure'.

16 Agranat Commission, *The Agranat Commission Report* (Hebrew; Tel Aviv: Am Oved, 1975), p. 19. A few students of the subject maintain that Israel was highly dependent on a warning from a specific source, which arrived only hours before war started: Eliot Cohen and John Gooch, *Military Misfortunes: The Anatomy of Failure in War* (New York: Vintage Books, 1991), pp. 126–7; Aharon Levran, 'Surprise and Warning – a Discussion of Fundamental Questions' (Hebrew) *Maarachot*, vol. 276–7 (October–November 1980), pp. 17–21, 18. As we know today, the warning from that source, which arrived in Israel about 10 hours before war broke out, had a major impact on policymakers' estimates, primarily those of the Chief of Staff and the Prime Minister, but hardly on Zeira and Bandman.

17 For example, Zeira, *October 73 War*, pp. 69–70.

18 Major General (ret.) Yisrael Tal, 'Warning in the War of Yom Kippur', lecture given to AMAN's officers on 12 July, 1993, *Symposiums on Intelligence in the War of Yom Kippur*, annex, pp. 7–8 (Hebrew). In 1973, Tal was the Deputy of the Chief of Staff.

19 Emanuel Wald, *The Nemesis of Broken Arms* (Hebrew; Tel-Aviv: Shoken, 1987), pp. 100–1; Moshe Dayan, *The Story of My Life* (Hebrew; Jerusalem: Edanim, 1976), pp. 684–5; Michael I. Handel, 'Technological Surprise in War', *Intelligence and National Security*, vol. 2, no. 1 (January 1987), pp. 1–53, 11–12; Richard K. Betts, 'Surprise Despite Warning: Why Sudden Attacks Succeed', *Political Science Quarterly*, vol. 95, no. 4 (1980–81), pp. 551–72, 568–9.

20 Office of the Director of Military Intelligence, 'Special Document on Warning', 16 June 1972, pp. 1–2 (private collection).

21 *Agranat*, p. 195; interview with Major-General (ret.) Yitzhak Hofi (the commander of the IDF Northern Command in 1973).

22 *Agranat*, p. 195.

23 Ibid., pp. 228, 232.

24 Wald, *Nemesis of Broken Arms*, pp. 100–1; Emanuel Rosen, 'Why the Barak Brigade Was Abandoned?', *Maariv*, 24 September 1973.

25 *Agranat*, pp. 210–1, 292–3, 328–33; interview with Colonel (ret.) Avner Shalev (military assistant to Chief of Staff David Elazar in 1973).

26 This is the estimate of Major General (ret.) Avraham Adan, who commanded Division 162 in the Canal front during the war. Quoted in Arie Braun, *Moshe Dayan and the Yom Kippur War* (Hebrew; Tel-Aviv: Edanim, 1992), p. 83.

27 A lecture by Lieutenant Colonel (ret.) Yossi Abudy, 'The IAF in the Yom Kippur War', Ramat Efal, 4 May 2000. The lecture is based on studies conducted by the history department of the IAF.

28 A lecture by the commander of the IAF in 1973, Major General (ret.) Benny Peled, Ramat Efal, 2 December 1999.

29 Michael I. Handel, 'War, Strategy and Intelligence: An Overview', in Michael I. Handel, *War, Strategy and Intelligence* (London: Frank Cass, 1989), pp. 3–50, 32–3.

30 Michael I. Handel, 'The Politics of Intelligence', *Intelligence and National Security*, vol. 2, no. 4 (October 1987), pp. 5–46.

31 Uri Bar-Joseph, *Intelligence Intervention in the Politics of Democratic States: The United States, Israel, and Britain* (University Park, PA: Pennsylvania State University Press, 1995), p. 72.

32 Michael I. Handel, *Perception, Deception, and Surprise: The Case of the Yom Kippur War*, Jerusalem Papers on Peace Problems, No. 19 (Jerusalem: Hebrew University of Jerusalem, Leonard Davis Institute for International Relations, 1976), pp. 7–8.

33 Ibid.

34 Handel, *War, Strategy and Intelligence*, p. 34. Despite this pessimistic conclusion, reality shows that there are exceptions, such as the Japanese failure to achieve surprise at Midway, and the German failures at Alam el Halfa and Kursk during World War II. In addition, a rare and a rather unknown case in which the victim was properly prepared for war because of intelligence warnings is that of the Egyptian–Israeli War of Attrition in 1969–70. After receiving warnings that Egypt intended to initiate a war in early spring, between December 1968 and March 1969, the IDF conducted intensive efforts – mainly the build-up of the Bar Lev line along the Suez Canal – to meet the coming challenge. Preparations were completed by 1 March and war started a few days later. The main Egyptian goal was to cause Israel the heaviest losses possible, but, due to its early preparations, the losses suffered by the IDF were relatively small. For a discussion of some of the variables that make the difference between surprise attack that begins a war and one that takes place while war is going on, see Uri Bar-Joseph, 'Methodological Magic', *Intelligence and National Security*, vol. 3, no. 4 (October 1988), pp. 134–55.

35 Among them, see Abraham Ben-Zvi, 'Hindsight and Foresight: A Conceptual Framework for the Analysis of Surprise Attacks', *World Politics*, vol. 28, no. 3 (April 1976), pp. 381–95; 'Threat Perception and Surprise: In Search of the Intervening Variable', in Frank P. Harvey and Ben D. Mor, eds, *Conflict in World Politics: Advances in the Study of Crisis, War and Peace* (New York: St. Martin's Press, 1998), pp. 241–71; Richard K. Betts, *Surprise Attack: Lessons for Defense Planning* (Washington, DC: Brookings Institution, 1982), pp. 68–9; Avi Shlaim, 'Failures in National Intelligence Estimates: The Case of the Yom Kippur War', *World Politics*, vol. 28, no. 3 (April 1976), pp. 348–80; Janice Gross Stein, 'The 1973 Intelligence Failure: A Reconsideration', *Jerusalem Quarterly*, vol. 24 (Summer 1982), pp. 41–5; 'Calculation, Miscalculation, and Conventional Deterrence II: The View from Jerusalem', in Robert Jervis, Richard Ned Lebow, and Janice Gross Stein, eds, *Psychology & Deterrence* (Baltimore, MD: Johns Hopkins University Press, 1985), pp. 60–88, 79; Yoel Ben-Porat, 'Estimates – Why Do they Collapse?', in Zvi Ofer and Avi Kober, eds, *Intelligence and National Security* (Hebrew; Tel-Aviv: Maarachot, 1987), pp. 223–50; Zvi Lanir, *Fundamental Surprise: The National Intelligence Crisis* (Hebrew; Tel-Aviv: Hakibutz HaMeuhad and Jaffee Center, 1983).

36 Unless otherwise noted, the evidence in this section is based on interviews that were conducted in connection with this chapter.

37 Avner Shalev's interview.

38 The most important discussion regarding this issue took place on 18 April 1973 in Golda Meir's residence, in a forum unofficially known as 'Golda's kitchen'. In addition to Meir herself, the other participants included Defense Minister Moshe Dayan, Minister without Portfolio Yisrael Galili, Chief of Staff David Elazar, DMI Zeira, and the Mossad's chief, Zvi Zamir. All those present, except for Zeira, estimated that war was highly probable in the coming summer. Hence, the IDF's 'blue-white' state of alert which took place between mid-May and mid-August 1973. The information presented here is based on a protocol of the meeting: 'A stenographic protocol of a consultation at the Prime Minister's residence on 18.4.73' (private collection).

39 Braun, *Moshe Dayan*, p. 29. Braun was Dayan's military assistant in 1973. His evidence is based on a protocol of the IDF GHQ meeting of 21 May 1973.
40 Dayan's interview in *Time* magazine, 30 July 1973.
41 Bandman's interview; Ben-Porat, 'Estimates', pp. 59–60.
42 Karl Popper, 'Of Clouds and Clocks: An Approach to the Problem of Rationality and the Freedom of Man', in Popper, *Objective Knowledge: An Evolutionary Approach* (Oxford: Clarendon Press, 1972), pp. 206–25, 207.
43 Directorate of Intelligence/Research Division, 'The Implication of Arab Arming with New Weapons – a Platform for GHQIDF (in Response to DMI Request)', 17 September 1973 (private collection). Zeira's decisiveness is vividly expressed also in his memoirs, written 20 years after the war. On many occasions he uses expressions such as 'there is no doubt' or 'certainly' even when doubts did exist and there was no certainty.
44 See, for example, the text of Dayan's speech in the graduation ceremony of the IDF Staff College, *Yedioth Ahronot*, 18 August 1972.
45 AMAN's 'Annual Intelligence Estimate: May–June 1972' (private collection).
46 'A stenographic protocol of a consultation at the Prime Minister's residence on 18.4.73' (private collection).
47 Hanoch Bartov, *Dado – 48 Years and Another 20 Days*, 2 vols (Hebrew; Tel-Aviv: Maariv, 1978), pp. 216–17.
48 Kanizher's interview.
49 *Agranat Commission Report*, p. 34.
50 The view of Bandman, see Bandman's interview.
51 *Agranat Commission Report*, p. 36.
52 The way that the message was interpreted when it arrived. Later, it became evident that the source warned that the Egyptian 'Tahrir 41' exercise, which was to start on 1 October, would turn into a real crossing and that the Syrians would join in. The source added additional information, which indicated that Egypt was gearing for war (Bartov, *Dado*, Vol. I, p. 299; Ben-Porat, 'Estimates', p. 23). *Post factum*, everything that the source said was proved to be right.
53 Braun, *Moshe Dayan*, p. 46.
54 *Agranat*, Vol. I, pp. 156–7. When learning about this piece of information after the war, the Chief of Staff said that had he known about it earlier, he would have mobilized the regular and the reserve army for war immediately, and this would have changed the course of the war (Ben-Porat, 'Estimates', p. 103). From what we know about Elazar's behavior on the eve of the war, there is no reason to doubt his word.
55 Avner Shalev's interview; Braun, *Moshe Dayan*, pp. 58–9; *Agranat Commission Report*, p. 46; Arie Shalev's interview; Chief of Staff, Major General Ehud Barak's interview to *Israeli TV*, 19 September 1993.
56 *Agranat Commission Report*, pp. 46–7.
57 Avner Shalev's interview.
58 Branch 3 + 5 + 6 + Israeli Air Force (IAF) Intelligence Division + Israeli Navy (IN) Intelligence Division, Immediate Military Intelligence Review, 'Alert Status and Activity in Syria and Egypt as of 051000 Oct. 7', para. 20 (private collection).
59 Ibid., para. 24.
60 *Agranat*, pp. 401–6.
61 Ibid., pp. 408–9.
62 Ibid., p. 414.
63 Bandman's interview.
64 *Agranat*, p. 76.
65 Braun, *Moshe Dayan*, p. 61. The notion that he, Zeira, knew better than the Soviets, tells us far more about the DMI's overconfidence than about the Soviets' real knowledge of Egyptian and Syrian war intentions.

66 Bartov, Vol. II, pp. 10–11.
67 *Agranat*, p. 32.
68 Braun, *Moshe Dayan*, p. 71.
69 Ibid., p. 74.
70 Interviews with Kanizer and Sudai.
71 Ibid.; Alex Fishman, 'Even Today He Does Not Believe that War Broke Out', *Hadashot*, 24 September 1993 (Hebrew).
72 Zeira, *October 73 War*, pp. 89, 95–7.
73 Bandman's interview.
74 *Agranat*, p. 268.
75 AMAN/Research Division, Branch 6, An Immediate Military Intelligence Review, 'Egypt: Emergency Deployment at the Canal Zone' (5 Oct., 05:45). The report summarized the results of an air-photograph sortie, which was carried out a day earlier. It was composed by the head of Egypt's military section in Branch 6, who, according to his own evidence, rejected all pressures to add calming assessment to the raw material (Rosenfeld interview).
76 Jonathan St B.T. Evans, *Bias in Human Reasoning: Causes and Consequences* (London: Lawrence Erlbaum, 1989), p. 41.
77 The classic work in this field is Leon Festinger, *A Theory of Cognitive Dissonance* (Stanford, CA: Stanford University Press, 1957).
78 See, for example, Daniel Kahneman and Amos Tversky, 'Subjective Probability: A Judgement of Representativeness', *Cognitive Psychology,* Vol. 3 (1972), pp. 430–51; Amos Tversky and Daniel Kahneman, 'Availability: A Heuristic for Judging Frequency and Probability', *Cognitive Psychology*, Vol. 5 (1973), pp. 207–32.
79 Arie W. Kruglanski, *Lay Epistemics and Human Knowledge: Cognitive and Motivational Biases* (New York: Plenum, 1989), p. 14. A semantic precursor for the term 'need for closure' is 'need for structure' (see A.P. Dijksterhuis, Ad van Knippenberg, Arie W. Kruglanski, and Carel Schaper, 'Motivated Social Cognition: Need for Closure Effects on Memory and Judgment', *Journal of Experimental Social Psychology*, Vol. 32 (1996), pp. 254–70, 255).
80 Arie W. Kruglanski and Donna M. Webster, 'Motivated Closing of the Mind: "Seizing" and 'Freezing'", *Psychological Review*, vol. 103, no. 2 (1996), pp. 263–83, 264; Donna M. Webster and Arie W. Kruglanski, 'Individual Differences in Need for Cognitive Closure', *Journal of Personality and Social Psychology*, vol. 67, no. 6 (1994), pp. 1049–62, 1050.
81 Webster and Kruglanski, 'Individual Differences', 1050.
82 Levran's interview. Notably, on Friday afternoon (the eve of Yom Kippur and less than 24 hours before war broke out) only one analyst remained on duty in the Research Division. The rest went home to prepare for Yom Kippur and to get some rest (Tehila's interview).
83 Tehila's interview; Sudai's interview; Rosenfeld's interview.
84 *Agranat*, pp. 156–7.
85 Zeira, *October 73 War*, p. 144.
86 For example, according to reliable evidence, the US Navy Director of War Plans in 1941, Admiral Richmond Turner, intervened in the naval intelligence process, thus contributing significantly to the distorted intelligence picture at Admiral Kimmel's headquarters in Pearl Harbor. For details, see Henry C. Clausen and Bruce Lee, *Pearl Harbor: Final Judgement* (New York: Crown Publishers, 1992), p. 294; E.T. Layton, '*And I Was There': Pearl Harbor and Midway – Breaking the Secrets*, pp. 138–45; Gordon W. Prange, with Donald M. Goldstein and Katherine V. Dillon, *Pearl Harbor: The Verdict of History* (New York: Penguin, 1991), p. 211.

7

Grant vs. Sherman: Paradoxes of Intelligence and Combat Leadership

Mark M. Lowenthal

It is already close to being trite to observe that the Persian Gulf War demonstrated a changed role for intelligence in warfare. As Lt General Kenneth Minihan (USAF, ret.), a former Director of the Defense Intelligence Agency and the National Security Agency, observed, intelligence went from being a contributor to being a participant. (Minihan pithily illustrated the difference between these two roles as follows: in a bacon and eggs breakfast, the hen is a contributor, the pig is a participant. Presumably, the outcome for intelligence as a participant is less dire.) Most observers also agree that US military operations against Iraq demonstrated the success of the Air Land Battle doctrine and vindicated those who had heralded a revolution in military affairs (RMA).

Even if these widely accepted views are true, there are many cautionary flags to be raised. The first is, in part, philosophical. Revolutions are *not*, by definition, necessarily beneficial, but are, rather, upsetting; that is why they are revolutions. Nor do revolutions necessarily benefit those who begin them. The French and Russian Revolutions are more illustrative of this point than is the American Revolution. As Talleyrand noted, a revolution is a monster that devours its children.

Moreover, revolutions tend to be leveling activities, and we have seen such a phenomenon in past military revolutions. For example, when the British Admiralty considered the development of the Dreadnought class of battleships in the late nineteenth century, it faced a dilemma. The Dreadnought would be superior to any other class of ship afloat in both firepower and armor. However, with one decision the Admiralty would be embarking on a new naval race with potential rivals – that is, Germany – from a position of parity instead of the long-required naval superiority. The first ship in this new class, HMS *Dreadnought*, was launched in 1906. By the outbreak of World War I in August 1914, Britain still greatly outclassed the German High Seas Fleet in older battleships as well as in cruisers and destroyers (40:22, 102:41, and 301:144, respectively) but the ratios were much closer for dreadnoughts and modern battle cruisers (20:13 and 8:5, respectively).[1]

We have also seen instances where military revolutions in terms of capabilities did not necessarily benefit the nation that invented them, but rather the nation that first was able to come up with a superior doctrine for their use. The tank is illustrative of this phenomenon. The British invented tanks in the latter part of World War I, but it was the Germans who came up with a superior doctrine – an earlier air land battle doctrine – in the blitzkrieg.

Finally, as successful as the US application of arms was in the Gulf War, and as much as it validated new doctrines, strategies, and tactics with a 'real-world' example (albeit against a greatly mismatched and inferior opponent), it was also an unfortunate proving ground to some degree. The Gulf War required that the United States demonstrate its new capabilities on a fairly minor battleground. And although its success may have over-awed some other would-be foes, it also allowed others very useful insights by which they could begin to plan counter-measures. A certain element of surprise was lost over a relatively minor foe. But nations do not always get to pick and choose their conflicts.

In all fairness, US combat doctrine has continued to develop since the Gulf War. The potential implications of that development, especially of the emphasis put on intelligence and its effect on combat leadership, are the main subjects of this chapter. But we must be cautious when we herald revolutions as unalloyed opportunities without potential risks.

Thus, we have the first of several paradoxes: the fact that military advantage does not necessarily accrue to the state that creates or introduces the innovation, but rather to the state that finds how to apply the most successful doctrine to this innovation.

The Joint Visions

In the decade since the Gulf War, the Joint Chiefs of Staff have produced two major statements of their warfighting concepts: Joint Vision 2010 (published in 1997) and Joint Vision 2020 (published in 2000).[2]

Early on, Joint Vision 2010 seeks to use 'the improved intelligence and command and control capabilities available in the information age' and then moves on to key operational concepts. A key theme throughout Joint Vision 2010 is that of 'dominance':

- Dominant maneuver;
- Full spectrum dominance;
- Dominant battlespace awareness.

In its somewhat didactic tone, Joint Vision 2010 asserts that improvements in information systems integration will 'provide accurate information in a timely manner'. Here is the first area of concern, an intellectual sloppiness that tends to use 'information systems' interchangeably with 'intelligence'. This is not surprising, given the predilection within the US Defense Department for housing intelligence with command, control, and communications, an arrangement guaranteed to give emphasis to the means for dissemination rather than the intelligence content itself. Interestingly, 'all source intelligence' (meaning a combination of signals intelligence, imagery, and perhaps espionage and some other sources) is taken as a given – how it happens is left unstated – but the emphasis is on the various technologies that will allow more intelligence to be made available to operations. The goal is the already-cited 'dominant battlespace awareness' (DBA), that is, a more accurate interactive 'picture' of the battle area, writ large. The definition of DBA in Joint Vision 2010 actually fails to do justice to the concept. In 1995, I had a meeting with Admiral William Owens, then Vice-Chairman of the Joint Chiefs of Staff. Admiral Owens described the 'battlespace' as a cube, stretching 200 meters along the front, 200 meters deep into the enemy's position, and 200 meters high above the front. The goal for intelligence, according to Admiral Owens, was to apply all of the intelligence resources necessary so that the commander would 'know everything' happening inside those eight million cubic meters.

As Admiral Owens and I discussed it, we quickly determined that although I was Clausewitzian, and believed in the inevitability of some fog of war, Admiral Owens believed that with sufficient intelligence resources that fog could be dissipated. Clausewitz believed that the very fact of combat operations produced a 'fog' of both known and unknown information in which the commanders are forced to operate. There will always be some aspect of the enemy's forces, dispositions, and plans that are unknown. It is obvious why a doctrine that relies so heavily on intelligence would claim that it can dissipate the fog of war. However, if we assume anything less than 'perfect' information – an unlikely state perhaps akin to omniscience – then we must assume that there will always be some level of fog. It may be thinner and wispier than in the past, but it is highly questionable as to whether it will disappear entirely.

Fortunately, Joint Vision 2010 is somewhat less grandiose in its claims for DBA. This document acknowledges that Clausewitz's famous fog of war will not be eliminated entirely, but does claim that DBA can make 'the battlespace considerably more transparent'.

Systems-integration improvements are also seen as combating yet another Clausewitzian dilemma, the friction of war. This concept is much less understood than the self-evident fog of war. By 'friction', Clausewitz meant all of the difficulties inherent in the operation of an armed force and the effect that two opposing armed forces have upon one another, even when they are not actually engaged in combat. Friction can be thought of as the entirety of impediments – bad terrain, units that do not arrive on time, various mechanical or logistical breakdowns, the sheer time it takes to get things done in any large organization – that interfere with the smooth execution of an operation, whether actual combat or other operations. Clausewitz devoted an entire (admittedly brief) chapter in *On War* to the concept of friction, noting that it was difficult to describe 'the unseen, all-pervading element' that made apparently simple acts in war become difficult.[3] Indeed, as Michael Handel points out, Clausewitz believed that the factors of uncertainty and friction led to doubts about the reliability of detailed military plans.[4] Interestingly, one of the compensating factors that Clausewitz saw as an antidote was the intuition of military genius, unfortunately a factor that cannot be supplied at will.[5]

Joint Vision 2010 claims, however, that at the higher echelons of command, 'these technologies will reduce the friction of war'. Joint Vision 2010 also concedes that these same improvements will result in a faster operational tempo, more stress and the need for more rapid decisions – in effect, more friction. So, here we have a second paradox: the various systems created to reduce operational friction can (and likely will at some level) also contribute to operational friction.

It is not difficult to think of potential examples. Anyone who has had a computer crash can imagine this happening in the more stressful milieu of a combat headquarters. Indeed, the greater the sophistication of the system, the higher the chance of some level of failure. It may not be crippling, but the failure and its attendant psychological effects will inevitably produce friction of their own.[6]

Interestingly, as Joint Vision 2010 examines the role of information, the standard becomes 'superiority', not 'dominance'. Information superiority is defined as, 'The capability to collect, process and disseminate an *uninterrupted* [emphasis added] flow of information while exploiting or denying an adversary's ability to do the same.'

As an aside, during the Cold War, Henry Kissinger once asked: 'What is nuclear superiority and what does one do with it?' One is tempted to rephrase the question here for information superiority: do we need *more* information, or the *right* information? Here is yet another paradox, this one related to the information age of which the Joint Visions are so firmly a part. It is now commonplace for managers in any organization of any appreciable size, whether in the public or private sector, to complain loudly and vigorously about 'information overload'. Millions of dollars are spent every month on hardware or software solutions that promise 'knowledge management' or 'information management' or 'data filters', and so on. Thus, we should recognize that added flows of information may bring some level of superiority, but they may also prove to be Achilles' heels.

More interesting is the fact that this portion of Joint Vision 2010 begins with a discussion of command, control, and intelligence, but quickly ends up with a discussion of information superiority. This odd segue stands the world of the intelligence officer on its head. In intelligence, one begins with 'information', which is basically anything that can be known, and ends up with 'intelligence' after that information has been collected with a specific requirement or policymaker in mind; and then has been processed, exploited, analyzed, and disseminated. In Joint Vision 2010, however, there is a passing nod to intelligence, which then becomes 'superior' information. What makes it 'superior' or what this quality entails are left unsaid. Even at its most benign interpretation, information and intelligence are being used interchangeably.

This flow gets reversed, however, in the ensuing discussion of joint operations. Here, Joint Vision 2010 states that the basis for joint operations is a new conceptual framework. This basis is, in turn, 'found in the improved command, control, and intelligence which can be assured by information superiority'.

The reasoning, in the end, is circular: improvements in command, control, and intelligence will allow information superiority, which will allow improved command, control, and intelligence. It is neat and it is self-fulfilling. Or, in the words of a former Assistant Secretary of Defense for Command, Control, Communications, and Intelligence: 'Intelligence is the ultimate self-licking ice cream cone.' Here we see the effects.

This cause-and-effect problem notwithstanding, Joint Vision 2010 goes on to cite information superiority as a key enabler of much that follows: precision engagement; force protection; and enhanced commander awareness of his area of responsibility.

In its latter section, Joint Vision 2010 acknowledges the importance of people, training, and leadership, 'regardless of how sophisticated technology becomes'. It also acknowledges 'the inevitable friction and fog of war'. It returns to the importance of education and training in employing these new technologies and also recognizes the need to train against 'both information saturation and total interruption of information flow'. Thus, Joint Vision 2010 is, from the perspective of a Clausewitzian intelligence professional, a mixed bag at best.

Joint Vision 2020 was completed three years after Joint Vision 2010, which is acknowledged as 'the conceptual template'. It is not surprising, therefore, that most of the same conceptual issues remain, although the emphasis on 'information superiority' has actually increased.

Joint Vision 2020 also makes the claim that 'Throughout history, military leaders have regarded information superiority as a key enabler of victory.' This may be little more than willful self-justification, for reasons that will be discussed below. Happily, Joint Vision 2020 also admits that information superiority does not mean 'perfect information' and that it will not eliminate the fog of war. There is also a much fuller discussion of friction and a further admission that the causes of friction cannot be eliminated. The new document also recognizes that the handling of information can produce its own fog and friction. Joint Vision 2020 also has a fuller development of information operations, including the important recognition that it will be very difficult to determine their effectiveness, that is, to conduct battle-damage assessments of information operations.

There are more intriguing effects that are not considered, however. First, how much of the enemy's C3I (Command, control, communications and intelligence) do we want to disrupt? There may be costs, both military and political, to a thorough or complete disruption. Militarily, suppose we are nearing the end of a successful campaign (as in the Gulf War) and seek to get the enemy to agree to a ceasefire. If we have degraded the enemy's C3I to an intense degree, will the enemy leadership be able to communicate this ceasefire order to his units?[7] Will these commanders, knowing that their communications have been disrupted or perhaps even commandeered by us, accept such an order as authentic? Politically, suppose we get a communication from the enemy suggesting a truce or a ceasefire, etc.; will we be able to authenticate that message, knowing how badly their C3I has been disrupted?

There is also an operational intelligence concern. If one's own information operations are successful in disrupting enemy information operations, one also faces the likelihood of less – or more fractured – intelligence to collect. Degradations in information operations capabilities also mean a decrease in that system's value as an intelligence collection source. There may be a distinct trade-off between information-operations targets and intelligence-collection targets.

The variables that may effect information operations are also noted in Joint Vision 2020, offering a complexity that is 'awesome' in the true sense of the word – overwhelming and a bit frightening. Indeed, there may be an information operations 'Sukhomlinov effect' to consider. (General Vladimir Sukhomlinov was the Russian Minister of War from 1909 to 1915, and bears great responsibility for Russia's decision to go to war in 1914 and for the serious lack of preparedness of the Russian Army. He gives his name to the somewhat tongue-in-cheek military-history theory that the army with the gaudier uniforms tends to lose.) In information operations, as in all other warfare, there is an advantage to simplicity: this holds true even amidst the complexities of twenty-first-century weaponry. It also raises the issue of asymmetries. In information warfare size may be a disadvantage, not an advantage. The very size of our information-operations capability may present a large number of targets to foes (or apparent bystanders but stealthy participants) to carry out what would be, in effect, computer guerrilla attacks. Indeed, in the world of information operations, one can have stealthy allies or enemies who operate remotely and randomly only in cyberspace, but who in the 'real' world appear to be neutral. For example, were Russia and China to become involved in a conflict, it would be in India's interest for China to suffer some level of loss. China is a threat to India; Russia is not. However, Indian leaders most likely would not want to risk direct involvement. But what would prevent India, which has a sophisticated computer industry of its own, from engaging in remote, untraceable cyber attacks on Chinese systems to aid Russia?

What Does it Matter? Grant vs. Sherman

One could dismiss the above discussion as no more than quibbles. However, doctrine matters. It underlies everything that the military does: what it buys, how it trains, how it proposes and expects to fight and win a war.

The concerns raised above about the Joint Visions are serious enough in their own right. Intelligence underpins a good deal of the structure of these Joint Visions. The information superiority that is repeatedly discussed should be more properly labeled 'good intelligence'. But, as has been noted, information and intelligence are not the same. Moreover, intelligence does not just happen, nor is it available in pre-determined quality and quantity, nor is the flow always uninterrupted. Granted, the United States intelligence collection array can produce volumes of intelligence. The sheer volume itself is another aspect of the information overload problem, as the system tries to determine which signals, images, and reports (both open and classified in all cases) should be processed and exploited first – or at all, and on a timely basis. Indeed, the gap between how much we collect and how much less we process, exploit, and analyze is large and growing, and has been a matter of serious concern for some time.

This raises the serious problem of 'paralysis by analysis'. One can have so much information that it will either be impossible to process or will bog one down in the processing. Decision points recede as analysts, or commanders, insist on going over the data yet again. Indeed, our information capabilities may make us susceptible to purposeful information overload on the part of an enemy who literally drowns us in information – most of it false but enough of it true to make the sorting more problematic. This is not a new technique. The Allies in World War II did much the same thing to the Germans in the days before the D-Day invasion in 1944, having created a phantom army under General George S. Patton, a deception plan that included streams of plausible but false radio messages. But in a system in which information management plays a much greater role, the opportunities for deception and for paralysis induced by information flooding also increase.

Sometimes even the obvious intelligence may also lead to the wrong decision. Imagine, for example, if the Founding Fathers in 1776 had done a fairly straightforward political-military analysis of their position vis-à-vis Britain before they made a decision about independence. They probably would have gone home and decided to pay their taxes.[8]

Thus, we possess tremendous collection capabilities but they have inherent vulnerabilities. As our capabilities become increasingly less covert and better known, rivals and adversaries develop improved means to deny or to deceive our collection. How well will this new doctrine operate on less-than-perfect intelligence – or intelligence that is fragmentary or contradictory? Can we be dominant in the face of operational uncertainty? We would do well to remember Admiral Horatio Nelson's admonition to his captains in the days before the Battle of Trafalgar: 'Something must be left to chance . . .'[9]

The place where this may be most important is in the area of combat-leadership training. Today's junior officers are tomorrow's senior commanders. How much intelligence will they come to expect? How reliant – or dependent – on it will they be?

During the Cold War, for example, one of the advantages we assumed we enjoyed over Soviet forces was the amount of initiative we left to NCOs and junior officers. We knew that the Soviet tank with the long antenna was the command tank. Given the tight control of units inherent in Red Army doctrine, we assumed that eliminating the command tank would greatly reduce the combat effectiveness of the tanks subordinate to it. In other words, are we creating an information doctrine that might, inadvertently, stifle initiative in combat leaders?

Let us return to the claim made by Joint Vision 2020 that 'Throughout history, military leaders have regarded information superiority as a key enabler of victory.' This belief assumes that good leaders will recognize good intelligence and will act on it. One hopes this is so, but the key element in the equation is good leaders. Combat leaders are not empty vessels into which one pours 'superior' information and then gets the appropriate response. Nor are they part of the 'machine' that produces this information; they are humans, flawed and limited. Their capability as commanders is far more important than the information/intelligence they will be receiving.

An illustrative example is General George McClellan and the Battle of Antietam in the American Civil War. Luck (one of the key attributes of a successful general, according to Napoleon) had delivered to McClellan a copy of General Robert E. Lee's orders, giving Lee's objectives and the fact that his command was still widely separated. McClellan gloated: 'Here is a paper with which if I cannot whip "Bobbie Lee", I will be willing to go home.'[10] McClellan certainly won the Battle of Antietam (or, at least he did not lose it) and it was a significant victory both militarily (ending Lee's first invasion of the North) and politically (precluding British and French diplomatic recognition of the Confederacy). But it was not the decisive victory it could have been. McClellan's innate caution and his constant preoccupation with phantom Confederate reserves deprived him of a decisive victory that might have destroyed Lee's army in detail, shortening the war considerably.

An opposite example is provided by Marshal Ferdinand Foch, during the second Battle of Marne in 1918, in World War I. Facing the final German offensive, Foch reported somewhat insouciantly: 'My center is giving way, my right is pushed back, situation excellent, I am attacking.'[11] Thus, Foch had information, little of which was good, but he was not diverted by it from his objective.

In other words, there is no substitute for a combat leader – at any echelon – who can take decisive action in the face of incomplete, minimal, or even vastly discomforting intelligence. This is not to suggest that commanders should rely entirely on their instincts and ignore available intelligence. Rather, it is recognition of the likely reality that the available intelligence will be incomplete and perhaps contradictory, and that it cannot be the sole or perhaps even the main basis for all decisions, especially in combat.

Reflections by the two most successful commanders in the American Civil War, Generals Ulysses S. Grant and William T. Sherman, bring this home graphically. Grant, in his *Memoirs*, describes his first Civil War engagement in which he exercised command, as colonel of the 21st Illinois Regiment:

> My sensations as we approached what I supposed might be 'a field of battle' were anything but agreeable. I had been in all the engagements in Mexico that it was possible for one person to be in; but not in command. If some one else had been colonel and I had been lieutenant colonel I do not think I would have felt any trepidation . . .
>
> As we approached the brow of the hill from which it was expected we could see [Confederate Colonel] Harris' camp, and possibly find his men ready to meet us, my heart kept getting higher and higher until it felt to me as though it was in my throat. I would have given anything then to have been back in Illinois, but I had not the moral courage to halt and consider what to do; I kept right on. When we reached a point from which the valley below was in full view I halted. The place where Harris had been encamped a few days before was still there and the marks of a recent encampment were plainly visible, but the troops were gone. My heart resumed its place. It occurred to me at once that Harris had been as much afraid of me as I had been of him. This was a view of the question I had never taken before; but it was one I never forgot afterwards. From that event to the close of the war, I never experienced trepidation upon confronting an enemy, though I always felt more or less anxiety. I never forgot that he had as much reason to fear my forces as I had his. The lesson was valuable.[12]

In other words, Grant determined to impose his will on the enemy, no matter what. This important attribute is evident in Grant's campaigns, particularly his decision to cut himself loose from his base and attack Vicksburg from the east, interposing himself between two Confederate forces; and in the tenacious hold he kept on Lee's army as they fought their way down towards Petersburg and Richmond.

Sherman, in correspondence, expressed a supporting view of the same issue:

> I'm a darned sight smarter than Grant; I know a great deal more about war, military histories, strategy and grand tactics than he does; I know more about organization, supply, and administration and about everything else than he does; but I'll tell you where he beats me and where he beats the world. He don't care a damn for what the enemy does out of his sight, but it scares me like hell.[13]

The difference is evident in Sherman's campaigns as an independent commander through Georgia and the Carolinas. For all of his considerable success, he did not display the same audacity as Grant. There was a caution to Sherman's battlefield preparations that one did not see in Grant. Sherman was successful, but he did not impose his will on the enemy in the way that Grant did.

Without taking anything away from Sherman, we clearly would like to have as many Grants as possible. But will the training inherent in the new doctrine produce more Shermans or – heaven forbid – McClellans? To what degree will the Joint Visions hold to their promise of training at less than optimal conditions – at either the high or low end of the 'information superiority' scale? To be fair, there are also political factors that now intrude, such as the American requirement for casualty-free and accident-free operations. These unrealistic imperatives will also breed caution, but they are not likely to be inbred in officers in the same way that doctrine is.

Conclusion

Thus, we have at least three paradoxes raised by the assertions of the Joint Visions. The first is that new military technologies do not necessarily accrue to the benefit of the first state to introduce them, but rather to the state that comes up with the best doctrine on how to use them. In this regard, the Joint Visions comes across as being more argumentative than persuasive. They do not lay out a successful doctrine so much as make assertions for the ability of the military to transform these new technologies into success. They are, too often, somewhat blithe about both the difficulties that are faced and the potential negative effects of this very same technology. Admittedly, this criticism may not be entirely fair; after all, these are *visions*, not strategic plans. But as visions, they do set forth a series of expectations and desired outcomes, many of which may be beyond the ability of either technology or doctrine to deliver.

The second paradox is that these new doctrines and their underlying technology may actually create more of the Clausewitzian problems of fog and friction that they were supposed to dissipate. There is no sure way of knowing this without testing systems out either in rigorous war games or, worse, on the battlefield. Here we encounter yet another admonition from Clausewitz, who noted: 'Friction is the only concept that more or less corresponds to the factors that distinguish real war from war on paper.'[14] In other words, only the reality of warfare will reveal the true frictions involved in any operation. Are we left with a new Heisenberg uncertainty principle that relates to military doctrines? Not really. What should be taken away from this is the likelihood that fog and friction will continue as realities on the battlefield, even if they can be diminished.

The third paradox is that these new technologies may also create new vulnerabilities. Information systems are potential conduits for *dis*information as well, especially from adversaries who have some understanding of the systems and have achieved a necessary level of technology of their own – not one that need be as sophisticated as ours, but only good enough to feed us what they want us to have.

Has the role of intelligence really changed? Perhaps not as much as some of its supporters might like to think. Even if we accept the fact that the role of intelligence in combat has changed and has become more participatory (and the Afghan campaign of 2001–2 would support this trend as well), the main goal of intelligence remains providing required information on a timely basis to help policymakers (civil or military) reduce their uncertainties as they make decisions. Note that the uncertainties can be *reduced*, not *eliminated*. Much still depends on the quality of the policymaker. The various technological improvements that buttress the Joint Visions are real, but they do not, in the end, guarantee 'better' intelligence. More intelligence is not, of necessity, better intelligence; it can be an impediment as much as an enabler. The Joint Visions err when they confuse means (command, control, and communications; or information technology) with ends (usable intelligence). They also err when they make unwarranted assumptions about how combat leaders will react to this intelligence.

Thus, we return to one of Clausewitz's antidotes for friction, the intuition of military genius. We need more Shermans than McClellans, but we also need more Grants than Shermans. A consistently successful commander must, on occasion, rise above what he sees and what he hears and rely on his intuition and his instinct. He is not likely to be right all of the time (Grant admitted that Cold Harbor was ill fought and very costly), but he is better able to react to the unexpected. After all, surprise, as Clausewitz noted, 'becomes the means to gain superiority, [and] lies at the root of all operations without exception'.[15] Thus, how we train our junior officers matters a great deal. In this case, teaching them to continue to think for themselves, to avoid becoming over-dependent on intelligence, is a key issue.

This brings us to a fourth paradox, the Handel Paradox, that high-risk operations become low-risk because their very riskiness gives them the advantage of surprise. But what is it that makes certain operations risky? It may be the relative sizes of the forces involved or the goals being sought, or conditions on the field, but these are all variables. The one invariable in all risky operations – and in all operations – is the uncertainty of outcome. Uncertainty, like risk, is unavoidable. But there are differences between accepting some level of uncertainty, even as we seek to limit it to whatever extent is practicable, and creating strategic visions that seek or claim to eliminate that uncertainty entirely. Not only is this an impractical goal, it is one that can have dire outcomes for leadership training and execution. We will, paradoxically, create new and unwarranted risks as we try to eliminate other risks.

For all of the changes that have occurred in warfare since Clausewitz wrote his unfinished classic in the aftermath of the Napoleonic Wars, much has remained the same and no series of revolutions in military affairs will reverse that. Clausewitz's principles of warfare have a transcendent aspect that the Joint Visions do not. Like Michael Handel, I believe that the closer we adhere to Clausewitz's broad principles about the nature and conduct of war, the more likely we are to be successful on the battlefield. Even as we seek to prepare the battlefield (to cite a currently vogue expression), we must accept the fact that some portion of the milieu in which we operate will always be beyond our control and beyond our ability to know it. States have, over the centuries, found ways to substitute new technologies, new tactics, and new strategies for old ones. But no one has found a way to substitute for what Clausewitz called 'the intuition of military genius'.

NOTES

1 R. Ernest Dupuy and Trevor N. Dupuy, *The Encyclopedia of Military History* (New York: Harper & Row, 1970), p. 934.
2 Joint Vision 2010 and Joint Vision 2020 are most easily found on the Worldwide Web at: http://www/dtic.mil/jv2010/jpub.htm and http://www.dtic.mil/jv2020/jvpub2.htm respectively.
3 'Friction in War' is Book I, Chapter 7 in *On War*. See Carl von Clausewitz, *On War*, ed. and trans. Michael Howard and Peter Paret (Princeton, NJ: Princeton University Press, 1976), pp. 119–21.
4 Michael Handel, *Masters of War*, 3rd edn (London: Frank Cass, 2001), p. 244.
5 Ibid., p. 245.
6 Interestingly, technological redundancy may actually increase the chance for failure, depending on the system and its use. Consider, as an example, Charles Lindbergh's decision to have his airplane, the *Spirit of St Louis*, powered by one

engine rather than three. Lindbergh calculated that although the engine he had selected was reliable, in a plane designed to fly on three engines there were three times as many chances that an engine failure would occur, dooming his flight. No single engine was likely to fail, but one engine failing in three was more likely. See John Noble Wilford, 'Man and Craft Were One, As a New Age Began', *The New York Times*, 21 May 2002, p. C1.

7   This problem was of great concern to US strategic planners during the Cold War as they debated the merits of 'decapitation', that is, direct attacks on the enemy's command-and-control authorities. The argument in favor of such nuclear strikes was the possibility that it would totally disrupt the enemy's ability to launch retaliatory strikes. The argument against was that a successful decapitation might leave a 'headless' enemy nuclear force over which no one had any control and that might continue fighting needlessly and pointlessly.

8   Britain had a standing army, part of which was already deployed in the colonies; the colonies had individual militias that had never fought together under their own command. Many senior British commanders had years of combat experience; no American had ever commanded a force of the size that was likely to be needed. Britain had the world's largest navy, allowing it to reinforce its army and to isolate the colonies; the colonies had no navy. Britain was already stirring up Indians on the frontier, thus creating a diversion for colonial forces. Britain was the wealthiest European state and had the means and infrastructure to finance a war; the colonies did not. Britain had the means to create the 'sinews of war' – arms and other necessary supplies; the colonies did not on a comparable basis. Finally, it was uncertain that the colonies would have any allies, even among Britain's enemies, all of which were still monarchies and might not favor supporting a republican rebellion against a lawful king.

9   Memorandum to the Fleet, off Cádiz, 9 October 1805. This is sometimes referred to as Nelson's Trafalgar Memorandum. See David Howarth, *Trafalgar: The Nelson Touch* (New York: Atheneum, 1969), pp. 71–3.

10 The original source is the memoirs of John Gibbon, *Personal Recollections of the Civil War* (New York: G.P. Putnam's, 1928), cited in James MacPherson, *Battle Cry of Freedom* (New York: Oxford University Press, 1988), p. 537.

11 *Bartlett's Familiar Quotations*, 14th edn (Boston, MA: Little Brown, 1968), p. 826, cites Basil H. Liddell Hart, *Reputations Ten Years After* ([1928] Freeport, NY: Books for Libraries Press, 1968 reprint) as the source for this quote.

12 Ulysses S. Grant, *Personal Memoirs* (New York: Library of America, 1990), pp. 163–5.

13 This quote from Sherman is cited in various places, but without reference to the correspondent or date. See, for example, http://saints.ces.edu/mkelsey/quotes.html.

14 Clausewitz, *On War*, p. 119.

15 Ibid., p. 198.

Index

CPSIA information can be obtained
at www.ICGtesting.com
Printed in the USA
BVHW090147010819
554828BV00004B/28/P